Saint Augustine

Biography - unabridged version

Louis Bertrand

Translated by
Vincent O'Sullivan

Alicia ÉDITIONS

Contents

TRANSLATOR'S NOTE 1
PROLOGUE 3

DAYS OF CHILDHOOD

1. AN AFRICAN FREE-TOWN SUBJECT TO ROME 13
2. THE FAMILY OF A SAINT 16
3. THE COMFORT OF THE MILK 25
4. THE FIRST GAMES 31
5. THE SCHOOLBOY OF MADAURA 37
6. THE HOLIDAYS AT THAGASTE 47

THE ENCHANTMENT OF CARTHAGE

1. CARTHAGO VENERIS 57
2. THE AFRICAN ROME 62
3. THE CARTHAGE STUDENT 70
4. THE SWEETNESS OF TEARS 81
5. THE SILENCE OF GOD 92

THE RETURN

1. THE CITY OF GOLD 107
2. THE FINAL DISILLUSION 115
3. THE MEETING BETWEEN AMBROSE AND AUGUSTINE 123
4. PLANS OF MARRIAGE 130
5. THE CHRIST IN THE GARDEN 140

THE HIDDEN LIFE

1. THE LAST SMILE OF THE MUSE — 155
2. THE ECSTASY OF SAINT MONNICA — 166
3. THE MONK OF THAGASTE — 175
4. AUGUSTINE A PRIEST — 183

THE APOSTLE OF PEACE AND OF CATHOLIC UNITY

1. THE BISHOP OF HIPPO — 193
2. WHAT WAS HEARD IN THE BASILICA OF PEACE — 204
3. THE BISHOP'S BURTHEN — 213
4. AGAINST "THE ROARING LIONS" — 222

FACE TO FACE WITH THE BARBARIANS

1. THE SACK OF ROME — 239
2. THE CITY OF GOD — 247
3. THE BARBARIAN DESOLATION — 257
4. SAINT AUGUSTINE — 271

TRANSLATOR'S NOTE

The quotations from Saint Augustine's *Confessions* are taken from Canon Bigg's scholarly version, which seems to me the best in English. But there are places where M. Bertrand's reading of the original text differs from Dr. Bigg's, and in such cases I have felt myself obliged to follow the author of this book. These differences never seriously affect the meaning of a passage; sometimes it is a mere matter of choice, as with the word *collactaneum* (I, 7) which Dr. Bigg translates "twin," and M. Bertrand, like Pusey, *frère de lait*, or "foster-brother." As a rule, Dr. Bigg chooses the quietest terms, and M. Bertrand the most forcible. Those curious in such matters may like to see an instance.

The original text runs:—

> Avulsa a latere meo tanquam impedimento conjugii, cum quâ cubare solitus eram, cor ubi adhaerebat, concisum et vulneratum mihi erat, et trahebat sanguinem.
>
> — (*Confessiones*, VI, 15.)

M. Bertrand translates:—

> Quand on arracha de mes flancs, sous prétexte qu'elle empêchait mon mariage, celle avec qui j'avais coutume de dormir, depuis si longtemps,

là où mon coeur était attaché au sien, il se déchira, et je traînais mon sang avec ma blessure.

Canon Bigg's version is:—

My mistress was torn from my side as an obstacle to my marriage, and my heart, which clung to her, was torn and wounded till it bled.

In this place, it will be observed that Dr. Bigg does not emphasize the word *ubi* which, as the reader will find on turning to page 185 of this volume, M. Bertrand thinks so significant.

The remaining English versions of the writings of Saint Augustine and of the other Latin authors quoted are my own, except the passages from *The City of God*, including the verse translation of Persius, which are taken, with some necessary alterations, from the Seventeenth century translation ascribed to John Healey.

V. O'S.

PROLOGUE

*Inquietum est cor nostrum,
donec requiescat in te !...*
Our heart finds no rest
until it rests in Thee...

— *Confessions*, I, i.

Painting of Saint Augustine in His Study *by Sandro Botticelli (1480), Ognissanti Church (Florence).*

Saint Augustine is now little more than a celebrated name. Outside of learned or theological circles people no longer read him. Such is true renown: we admire the saints, as we do great men, on trust. Even his *Confessions* are generally spoken of only from hearsay. By this neglect, is he atoning for the renewal of glory in which he shone during the seventeenth century, when the Jansenists, in their inveterate obstinacy, identified him with the defence of their cause? The reputation of sour austerity and of argumentative and tiresome prolixity which attaches to the remembrance of all the writers of Port-Royal, save Pascal—has that affected too the work of Augustine, enlisted in spite of himself in the ranks of these pious schismatics? And yet, if there have ever been any beings who do not resemble Augustine, and whom probably he would have attacked with all his eloquence and all the force of his dialectic, they are the Jansenists. Doubtless he would have said with contempt: "The party of Jansen," even as in his own day, with his devotion to Catholic unity, he said: "The party of Donatus."

It must be acknowledged also that the very sight of his works is terrifying, whether we take the enormous folios in two columns of the Benedictine edition, or the volumes, almost as compact, and much more numerous, of recent editions. Behind such a rampart of printed matter he is well defended against profane curiosity. It needs courage and perseverance to penetrate into this labyrinth of text, all bristling with theology and exegesis and metaphysics. But only cross the threshold of the repellent enclosure, grow used to the order and shape of the building, and it will not be long ere you are overcome by a warm sympathy, and then by a steadily increasing admiration for the host who dwells there. The hieratic face of the old bishop lights up, becomes strangely living, almost modern, in expression. You discover under the text one of the most passionate lives, most busy and richest in instruction, that history has to shew. What it teaches is applicable to ourselves, answers to our interests of yesterday and to-day. This existence, and the century in which it was passed, recall our own century and ourselves. The return of similar circumstances has brought similar situations and characters; it is almost our portrait. And we feel half ready to conclude that at the present moment there is no subject more actual than St. Augustine.

At least he is one of the most interesting. What, indeed, is more romantic than this wandering life of rhetorician and student that the youthful Augustine led, from Thagaste to Carthage, from Carthage to Milan and to Rome—begun in the pleasures and tumult of great cities, and ending in the penitence, the silence, and recollection of a monastery? And again, what drama is more full of colour and more profitable to consider than that last agony of the Empire, of which Augustine was a spectator, and, with all his heart faithful to Rome, would have prevented if he could? And then, what tragedy more stirring and painful than the crisis of soul and conscience which tore his life? Well may it be said that, regarded as a whole, the life of Augustine was but a continual spiritual struggle, a battle of the soul. It is the battle of every moment, the never-ceasing combat of body and spirit, which the poets of that time dramatized, and which is the history of the Christian of all times. The stake of the battle is a soul. The upshot is the final triumph, the redemption of a soul.

What makes the life of Augustine so complete and so truly typical is that he fought the good fight, not only against himself, but against all the enemies of the Church and the Empire. If he was a doctor and a saint, so was he too the type of the man of action in one of the most disheartened periods. That he triumphed over his passions—this, in truth, concerns only God and himself. That he preached, wrote, shook crowds, disturbed minds, may seem without importance to those who reject his doctrine. But that across the centuries his soul, afire with charity, continues to warm our own; that without our knowledge he still shapes us; and that, in a way more or less remote, he is still the master of our hearts, and, in certain aspects, of our minds—there is what touches each and all of us, without distinction. Not only has Augustine always his great place in the living communion of all christened people, but the Western soul is marked with the stamp of his soul.

First of all, his fate is confused with that of the dying Empire. He witnessed, if not the utter disappearance, at least the gradual swooning away of that admirable thing called the Roman Empire, image of Catholic unity. Well, we are the wreckage of the Empire. Usually, we turn away with contempt from those wretched centuries which underwent the descents of the Barbarians. For us, that is the Lower-Empire, a time of shameful decadence which deserves nothing but our scorn. However, it is out of this chaos and this degradation that we have arisen.

The wars of the Roman republic concern us less than the outlawry of the Barbarian chiefs who separated our Gaul from the Empire, and without knowing it, prepared the dawn of France. After all, what are the rivalries of Marius and Sylla to us? The victory of Aëtius over the Huns in the plains of Chalons concerns us a good deal more. Further, it is unfair to the Lower-Empire to view it only as a time of feebleness and cowardice and corruption. It was also an epoch of immense activity, prolific of daring and high-flying adventurers, some of them heroic. Even the most degenerate of the last Emperors never lost the conviction of Roman majesty and grandeur. Unto the very end, they employed all the ruses of their diplomacy to prevent the Barbarian chiefs from imagining themselves anything else but vassals of the Empire. Honorius, at bay in Ravenna, persisted in refusing Alaric the title of commander of the *Cohortes Urbanæ*, even though his refusal were to lead to the sack of Rome and imperil his own life.

Simply by his fidelity to the Empire, Augustine shews himself one like ourselves—a Latin of Occitania. But still closer resemblances draw him near to us. His time was very like our own time. Upon even a slight familiarity with his books we recognize in him a brother-soul who has suffered, felt, thought, pretty nearly like us. He came into an ending world, on the eve of the great cataclysm which was going to carry away an entire civilization—a tragic turning-point of history, a time troubled and often very grievous, which was hard to live in for all, and to even the most determined minds must have appeared desperate. The peace of the Church was not yet settled; consciences were divided. People hesitated between the belief of yesterday and the belief of to-morrow. Augustine was among those who had the courage to choose, and who, having once chosen their faith, proclaimed it without weakening. The belief of a thousand years was dying out, quenched by a young belief to which was promised an eternal duration. How many delicate souls must have suffered from this division, which cut them off from their traditions and obliged them, as they thought, to be false to their dead along with the religion of their ancestors! All the irritations which the fanatics of to-day inflict upon believing souls, many must have had to suffer then. The sceptics were infused by the intolerance of the others. But the worst (even as it is to-day) was to watch the torrent of foolishness which, under cover of religion, philosophy, or miracle-working, pretended to the conquest of mind and will. Amid this mass of wildest doctrines and heresies, in this orgy of vapid intellectualism, they had indeed solid heads who were able to resist the general intoxication. And among all these people talking nonsense, Augustine appears admirable with his good sense.

This "intellectual," this mystic, was not only a man of prayer and meditation. The prudence of the man of action and the administrator balanced his outbursts of dialectical subtlety, often carried too far. He had that sense of realities such as we flatter ourselves that we have; he had a knowledge of life and passion. Compared to the experience of, say, Bossuet, how much wider was Augustine's! And with all that, a quivering sensitiveness which is again like our own—the sensitiveness of times of intense culture, wherein the abuse of thought has multiplied the ways of suffering in exasperating the desire for pleasure. "The soul of antiquity was rude and vain." It was, above all, limited. The soul of Augustine is tender and serious, eager for certainties and those enjoyments which do not betray. It is vast and sonorous; let it be stirred ever so little, and from it go forth deep vibrations which render the sound of the infinite. Augustine, before his conversion, had the apprehensions of our Romantics, the causeless melancholy and sadness, the immense yearnings for "anywhere but here," which overwhelmed our fathers. He is really very close to us.

He has broadened our Latin souls by reconciling us with the Barbarian. The Latin, like the Greek, only understood himself. The Barbarian had not the right to express himself in the language of the Empire. The world was split into two parts which endeavoured to ignore each other, Augustine has made us conscious of the nameless regions, the vague countries of the soul, which hitherto had lain shrouded in the darkness of barbarism. By him the union of the Semitic and the Occidental genius is consummated. He has acted as our interpreter for the Bible. The harsh Hebraic words become soft to our ears by their passage through the cultivated mouth of the rhetorician. He has subjugated us with the word of God. He is a Latin who speaks to us of Jehovah.

Others, no doubt, had done it before him. But none had found a similar emotion, a note of tenderness so moving. The gentle violence of his charity wins the adherence of hearts. He breathes only charity. After St. John, it is he who is the Apostle of Love.

His tireless voice dominated the whole of the West. The Middle Ages still heard it. For centuries his sermons and treatises were copied over and over again; they were repeated in cathedrals, commented in abstracts of theology. People came to accept even his theory of the fine arts. All that we have inherited from the ancients reaches us through Augustine. He is the great teacher. In his hands the doctrinal demonstration of the Catholic religion takes firm shape. To indicate the three great stages of the onward march of the truth, one may say: Jesus Christ, St. Paul, St. Augustine. Nearest to our weakness is the last. He is truly our spiritual father. He has taught us the language of prayer. The words of Augustine's prayers are still upon the lips of the devout.

This universal genius, who during forty years was the speaking-trumpet of Christendom, was also the man of one special century and country. Augustine of Thagaste is the great African.

Well may we be proud of him and adopt him as one of our glories—we who have kept up, for now almost a century, a struggle like to that which he maintained for the unity of the Roman Empire, we who consider Africa as an extension of France. More than any other writer, he has expressed the temperament and the genius of his country. This motley Africa, with its eternal mixture of races at odds with one another, its jealous sectarianism, the variety of its scenery and climate, the violence of its sensations and passions, its seriousness of character and its quick-changing humour, its mind at once practical and frivolous, its materialism and its mysticism, its austerity and its luxury, its resignation to servitude and its instincts of independence, its hunger to rule—all that comes out with singularly vivid touches in the work of Augustine. Not only was he his country's voice, but, as far as he could, he realized its old dream of dominion. The supremacy in spiritual matters that Carthage disputed so long and bitterly with Rome, it ended by obtaining, thanks to Augustine. As long as he lived, the African Church was the mistress of the Churches of the West.

As for me—if I may venture to refer to myself in such a matter—I have had the joy to recognize in him, besides the Saint and Teacher whom I revere, the ideal type of the Latin of Africa. The image of which I descried the outline long ago through the mirages of the South in following the waggons of my rugged heroes, I have seen at last become definite, grow clear, wax noble and increase to the very heaven, in following the traces of Augustine.

And even supposing that the life of this child of Thagaste, the son of Monnica, were not intermingled so deeply with ours, though he were for us only a foreigner born in a far-off land, nevertheless he would still remain one of the most fascinating and luminous souls who have shone amid our darkness and warmed our sadness—one of the most human and most divine creatures who have trod our highways.

DAYS OF CHILDHOOD

Sed delectabat ludere.
Only, I liked to play.

— *Confessions*, I, 4.

Chapter 1
AN AFRICAN FREE-TOWN SUBJECT TO ROME

Little streets, quite white, which climb up to clay-formed hills deeply furrowed by the heavy winter rains; between the double row of houses, brilliant in the morning sun, glimpses of sky of a very tender blue; here and there, in the strip of deep shade which lies along the thresholds, white figures crouched upon rush-mats—indolent outlines, draped with bright colours, or muffled in rough and sombre wool-stuffs; a horseman who passes, bent almost in two in his saddle, the big hat of the South flung back over his shoulders, and encouraging with his heel the graceful trot of his horse—such is Thagaste as we see it today, and such undoubtedly it appeared to the traveller in the days of Augustine.

Like the French town built upon its ruins, the African free-city lay in a sort of plain taken between three round hills. One of them, the highest one, which is now protected by a *bordj*, must have been defended in old days by a *castellum*. Full-flowing waters moisten the land. To those coming from the stony regions about Constantine and Setif, or the vast bare plain of the Medjerda, Thagaste gives an impression of freshness and cool. It is a laughing place, full of greenery and running water. To the Africans it offers a picture of those northern countries which they have never seen, with its wooded mountains covered by pines and cork trees and ilex. It presents itself as a land of mountain and forest—especially forest. It is a hunter's country. Game is plentiful there

—boar, hare, redwing, quail, partridge. In Augustine's time, wild beasts were apparently more numerous in the district than they are to-day. When he compares his adversaries, the Donatists, to roaring lions, he speaks like a man who knows what a lion is.

To the east and west, wide stretches of woodland, rounded hill-summits, streams and torrents which pour through the valleys and glens —there you have Thagaste and the country round about—the world, in fact, as it revealed itself to the eyes of the child Augustine. But towards the south the verdure grows sparse; arid mountain-tops appear, crushed down as blunted cones, or jutted in slim Tables of the Law; the sterility of the desert becomes perceptible amid the wealth of vegetation. This full-foliaged land has its harsh and stern localities. The African light, however, softens all that. The deep green of the oaks and pines runs into waves of warm and ever-altering tints which are a caress and a delight for the eye. A man has it thoroughly brought home to him that he is in a land of the sun.

To say the least, it is a country of strongly marked features which affords the strangest contrast with the surrounding districts. This wooded Numidia, with its flowing brooks, its fields where the cattle graze, differs in the highest degree from the Numidia towards Setif—a wide, desolate plain, where the stubble of the wheat-fields, the sandy *steppes*, roll away in monotonous undulations to the cloudy barrier of Mount Atlas which closes the horizon. And this rough and melancholy plain in its turn offers a striking contrast with the coast region of Boujeiah and Hippo, which is not unlike the Italian Campania in its mellowness and gaiety. Such clear-cut differences between the various parts of the same province doubtless explain the essential peculiarities of the Numidian character. The bishop Augustine, who carried his pastoral cross from one end to the other of this country, and was its acting and thinking soul, may perhaps have owed to it the contrasts and many-sidedness of his own rich nature.

Of course, Thagaste did not pretend to be a capital. It was a free-town of the second or third order; but its distance from the great centres gave it a certain importance. The neighbouring free-towns, Thubursicum, Thagura, were small. Madaura and Theveste, rather larger, had not perhaps the same commercial importance. Thagaste was placed at the junction of many Roman roads. There the little Augustine, with other children of his age, would have a chance to admire the out-riders and equipages of the Imperial Mail, halted before the inns of the town. What we can be sure of is that Thagaste, then as now, was a town of passage and of traffic, a half-way stopping-place for the southern and coast towns, as well as for those of the Proconsulate and Numidia. And like the present Souk-Ahras, Thagaste must have been above all a market. Bread-stuffs and Numidian wines were bartered for the flocks of the Aures, leather, dates, and the esparto basket-work of the regions of Sahara. The marbles of Simitthu, the citron-wood of which they made precious tables, were doubtless handled there. The neighbouring forests could furnish building materials to the whole country. Thagaste was the great mart of woodland Numidia, the warehouse and the bazaar, where to this day the nomad comes to lay in a stock of provisions, and stares with childish delight at the fine things produced by the inventive talent of the workers who live in towns.

Thus images of plenty and joy surrounded the cradle of Augustine. The smile of Latin beauty welcomed him also from his earliest steps. It is true that Thagaste was not what is called a fine city. The fragments of antiquity which have been unearthed there are of rather inferior workmanship. But how little is needed to give wings to the imagination of an intelligent child! At all events, Thagaste had a bathing-hall paved with mosaics and perhaps ornamented with statues; Augustine used to bathe there with his father. And again, it is probable that, like the neighbouring Thubursicum and other free-cities of the same level, it had its theatre, its forum, its nymph-fountains, perhaps even its amphitheatre. Of all that nothing has been found. Certain inscribed stone tablets, capitals and shafts of columns, a stone with an inscription which belonged to a Catholic church—that is all which has been discovered up to this present time.

Let us not ask for the impossible. Thagaste had columns—nay, perhaps a whole street between a double range of columns, as at Thimgad. That would be quite enough to delight the eyes of a little wondering boy. A column, even injured, or scarcely cleansed from wrack and rubbish, has about it something impressive. It is like a free melody singing among the heavy masses of the building. To this hour, in our Algerian villages, the mere sight of a broken column entrances and cheers us—a white ghost of beauty streaming up from the ruins among the modern hovels.

There were columns at Thagaste.

Chapter 2
THE FAMILY OF A SAINT

It was in this pleasant little town, shaded and beautified for many years now by the arts of Rome, that the parents of Augustine lived.

His father, Patricius, affords us a good enough type of the Romanized African. He belonged to the order of *Decuriones*, to the "very brilliant urban council of Thagaste" (*splendidissimus ordo Thagastensis*), as an inscription at Souk-Ahras puts it. Although these strong epithets may be said to be part of the ordinary official phraseology, they indicate, just the same, the importance which went with such a position. In his township, Patricius was a kind of personage. His son assures us that he was poor, but we may suspect the holy bishop of exaggerating through Christian humility. Patricius must certainly have owned more than twenty-five acres of land, for this was made a condition of being elected to the *curia*. He had vineyards and orchards, of which Augustine later on recalled the plentiful and sweet-tasting fruits. In short, he lived in considerable style. It is true that in Africa household expenses have never at any time been a great extravagance. Still, the sons of Patricius had a pedagogue, a slave specially engaged to keep them under his eye, like all the children of families comfortably off.

It has been said that as Augustine's father was a member of the *curia*, he must have been a ruined man. The Decurions, who levied taxes and made themselves responsible for their collection, were obliged to supply any deficiency in the revenue out of their own money. Patricius, it is thought, must have been one of the numerous victims of this disastrous system. But no doubt there were a good many exceptions. Besides, there is nothing in Augustine's reminiscences which authorizes us to believe that his father ever knew embarrassment, to say nothing of actual poverty. What seems by far the most probable is that he lived as well as he could upon the income of his estate as a small country landowner. In Africa people are satisfied with very little. Save for an unusually bad year following a time of long drought, or a descent of locusts, the land always gives forth enough to feed its master.

To hunt, to ride horseback, now and then to go on parade, to look after his small-holders and agricultural slaves, to drive one of those bargains in which African cunning triumphs—such were the employments of Patricius. In short, he drifted through life on his little demesne. Sometimes this indolent man was overcome by a sudden passion for work; or again he was seized by furious rages. He was violent and brutal. At such moments he struck out right and left. He would even have hit his wife or flogged the skin off her back if the quietude of this woman, her dignity and Christian mildness, had not overawed him. Let us not judge this kind of conduct by our own; we shall never understand it. The ancient customs, especially the African customs, were a disconcerting mixture of intense refinement and heedless brutality.

That is why it will not do to exaggerate the outbursts of Patricius, which his son mentions discreetly. Although he may not have been very faithful to his wife, that was in those days, more than in ours, a venial sin in the eyes of the world. At heart the African has always longed for a harem in his house; he inclines naturally to the polygamy of Muslemism. In Carthage, and elsewhere, public opinion was full of indulgence for the husband who allowed himself liberties with the serving-women. People laughed at it, and excused the man. It is true they were rather harder on the matron who took the same kind of liberty with her men-slaves. However, that went on too. The Bishop of Hippo, in his sermons, strongly rebuked the Christian married couples for these frequent adulteries which were scarcely regarded as errors.

Patricius was a pagan, and this partly explains his laxity. It would doubtless be going too far to say that he remained faithful to paganism all his life. It is not likely that this urban councillor of Thagaste was a particularly assured pagan. Speculative and intellectual considerations made a very moderate appeal to him. He was not an arguer like his son.

He was pagan from habit, from that instinctive conservatism of the citizen and landowner who sticks obstinately to his class and family traditions. Prudence and diplomacy had also something to do with it. Many great landlords continued to defend and practise paganism, probably from motives similar to those of Patricius himself. As for him, he had no desire to get wrong with the important and influential people of the country; he might have need of their protection to save his small property from the ravenous public treasury. Moreover, the best-paid posts were still controlled by the pagan priesthood. And so Augustine's father thought himself very wise in dealing cautiously with a religion which was always so powerful, and rewarded its adherents so well.

But for all that, it is undeniable that paganism about this time was in an awkward position from a political point of view. The Government eyed it with disapproval. Since the death of Constantine, the "accursed emperors" had waged against it a furious war. In 353, just before the birth of Augustine, Constantius promulgated an edict renewing the order for the closing of the temples and the abolition of sacrifices—and that too under pain of death and confiscation. But in distant provinces, such as Numidia, the action of the central power was slow and irregular. It was often represented by officials who were hostile or indifferent to Christianity. The local aristocracy and their following scoffed at it more or less openly. In their immense villas, behind the walls of their parks, the rich landowners offered sacrifices and organized processions and feasts as if there were no law at all. Patricius knew all that. And, on the other side, he could take note of the encroachments of the new religion. During the first half of the fourth century Thagaste had been conquered by the Donatists. Since the edict of Constans against these schismatics, the inhabitants of the little city had come back to Catholicism out of fear of the severity of the imperial government. But the settlement was far from being complete and final. As a consequence of the edict, the whole region of the Aures had been in revolution. The Bishop of Bagai, fortified in his episcopal city and basilica, had stood an actual siege from the Roman troops. Almost everywhere the struggle between Donatists and Catholics still went on below the surface. There cannot be the least doubt that Thagaste took its share in these quarrels. To those who urged him to be baptized, the father of Augustine might well answer with ironic politeness: "I am only waiting till you agree among yourselves, to see where the truth lies." In his heart this rather lukewarm pagan had no inveterate dislike to Christianity.

What proves it at once is that he married a Christian.

How did Monnica become the wife of Patricius? How did these two beings, so little alike, between whom there was such a great difference of age, not to mention all the rest, come to join their fate? Those are questions which it would never have occurred to the people of Thagaste to ask. Patricius married to be like everybody else—and also because he was well over forty, and his mother an old woman who would soon be no longer able to run his house.

Monnica also had her mother. The two old women had a meeting, with many politenesses and ceremonious bowings, and because the thing appeared to them reasonable and most suitable, they settled the marriage. Had Patricius ever seen the girl that he was going to take, according to custom, so as to have a child-bearer and housewife? It is quite likely he had not. Was she pretty, rich, or poor? He considered such matters as secondary, since the marriage was not a love-match but a traditional duty to fulfil. If the union was respectable, that was quite enough. But however the matter fell out, what is certain is that Monnica was very young. She was twenty-two when Augustine was born, and he was probably not her first child. We know that she was hardly marriageable when she was handed over, as Arab parents do to-day with their adolescent or little girls, to the man who was going to marry her. Now in Africa girls become marriageable at a very early age. They are married at fourteen, sometimes even at twelve. Perhaps she was seventeen or eighteen at most when she married Patricius. She must have had first a son, Navigius, whom we shall meet later on at Milan, and also a daughter, of whom we do not even know the name, but who became a nun, and superior of a convent in the diocese of Hippo. For us the features of these two other children of Monnica and Patricius are obliterated. They are concealed by the radiance of their illustrious great brother.

Monnica was fond of telling stories of her girlhood to her son. He has handed down some of them to us.

She was brought up strictly, according to the system of that time. Both her parents came of families which had been Christian, and Catholic-Christian, for many generations. They had never been carried away by the Donatist schism; they were people very obstinate in their convictions—a character quite as frequent in Africa as its opposite, the kind of Numidian or Moor, who is versatile and flighty. It is not unimportant that Augustine came from this hard-headed race, for this it was, with the aid of God's grace, that saved him—the energetic temper of his will.

Still, if the faith of the young Monnica was confirmed from her earliest years, it is not so much to the lessons of her mother that she owed it, as to the training of an old woman-servant of whom she always spoke with gratitude. In the family of her master, this old woman had a place like the one which to-day in a Turkish family is held by the nurse, the *dada*, who is respected by all the harem and all the household. Doubtless she herself was born in the house and had seen all the children born. She had carried Monnica's father on her back when he was little, just as the Kabylian women or the Bedouin nomads carry their babies still. She was a devoted slave, just a bit unreasonable—a veritable housedog who in the zeal of guardianship barks more than is necessary at the stranger who passes. She was like the negress in the Arab houses to-day, who is often a better Muslem, more hostile to the Christian, than her employers. The old woman in Monnica's family had witnessed the last persecutions; she had perhaps visited the confessors in prison; perhaps she had seen flow the blood of the martyrs. These exciting and terrible scenes would have been graven on her memory. What inflamed stories the old servant must have told her young mistresses, what vital lessons of constancy and heroism! Monnica listened to them eagerly.

Because of her great faith, this simple slave was revered as a saint by her owners, who entrusted her with the supervision of their daughters. She proved a stern governess, who would stand no trifling with her rules. She prevented these girls from drinking even water except at meals. Cruel suffering for little Africans! Thagaste is not far from the country of thirst. But the old woman said to them:

"You drink water now because you can't get at the wine. In time to come, when you are married and have bins and cellars of your own, you'll turn up your nose at water, and your habit of drinking will be too much for you."

Monnica came near fulfilling the prophecy of the honest woman. It was before she was married. As she was very well-behaved and very temperate, she used to be sent to the cellar to draw the wine from the cask. Before pouring it into the flagon she would sip just a little. Being unaccustomed to wine, she was not able to drink more; it was too strong for her gullet. She did this, not because she liked the wine, but from naughtiness, to play a trick on her parents who trusted her, and also, of course, because it was prohibited. Each time she swallowed a little more, and so it went on till she ended by finding it rather nice, and came to drinking greedily one cup after another. One day a slave-girl, who went with her to the cellar, began to grumble. Monnica gave her a sharp answer. Upon this the girl called Monnica a drunkard... Drunkard! This bitter taunt so humiliated the self-respect of the future saint, that she got the better of her taste for drink. Augustine does not say it was through piety she did this, but because she felt the ugliness of such a vice.

There is a certain roughness in this story of childhood, the roughness of ancient customs, with which is always mingled some decency or dignity. Christianity did the work of polishing the soul of Monnica. At the time we are dealing with, if she was already a very devout young girl, she was far as yet from being the grand Christian that she became afterwards.

When she married Patricius she was a girl very reserved and cold to all appearances (in reality, she was very passionate), precise in attending to her religious duties, even a little strict, with her exaggeration of the Christian austerity in her hate of all the brutalities and all the careless morals that paganism condoned. Nevertheless, this rigid soul knew how to bend when it was necessary. Monnica had tact, suppleness, and, when it was needed, a very acute and very reasonable practical sense of which she gave many a proof in the bringing up and management of her son Augustine. This soul, hard for herself, veiled her uncompromising religion under an unchangeable sweetness which was in her rather the work of grace than a natural gift.

There can be little doubt that her behaviour and character greatly disturbed Patricius at the beginning of their married life. Perhaps he regretted the marriage. What use had he for this nun alongside of him! Both of them must have suffered the usual annoyances which always appeared before long in unions of this kind between pagan and Christian. True, it was no longer the time of Tertullian, the heroic century of persecutions, when the Christian women glided into the prisons to kiss the shackles of the martyrs. (What a revenge did woman take then for her long and enforced confinement to the women's apartments! And how outrageous such conduct must have seemed to a husband brought up in the Roman way!) But the practices of the Christian life established a kind of intermittent divorce between husbands and wives of different religion. Monnica often went out, either alone, or accompanied by a faithful bondwoman. She had to attend the services of the Church, to go about the town visiting the poor and giving alms. And there were the fast-days which occurred two or three times a week, and especially the long fast of Lent—a grievous nuisance when the husband wanted to give a dinner-party just on those particular days! On the vigil of festivals, Monnica would spend a good part of the night in the Basilica. Regularly, doubtless on Sundays, she betook herself to the cemetery, or to some chapel raised to the memory of a martyr who was often buried there—in fact, they called these chapels "Memorials" (*memoriæ*).

There were many of these chapels—even too many in the opinion of austere Christians. Monnica went from one to another carrying in a large basket made of willow branches some pieces of minced meat, bread, and wine mixed with water. She met her friends in these places. They would sit down around the tombs, of which some were shaped like tables, unpack the provisions, and eat and drink piously in honour of the martyr. This was a residue of pagan superstition among the Christians. These pious *agapæ*, or love-feasts, often turned into disgusting orgies. When Augustine became Bishop of Hippo he had considerable trouble to get his people out of the habit of them. Notwithstanding his efforts, the tradition still lasts. Every Friday the Muslim women keep up the custom of visiting the cemeteries and the marabouts. Just as in the time of St. Monnica, they sit around the tombs, so cool with their casing of painted tiles, in the shade of the cypress and eucalyptus. They gobble sweetmeats, they gossip, they laugh, they enjoy themselves—the husbands are not there.

Monnica made these visits in a really pious state of mind, and was far from trying to find in them opportunities for lewdness or carouse. She was content to drink a little wine very carefully—she always bore in mind her youthful sin. Besides, this wine weakened with water that she brought from the house, was tepid by the time she reached the cemetery; it would be a drink of very moderate relish, little likely to stimulate the senses. She distributed what was left of it among the needy, together with the contents of her basket, and came back modestly to her house.

But however staid and reserved she might be, still these outings gave rise to scandalous talk. They annoyed a suspicious husband. All the Africans are that. Marital jealousy was not invented by Islam. Moreover, in Monnica's time men and women took part in these funeral love-feasts and mingled together disturbingly. Patricius got cross about it, and about a good many other things too. His old mother chafed his suspicions by carrying to him the ugly gossip and even the lies of the servants about his wife. By dint of patience and mildness and attentions, Monnica ended by disarming her mother-in-law and making it clear that her conduct was perfect. The old woman flew into a rage with the servants who had lied to her, and denounced them to her son. Patricius, like a good head of a household, had them whipped to teach them not to lie any more. Thanks to this exemplary punishment, and the good sense of the young wife, peace reigned once more in the family.

Women, friends of Monnica, were amazed that the good understanding was not oftener upset, at least in an open manner, between husband and wife. Everybody in Thagaste knew the quick-tempered and violent character of Patricius. And yet there were no signs that he beat his wife. Nor did any one say he did. Other women who had less passionate husbands were nevertheless beaten by them. When they came to Monnica's house they shewed her the marks of the whacks they had got, their faces swollen from blows, and they burst out in abuse of men, clamouring against their lechery, which, said these matrons, was the cause of the ill-treatment they had to endure.

"Blame your own tongue," retorted Monnica.

According to her, women should close their eyes to the infidelities of their husbands and avoid arguing with them when they were angry. Silence, submissiveness, were the all-powerful arms. And since, as a young woman, she had a certain natural merriment, she added, laughing:

"Remember what was read to you on your wedding-day. You were told that you are the handmaids of your husbands. Don't rebel against your masters!..."

Possibly this was a keen criticism of the pagan code, so hard in its rules. Still, in this matter, the Roman law was in agreement with the Gospel. Sincere Christian as she was, the wife of Patricius never had any quarrel with him on account of his infidelities. So much kindness and resignation touched the dissolute and brutal husband, who besides was an excellent man and warm-hearted. The modesty of his wife, after a while, made her attractive in his eyes. He loved her, so to speak, on the strength of his respect and admiration for her. He would indeed have been a churl to find fault with a wife who interfered with him so little and who was a perfect housekeeper, as we shall see later on when we come to her life at Cassicium. In one point, where even she did not intend it, she forwarded the interests of her husband by gaining him the good-will of the Christians in Thagaste; while he, on his side, could say to the pagans who looked askance at his marriage: "Am I not one of yourselves?"

In spite of all the differences between him and Monnica, Patricius was a contented husband.

Chapter 3
THE COMFORT OF THE MILK

Augustine came into this world the thirteenth of November of the year of Christ 354.

It was just one little child more in this sensual and pleasure-loving Africa, land of sin and of carnal productiveness, where children are born and die like the leaves. But the son of Monnica and Patricius was predestined: he was not to die in the cradle like so many other tiny Africans.

Even if he had not been intended for great things, if he had been only a head in the crowd, the arrival of this baby ought, all the same, to affect us, for to the Christian, the destiny of the obscurest and humblest of souls is a matter of importance. Forty years afterwards, Augustine, in his *Confessions*, pondered this slight ordinary fact of his birth, which happened almost unnoticed by the inhabitants of Thagaste, and in truth it seems to him a great event, not because it concerns himself, bishop and Father of the Church, but because it is a soul which at this imperceptible point of time comes into the world.

Let us clearly understand Augustine's thought. Souls have been ransomed by a Victim of infinite value. They have themselves an infinite value. Nothing which goes on in them can be ignored. Their most trifling sins, their feeblest stirrings towards virtue, are vital for the eternity of their lot. All shall be attributed to them by the just Judge. The theft of an apple will weigh perhaps as heavily in the scales as the seizure of a province or a kingdom. The evil of sin is in the evil intention. Now the fate of a soul, created by God, on Him depends. Hence everything in a human life assumes an extreme seriousness and importance. In the history of a creature, all is worthy of being examined, weighed, studied, and perhaps also, for the edification of others, told.

Here is an altogether new way of regarding life, and, proceeding from that, of understanding art. Even as the slaves, thanks to Christianity, came into the spiritual city, so the most minute realities by this outlook are to be included in literature. The *Confessions* will be the first model of the art of the new era. A deep and magnificent realism, because it goes even to the very depths of the divine—utterly distinct, at any rate, from our surface realism of mere amusement—is about to arise from this new conception. Without doubt, in Augustine's eyes, beauty dwells in all things, in so far forth as beauty is a reflection of the order and the thought of the Word. But it has also a more essential character—it has a moral signification and value. Everything, in a word, can be the instrument of the loss or the redemption of a soul. The most insignificant of our actions reverberates to infinitude on our fate. Regarded from this point, both things and beings commence to live a life more closely leagued together and at the same time more private; more individual and more general. All is in the lump, and nevertheless all is separate. Our salvation concerns only ourselves, and yet through charity it becomes involved with the salvation of our fellows.

In this spirit let us look at the cradle of Augustine. Let us look at it with the eyes of Augustine himself, and also, perchance, of Monnica. Bending over the frail body of the little child he once was, he puts to himself all the great desperate questions which have shaken humanity for thousands of years. The mystery of life and death rises before him, formidable. It tortures him to the point of anguish, of confusion: "Yet suffer me to speak before Thy mercy, me who am but dust and ashes. Yea, suffer me to speak, for, behold, I speak not to man who scorns me, but to Thy mercy. Even Thou perhaps dost scorn me, but Thou wilt turn and have pity. For what is it that I would say, O Lord my God, save that I know not whence I came hither into this dying life, shall I call it, or living death?... And, lo, my infancy has long been dead, and I live. But Thou, O Lord, who ever livest and in whom nothing ever dies—tell me, I beseech Thee, O God, and have mercy on my misery, tell me whether another life of mine died before my infancy began."

One is reminded here of Pascal's famous prosopopoeia: "I know not who has put me into the world, nor what the world is, nor myself. I am in a terrible ignorance about everything... All I know is that I must soon die, but what I know least of all is this very death which I cannot escape."

The phrases of the *Pensées* are only the echo of the phrases of the *Confessions*. But how different is the tone! Pascal's charge against human ignorance is merciless. The God of Port-Royal has the hard and motionless face of the ancient Destiny: He withdraws into the clouds, and only shews Himself at the end to raise up His poor creature. In Augustine the accent is tender, trusting, really like a son, and though he be harassed, one can discern the thrill of an unconquerable hope. Instead of crushing man under the iron hand of the Justice-dealer, he makes him feel the kindness of the Father who has got all ready, long before its birth, for the feeble little child: "The comforts of Thy pity received me, as I have heard from the father and mother of my flesh... And so the comfort of woman's milk was ready for me. For my mother and my nurses did not fill their own bosoms, but Thou, O Lord, by their means gavest me the food of infancy, according to Thy ordinance..."

And see! his heart overflows at this remembrance of his mother's milk. The great doctor humbles his style, makes it simple and familiar, to tell us of his first mewlings, and of his baby angers and joys. He too was a father; he knew what is a new-born child, and a young mother who gives it suck, because he had seen that with his own eyes close beside him. All the small bothers which mingle with the pleasures of fatherhood he had experienced himself. In his own son he studied himself.

This child, born of a Christian mother, and who was to become the great defender of the faith, was not christened at his birth. In the early Church, and especially in the African Church, it was not usual to do so. The baptismal day was put as far off as possible, from the conviction that the sins committed after the sacrament were much more serious than those which went before. The Africans, very practical folk, clearly foresaw that they would sin again even after baptism, but they wanted to sin at a better rate, and lessen the inflictions of penance. This penance in Augustine's time was far from being as hard as in the century before. Nevertheless, the remembrance of the old severity always remained, and the habit was taken to put off baptism so as not to discourage sinners overmuch.

Monnica, always sedulous to conform with the customs of her country and the traditions of her Church, fell in with this practice. Perhaps she may have had also the opposition of her husband to face, for he being a pagan would not have cared to give too many pledges to the Christians, nor to compromise himself in the eyes of his fellow-pagans by shewing that he was so far under the control of Christian zealots as to have his child baptized out of the ordinary way. There was a middle course, and this was to inscribe the child among the catechumens. According to the rite of the first admission to the lowest order of catechumens, the sign of the cross was made on Augustine's forehead, and the symbolic salt placed between his lips. And so they did not baptize him. Possibly this affected his whole life. He lacked the baptismal modesty. Even when he was become a bishop, he never quite cast off the old man that had splashed through all the pagan uncleannesses. Some of his words are painfully broad for chaste ears. The influence of African conditions does not altogether account for this. It is only too plain that the son of Patricius had never known entire virginity of soul.

They named him Aurelius Augustineus. Was Aurelius his family name? We cannot tell. The Africans always applied very fantastically the rules of Roman nomenclature. Anyhow, this name was common enough in Africa. The Bishop of Carthage, primate of the province and a friend of Augustine, was also called Aurelius. Pious commentators have sought to find in this name an omen of Augustine's future renown as an orator. They have remarked that the word *aurum*, gold, is contained in Aurelius—a prophetic indication of the golden mouth of the great preacher of Hippo.

Meanwhile, he was a baby like any other baby, who only knew, as he tells us, how to take his mother's breast. However, he speaks of nurses who suckled him; no doubt these were servants or slaves of the household. They gave him their milk, like those Algerian women who, to-day, if their neighbour is called away, take her child and feed it. Besides, with them children are weaned much later than with us. You can see mothers sitting at their doors put down their work and call to a child of two or three playing in the street for him to come and take the breast. Did Augustine remember these things? At least he recalled his nurses' games, and the efforts they made to appease him, and the childish words they taught him to stammer. The first Latin words he repeated, he picked up from his mother and the servants, who must also have spoken Punic, the ordinary tongue of the populace and small trader class. He learned Punic without thinking about it, in playing with other children of Thagaste, just as the sons of our colonists learn Arab in playing with little boys who wear chechias on their heads.

He is a Christian, a bishop, already a venerated Father, consulted by the whole Catholic world, and he tells us all that. He tells it in a serious and contrite way, with a manifest anxiety to attribute to God, as the sole cause, all the benefits which embellished his childhood, as well as to deplore his faults and wretchedness, fatal consequence of the original Fall. And still, we can make out clearly that these suave and far-off memories have a charm for him which he cannot quite guard himself against. The attitude of the author of the *Confessions* is ambiguous and a little constrained. The father who has loved his child, who has joined in his games, struggles in him against the theologian who later on was to uphold the doctrine of Grace against the heretics. He feels that he must shew, not only that Grace is necessary for salvation and that little children ought to be baptized, but that they are capable of sinning. Yes, the children sin even at nurse. And Augustine relates this story of a baby that he had seen: "I know, because I have seen, jealousy in a babe. It could not speak, yet it eyed its foster-brother *with pale cheeks and looks of hate.*" Children are already men. The egoism and greediness of the grown man may be already descried in the newly born.

However, the theologian of Grace was not able to drive from his mind this verse of the Gospel: *Sinite ad me parvulos venire*—"Suffer little children to come unto Me." But he interprets this in a very narrow sense, luring it into an argument which furthers his case. For him, the small height of children is a symbol of the humility without which no one can enter God's kingdom. The Master, according to him, never intended us to take children as an example. They are but flesh of sin. He only drew from their littleness one of those similitudes which He, with His fondness for symbols, favoured.

Well, let us dare to say it: Augustine goes wrong here. Such is the penalty of human thought, which in its justest statements always wounds some truth less clear or mutilates some tender sentiment. Radically, Augustine is right. The child is wicked as man is. We know it. But against the relentlessness of the theologian we place the divine gentleness of Christ: "Suffer little children to come unto Me, for of such is the Kingdom of God."

Chapter 4
THE FIRST GAMES

"I loved to play," Augustine says, in telling us of those far-off years.
Is it surprising if this quick and supple intelligence, who mastered without effort, and as if by instinct, the encyclopædic knowledge of his age, who found himself at his ease amidst the deepest abstractions, did, at the beginning, take life as a game?

The amusements of the little Africans of to-day are not very many, nor very various either. They have no inventive imagination. In this matter their French playfellows have taught them a good deal. If they play marbles, or hopscotch, or rounders, it is in imitation of the *Roumis*. And yet they are great little players. Games of chance attract them above all. At these they spend hour after hour, stretched out flat on their stomachs in some shady corner, and they play with an astonishing intensity of passion. All their attention is absorbed in what they are about; they employ on the game all the cunning of their wits, precociously developed, and so soon stuck fast in material things.

When Augustine recalls the games of his childhood, he only mentions "nuts," handball, and birds. To capture a bird, that winged, light, and brilliant thing, is what all children long to do in every country on earth. But in Africa, where there are plenty of birds, big people as well as little love them. In the Moorish cafés, in the wretchedest *gourbis*, cages made of reeds are hung on the walls, all rustling with trills and fluttering of wings. Quail, thrushes, nightingales are imprisoned in them.

The nightingale, the singing-bird beyond all others, so difficult to tame, is the honoured guest, the privileged dweller in these rustic cages. With the rose, he is an essential part of Arab poetry. The woods round about Thagaste were full of nightingales. Not the least doubt that the child Augustine had felt the little musical throats of these singing-birds throb between his hands. His sermons, his heaviest treatises, have a recollection of them. He draws from them an evidence in favour of the creating Word who has put beauty and harmony everywhere. In the song of the nightingale he finds, as it were, an echo of the music of the spheres.

If he loved birds, as a poet who knows not that he is a poet, did he love as well to play at "nuts"? "Nuts," or thimble-rigging, is only a graceful and crafty game, too crafty for a dreaming and careless little boy. It calls for watchfulness and presence of mind. Grown men play at it as well as children. A step of a staircase is used as a table by the players, or the pavement of a courtyard. Three shells are laid on the stone and a dried pea. Then, with rapid baffling movements, hands brown and alert fly from one shell to another, shuffle them, mix them up, juggle the dried pea sometimes under this shell, sometimes under that,—and the point is to guess which shell the pea has got under. By means of certain astute methods, an artful player can make the pea stick to his fingers, or to the inside of the shell, and the opponent loses every time. They cheat with a calm shamelessness. Augustine cheated too—which did not prevent him from bitterly denouncing the cheating of his fellow-players.

The truth is, that he would not have quite belonged to his country if he had not lied and stolen now and then. He lied to his tutor and to his schoolmasters. He stole at his parents' table, in the kitchen, and in the cellar. But he stole like a man of quality, to make presents and to win over his playfellows: he ruled the other boys by his presents—a noteworthy characteristic in this future ruler of souls. Morals like these, a little rough, shape free and bold natures. Those African children were much less coddled, much less scolded, than to-day. Monnica had something else to do than to look after the boys. So for them it was a continual life in the open air, which makes the body strong and hard. Augustine and his companions should be pictured as young wild-cats.

This roughness came out strong at games of ball, and generally at all the games in which there are two sides, conquerors and prisoners, or fights with sticks and stones. Stone-throwing is an incurable habit among the little Africans. Even now in the towns our police are obliged to take measures against these ferocious children. In Augustine's time, at Cherchell, which is the ancient *Cæsarea Mauretaniæ*, the childish population was split into two hostile camps which stoned each other. On certain holidays the fathers and big brothers joined the children; blood flowed, and there were deaths.

The bishop Augustine recalls with severity the "superb victories" he won in jousts of this kind. But I find it hard to believe that such a delicate child (he was sickly almost all his life) could have got much pleasure out of these brutal sports. If he was drawn into them by the example of others, it must have been through the imagination they appealed to him. In these battles, wherein sides took the field as Romans against Carthaginians, Greeks against Trojans, he believed himself Scipio or Hannibal, Achilles or Hector. He experienced beforehand, as a rhetorician, the intoxication of a triumph which playfellows who were stronger and better provided with muscles gave him a hard fight for. He did not always get the upper hand, except perhaps when he bribed the enemy. But an eager young soul, such as he was, can hardly be content with half-victories; he wants to excel. Accordingly, he sought his revenge in those games wherein the mind has the chief part. He listened to stories with delight, and in his turn repeated them to his little friends, thus trying upon an audience of boys that charm of speech by which later he was to subdue crowds. They also played at acting, at gladiators, at drivers and horses. Some of Augustine's companions were sons of wealthy citizens who gave splendid entertainments to their fellow-countrymen. As these dramatic representations, or games of the arena or circus, drew near, the little child-world was overcome by a fever of imitation. All the children of Thagaste imitated the actors, the *mirmillones*, or the horsemen in the amphitheatre, just as the young Spaniards of to-day imitate the *toreros*.

In the midst of these amusements Augustine fell ill; he had fever and violent pains in the stomach. They thought he was going to die. It appears that it was himself who in this extreme situation asked for baptism. Monnica was making all haste to have the sacrament administered, when suddenly, against all expectation, the child recovered. Again was baptism postponed, and from the same reason: to lessen the gravity of the sins which young Augustine was bound to commit. His mother, who no doubt foresaw some of them, again fell in with the custom.

It is possible that Patricius interfered this time in a more decided way. Just at this period Catholicism was in an unfavourable situation. The short reign of Julian had started a violent pagan reaction. Everywhere the temples were reopening, the sacrifices beginning again. Moreover, the Donatists secretly aided the pagans. Their *Seids*, more or less acknowledged, the Circoncelliones, bands of fanatical peasants, scoured through the Numidian country, attacking the Catholics, ravaging and pillaging, and burning their farms and villas. Was this a good time to make a noisy profession of faith, to be enrolled among the ranks of the conquered party?

Little Augustine knew nothing of all these calculations of motherly prudence and fatherly diplomacy: he begged for baptism, so he tells us. This seems very remarkable in so young a child. But he lived in a house where all the service was done by Christians. He heard the talk of Monnica's friends; perhaps, too, of his grandparents, who were Catholics faithful and austere. And then, his soul was naturally religious. That explains everything: he asked for baptism to be like grown-up people, and because he was predestined. Among children, the chosen have these sudden flashes of light. At certain moments they feel what one day they shall be. Anyhow, Monnica must have seen this sign with joy.

He got well, and took up again his little boy's life, divided between play, and dawdling, and school.

School! painful memory for Augustine! They sent him to the *primus magister*, the elementary teacher, a real terror, armed with a long switch which came down without pity on idle boys. Seated on benches around him, or crouched on mats, the boys sang out all together: "One and one are two, two and two are four"—horrible refrain which deafened the whole neighbourhood. The school was often a mere shed, or a *pergola* in the fields which was protected fairly well from sun and rain by cloths stretched overhead—a hut rented for a trifle, wide open to the winds, with a mosquito-net stretched out before the entrance. All who were there must have frozen in winter and broiled in summer. Augustine remembered it as a slaves' chain-prison (*ergastulum*) of boyhood.

He hated school and what they taught there—the alphabet, counting, and the rudiments of Latin and Greek grammar. He had a perfect horror of lessons—of Greek above all. This schoolboy, who became, when his turn came, a master, objected to the methods of school. His mind, which grasped things instinctively at a single bound, could not stand the gradual procedure of the teaching faculty. He either mastered difficulties at once, or gave them up. Augustine was one of the numerous victims of the everlasting mistake of schoolmasters, who do not know how to arrange their lessons to accord with various kinds of mind. Like most of those who eventually become great men, he was no good as a pupil. He was often punished, thrashed—and cruelly thrashed. The master's scourge filled him with an unspeakable terror. When he was smarting all over from cuts and came to complain to his parents, they laughed at him or made fun of him—yes, even the pious Monnica. Then the poor lad, not knowing whom to turn to, remembered hearing his mother and the servants talk of a Being, very powerful and very good, who defends the orphan and the oppressed. And he said from the depths of his heart:

"O my God, please grant that I am not whipped at school."

But God did not hear his prayer because he was not a good boy. Augustine was in despair.

It is evident that these punishments were cruel, because forty years afterwards he denounces them with horror. In his mind, they are tortures comparable to the wooden horse or the iron pincers. Nothing is small for children, especially for a sensitive child like Augustine. Their sensitiveness and their imagination exaggerate all things out of due measure. In this matter, also, schoolmasters often go wrong. They do not know how to handle delicate organizations. They strike fiercely, when a few words said at the right moment would have much more effect on the culprit... Monnica's son suffered as much from the rod as he took pride in his successes at games. If, as Scipio, he was filled with a sensation of glory in his battles against other boys, no doubt he pictured himself a martyr, a St. Laurence or St. Sebastian, when he was swished. He never pardoned—save as a Christian—his schoolmasters for having brutalized him.

Nevertheless, despite his hatred for ill-ordered lessons, his precocious intelligence was remarked by everybody. It was clear that such lucky gifts should not be neglected. Monnica, no doubt, was the first to get this into her head, and she advised Patricius to make Augustine read for a learned profession.

The business of the *curia* was not exactly brilliant, and so he may have perceived that his son might raise their fortunes if he had definite employment. Augustine, a professor of eloquence or a celebrated pleader, might be the saviour and the benefactor of his family. The town councils, and even the Imperial treasury, paid large salaries to rhetoricians. In those days, rhetoric led to everything. Some of the professors who went from town to town giving lectures made considerable fortunes. At Thagaste they pointed with admiration to the example of the rhetorician Victorinus, an African, a fellow-countryman, who had made a big reputation over-seas, and had his statue in the Roman Forum. And many years before, had not M. Cornelius Fronto, of Cirta, another African, become the tutor of Marcus Aurelius, who covered him with honours and wealth and finally raised him to the Consulship? Pertinax himself, did he not begin as a simple teacher of grammar, and become Proconsul of Africa and then Emperor of Rome? How many stimulants for provincial ambition!...

Augustine's parents reasoned as the middle-class parents of to-day. They discounted the future, and however hard up they were, they resolved to make sacrifices for his education. And as the schools of Thagaste were inadequate, it was decided to send this very promising boy to Madaura.

Chapter 5
THE SCHOOLBOY OF MADAURA

A new world opened before Augustine. It was perhaps the first time he had ever gone away from Thagaste.

Of course, Madaura is not very far off; there are about thirty miles at most between the two towns. But there are no short journeys for children. This one lay along the military road which ran from Hippo to Theveste—a great Roman causeway paved with large flags on the outskirts of towns, and carefully pebbled over all the rest of the distance. Erect upon the high saddle of his horse, Augustine, who was to become a tireless traveller and move about ceaselessly over African roads during all his episcopal life—Augustine got his first glimpse of the poetry of the open road, a poetry which we have lost for ever.

How amusing they were, the African roads of those days, how full of sights! Pauses were made at inns with walls thick as the ramparts of citadels, their interiors bordered by stables built in arcades, heaped up with travellers' packs and harness. In the centre were the trough and cistern; and to the little rooms opening in a circle on to the balcony, drifted up a smell of oil and fodder, and the noise of men and of beasts of burthen, and of the camels as they entered majestically, curving their long necks under the lintel of the door. Then there was talk with the merchants, just arrived from the south, who brought news of the nomad countries, and had stories to tell. And then, without hurrying, a start was made again for the next stage. Long files of chariots were encountered carrying provisions to soldiers garrisoned on the frontier, or the State-distributed corn of the Roman people to the sea-ports; or again, from time to time, the *lectica*, brought along by slaves or mules, of a bishop on a visitation; and then the litter, with close-drawn curtains, of a matron or some great personage. Of a sudden all pulled sharp to one side; the vehicles lined up on the edge of the road; and there passed at full speed, in a cloud of dust, a messenger of the Imperial Post...

Certainly this road from Hippo to Theveste was one of the busiest and most picturesque in the province: it was one of its main arteries.

At first the look of the country is rather like the neighbourhood of Thagaste. The wooded and mountainous landscape still spreads out its little breast-shaped hills and its sheets of verdure. Here and there the road skirts the deeply-ravined valley of the Medjerda. At the foot of the precipitous slopes, the river can be heard brawling in a torrent over its stony bed, and there are sharp descents among thickets of juniper and the fringed roots of the dwarf-pines. Then, as the descent continues, the land becomes thinner and spaces bare of vegetation appear oftener. At last, upon a piece of tableland, Madaura comes into view, all white in the midst of the vast tawny plain, where to-day nothing is to be seen but a mausoleum in ruins, the remains of a Byzantine fortress, and vague traces vanishing away.

This is the first rise of the great plain which declines towards Theveste and the group of the Aures Mountains. Coming from the woodland country of Thagaste, the nakedness of it is startling. Here and there, thin cows crop starveling shrubs which have grown on the bank of some *oued* run dry. Little asses, turned loose, save themselves at a gallop towards the tents of the nomads, spread out, black and hairy, like immense bats on the whiteness of the land. Nearer, a woman's red *haick* interposes, the single stain of bright colour breaking the indefinite brown and grey of the plain. Here is felt the harshness of Numidia; it is almost the stark spaces of the desert world. But on the side towards the east, the architecture of mountains, wildly sculptured, stands against the level reaches of the horizon. Upon the clear background of the sky, shew, distinctly, lateral spurs and a cone like to the mystic representation of Tanit. Towards the south, crumbling isolated crags appear, scattered about like gigantic pedestals uncrowned of their statues, or like the pipes of an organ raised there to capture and attune the cry of the great winds of the *steppe*.

This country is characterized by a different kind of energy from Thagaste. There is more air and light and space. If the plantation is sparse, the beautiful shape of the land may be observed all the better. Nothing breaks or lessens the grand effects of the light... And let no one say that Augustine's eyes cared not for all that, he who wrote after his conversion, and in all the austerity of his repentance: "If sentient things had not a soul, we should not love them so much."

It is here, between Madaura and Thagaste, during the eager years of youth, that he gathered together the seeds of sensations and images which, later on, were to burst forth into fiery and boiling metaphors in the *Confessions*, and in his homilies and paraphrases of Holy Scripture. Later on, he will not have the time to observe, or he will have lost the power. Rhetoric will stretch its commonplace veil between him and the unceasing springtide of the earth. Ambition will turn him away from those sights which reveal themselves only to hearts unselfish and indifferent. Then, later on, Faith will seize hold of him to the exclusion of all else. He will no longer perceive the creation save at odd moments in a kind of metaphysical dream, and, so to speak, across the glory of the Creator. But in these youthful years all things burst upon him with extraordinary violence and ecstasy. His undulled senses swallowed greedily the whole banquet offered by this wide world to his hunger for pleasure. The fugitive beauty of things and beings, with all their charms, revealed itself to him in its newness: *novissimarum rerum fugaces pulchritudines, earumque suavitates.* This craving for sensation will still exist in the great Christian teacher, and betray itself in the warm and coloured figures of his style. Of course, he was not as a worldly describer, who studies to produce phrases which present an image, or arranges glittering pictures—all such endeavours he knew nothing about. But by instinct, and thanks to his warm African temperament, he was a kind of impressionist and metaphysical poet.

If the rural landscape of Thagaste is reflected in certain passages—the pleasantest and most well known—of the *Confessions*, all the intellectual part of Augustine's work finds its symbolical commentary here in this arid and light-splashed plain of Madaura. Like it, the thought of Augustine has no shadows. Like it too, it is lightened by strange and splendid tints which seem to come from far off, from a focal fire invisible to human eyes. No modern writer has better praised the light—not only the immortal light of the blessed, but that light which rests on the

African fields, and is on land and sea; and nobody has spoken of it with more amplitude and wonder. The truth is, that in no country in the world, not even in Egypt, in the rose-coloured lands of Karnak and Luxor, is the light more pure and admirable than in these great bare plains of Numidia and the region of the Sahara. Is there not enchantment for the eyes of the metaphysician in this play of light, these nameless interfulgent colours which appear flimsy as the play of thought? For the glowing floating haze is made of nothing—of lines, of gleam, of unregulated splendour. And all this triumph of fluctuating light and elusive colour is quenched with the sun, smoulders into darkness, even as ideas in the obscure depths of the intelligence which reposes...

Not less than this land, stern even to sadness, but hot and sumptuous, the town of Madaura must have impressed Augustine.

It was an old Numidian city, proud of its antiquity. Long before the Roman conquest, it had been a fortress of King Syphax. Afterwards, the conquerors settled there, and in the second century of our era, Apuleius, the most famous of its children, could state before a proconsul, not without pride, that Madaura was a very prosperous colony. It is probable that this old town was not so much Romanized as its neighbours, Thimgad and Lambesa, which were of recent foundation and had been built all at once by decree of the Government. But it may well have been as Roman as Theveste, a no less ancient city, where the population was probably just as mixed. Madaura, like Theveste, had its temples with pillars and Corinthian porticoes, its triumphal arches (these were run up everywhere), its forum surrounded by a covered gallery and peopled with statues. Statues also were very liberally distributed in those days. We know of at least three at Madaura which Augustine mentions in one of his letters: A god Mars in his heroic nakedness, and another Mars armed from head to foot; opposite, the statue of a man, in realistic style, stretching out three fingers to neutralize the evil eye. These familiar figures remained very clear in the recollection of Augustine. In the evening, or at the hour of the siesta, he had stretched himself under their pedestals and played at dice or bones in the cool shade of the god Mars, or of the Man with outstretched fingers. The slabs of marble of the portico made a good place to play or sleep.

Among these statues, there was one perhaps which interested the lad and stimulated all his early ambitions—that of Apuleius, the great man of Madaura, the orator, philosopher, sorcerer, who was spoken of from one end to the other of Africa. By dint of gazing at this, and listening to the praises of the great local author, did the young scholar become aware of his vocation? Did he have from this time a confused sort of wish to become one day another Apuleius, a Christian Apuleius —to surpass the reputation of this celebrated pagan? These impressions and admirations of youth have always a more or less direct influence upon what use a boy makes of his talents.

Be that as it will, Augustine could not take a step in Madaura without running against the legend of Apuleius, who was become almost a divinity for his fellow-countrymen. He was looked upon not only as a sage, but as a most wily nigromancer. The pagans compared him to Christ—nay, put him higher than Christ. In their view he had worked much more astonishing miracles than those of Jesus or of Apollonius of Tyana. And people told the extravagant stories out of his *Metamorphoses* as real, as having actually happened. Nothing was seen on all sides but wizards, men changed into animals, animals, or men and women, under some spell. In the inns, a man watched with a suspicious look the ways of the maidservant who poured out his drink or handed him a dish. Perhaps some magic potion was mingled with the cheese or bread that she was laying on the table. It was an atmosphere of feverish and delirious credulity. The pagan madness got the better of the Christians themselves. Augustine, who had lived in this atmosphere, will later find considerable trouble in maintaining his strong common sense amid such an overflow of marvels.

For the moment, the fantasy of tales filled him with at least as much enthusiasm as the supernatural. At Madaura he lived in a miraculous world, where everything charmed his senses and his mind, and everything stimulated his precocious instinct for Beauty.

More than Thagaste, no doubt, Madaura bore the marks of the building genius of the Romans. Even to-day their descendants, the Italians, are the masons of the world, after having been the architects. The Romans were the building nation above all others. They it was who raised and established towns upon the same model and according to the same ideal as an oration or a poem. They really invented the house, *mansio*, not only the shelter where one lives, but the building which itself lives, which triumphs over years and centuries, a huge construction ornamental and sightly, existing as much—and perhaps more—for the delight of the eyes as for usefulness. The house, the *Town-with-deep-*

streets, perfectly ordered, were a great matter of amazement for the African nomad—he who passes and never settles down anywhere. He hated them, doubtless, as the haunts of the soldier and the publican, his oppressors, but he also regarded them with admiration mixed with jealousy as the true expression of a race which, when it entered a country, planted itself for eternity, and claimed to join magnificence and beauty to the manifestation of its strength. The Roman ruins which are scattered over modern Algeria humiliate ourselves by their pomp—us who flatter ourselves that we are resuming the work of the Empire and continuing its tradition. They are a permanent reproach to our mediocrity, a continual incitement to grandeur and beauty. Of course, the Roman architecture could not have had on Augustine, this still unformed young African, the same effect as it has to-day on a Frenchman or a man from Northern Europe. But it is certain that it formed, without his knowledge, his thought and his power of sensation, and extended for him the lessons of the Latin rhetoricians and grammarians.

All that was not exactly very Christian. But from these early school years Augustine got further and further away from Christianity, and the examples he had under his eyes, at Madaura were hardly likely to strengthen him in his faith. It was hardly an edifying atmosphere there for a Catholic youth who had a lively imagination, a pleasure-loving temperament, and who liked pagan literature. The greatest part of the population were pagans, especially among the aristocrats. The Decurions continued to preside at festivals in honour of the old idols.

These festivals were frequent. The least excuse was taken to engarland piously the doors of houses with branches, to bleed the sacrificial pig, or slaughter the lamb. In the evening, squares and street corners were illuminated. Little candles burned on all the thresholds. During the mysteries of Bacchus, the town councillors themselves headed the popular rejoicings. It was an African carnival, brutal and full of colour. People got tipsy, pretended they were mad. For the sport of the thing, they assaulted the passers and robbed them. The dull blows on tambourines, the hysterical and nasal preludes of the flutes, excited an immense elation, at once sensual and mystic. And all quieted down among the cups and leather flagons of wine, the grease and meats of banquets in the open air. Even in a country as sober as Africa, the pagan feasts were never much else than excuses for gorging and orgies. Augustine, who after his conversion had only sarcasms for the carnival of Madaura, doubtless went with the crowd, like many other Christians. Rich and influential people gave the example. There was danger of annoying them by making a group apart. And then, there was no resisting the agreeableness of such festivals.

Perhaps he was even brought to these love-feasts by those in whose charge he was. For, in fact, to whom had he been entrusted? Doubtless to some host of Patricius, a pagan like himself. Or did he lodge with his master, a grammarian, who kept a boarding-house for the boys? Almost all these schoolmasters were pagan too. Is it wonderful that the Christian lessons of Monnica and the nurses at Thagaste became more and more blurred in Augustine's mind? Many years after, an old Madaura grammarian, called Maximus, wrote to him in a tone of loving reproach: "Thou hast drawn away from us"—*a secta nostra deviasti*. Did he wish to hint that at this time Augustine had glided into paganism? Nothing is more unlikely. He himself assures us that the name of Christ remained always "graven on his heart." But while he was at Madaura he lived indifferently with pagans and Christians.

Besides that, the teaching he got was altogether pagan in tone. No doubt he picked out, as he always did, the subjects which suited him. Minds such as his fling themselves upon that which is likely to nourish them: they throw aside all the rest, or suffer it very unwillingly. Thus Augustine never wavered in his dislike for Greek: he was a poor Greek scholar. He detested the Greeks by instinct. According to Western prejudice, these men of the East were all rascals or amusers. Augustine, as a practical African, always regarded the Greeks as vain, discoursing wits. In a word, they were not sincere people whom it would be safe to trust. The entirely local patriotism of the classical Greek authors further annoyed this Roman citizen who was used to regard the world as his country: he thought them very narrow-minded to take so much interest in the history of some little town. As for him, he looked higher and farther. It must be remembered that in the second half of the fourth century the Greek attitude, broadened and fully conscious of itself, set itself more and more against Latinism, above all, politically. There it lay, a hostile and impenetrable block before the Western peoples. And here was a stronger reason for a Romanized African to dislike the Greeks.

So he painfully construed the *Iliad* and *Odyssey*, very cross at the difficulties of a foreign language which prevented him from grasping the plots of the fine, fabulous narratives. There were, however, abridgments used in the schools, a kind of summaries of the Trojan War, written by Latin grammarians under the odd pseudonyms of Dares the Phrygian and Dictys of Crete. But these abridgments were very dry for an imagination like Augustine's. He much preferred the *Æneid*, the poem admired above all by the Africans, on account of the episode devoted to the foundation of Carthage. Virgil was his passion. He read and re-read him continually; he knew him by heart. To the end of his life, in his severest writings, he quoted verses or whole passages out of his much-loved poet. Dido's adventure moved him to tears. They had to pluck the book out of his hands.

Now the reason is that there was a secret harmony between Virgil's soul and the soul of Augustine. Both were gracious and serious. One, the great poet, and one, the humble schoolboy, they both had pity on the Queen of Carthage, they would have liked to save her, or at any rate to mitigate her sadness, to alter a little the callousness of Æneas and the harshness of the Fates. But think of it! Love is a divine sickness, a chastisement sent by the gods. It is just, when all's said, that the guilty one should endure her agony to the very end. And then, such very great things are going to arise out of this poor love! Upon it depends the lot of two Empires. What counts a woman before Rome and Carthage? Besides, she was bound to perish: the gods had decreed it... There was in all that a concentrated emotion, a depth of sentiment, a religious appeal which stirred Augustine's heart, still unaware of itself. This obedience of the Virgilian hero to the heavenly will, was already an adumbration of the humility of the future Christian.

Certainly, Augustine did not perceive very plainly in these turbid years of his youth the full religious significance of Virgil's poem. Carried away by his headstrong nature, he yielded to the heart-rending charm of the romantic story: he lived it, literally, with the heroine. When his schoolmasters desired him to elaborate the lament of the dying Queen Dido in Latin prose, what he wrote had a veritable quiver of anguish. Without the least defence against lust and the delusions of the heart, he spent intellectually and in a single outburst all the strength of passion.

He absorbed every love-poem with the eagerness of a participating soul. If he took pleasure in the licentiousness of Plautus and Terence, if he read delightfully those comedies wherein the worst weaknesses are excused and glorified, I believe that he took still more pleasure in the

Latin Elegiacs who present without any shame the romantic madness of Alexandrine love. For what sing these poets even to weariness, unless it be that no one can resist the Cyprian goddess, that life has no other end but love? Love for itself, to love for the sake of loving—there is the constant subject of these sensualists, of Catullus, Propertius, Tibullus, Ovid. After the story of Dido, the youthful reader was ravished by the story of Ariadne, even more disturbing, because no remorse modifies the frenzy of it. He read:

Now while the careless hero flees, beating the wave with his and casting to the gales of the open sea his idle promises,—there, standing among the shingle of the beach, the daughter of Minos follows him, alas! with her beautiful sad eyes: she stares, astonied, like to a Bacchante changed into a statue. She looks forth, and her heart floats upon the great waves of her grief. She lets slip from her head her fine-spun coif, she tears away the thin veils which cover her bosom, and the smooth cincture which supports her quivering breasts. All that slips from her body into the salt foam which ripples round her feet. But little she cares for her coif or for her apparel carried away by the tide! Lost, bewildered, with all her heart and all her soul, she is clinging to thee, O Theseus.

And if Augustine, when he had read these burning verses of Catullus, looked through the Anthologies which were popular in the African schools, he would come upon "The Vigil of Venus," that eclogue which ends with such a passionate cry:

O my springtime, when wilt thou come? When shall I be as the swallow? When shall I cease to be silent?... May he love to-morrow, he has not loved yet. And he who has already loved, may he love again to-morrow.

Imagine the effect of such exhortations on a youth of fifteen! Truly, this springtide of love, which the poet cries for in his distress, the son of Monnica knew well was come for him. How he must have listened to the musical and melancholy counsellor who told his pain to the leaves of the book! What stimulant and what food for his boyish longings and dreams! And what a divine chorus of beauties the great love-heroines of ancient epic and elegy, Helen, Medea, Ariadne, Phædra, formed and reformed continually in his dazzled memory! When we of to-day read such verses at Augustine's age, some bitterness is mixed with our delight. These heroes and heroines are too far from us. These almost chimerical beings withdraw from us into outlying lands, to a vanished world which will never come again. But for Augustine, this was the world he was born into—it was his pagan Africa where pleasure was the whole of life, and one lived only for the lusts of the flesh. And the race of fabulous princesses—they were not dead, those ladies: they were ever waiting for the well-beloved in the palaces at Carthage. Yes, the scholar of Madaura lived wonderful hours, dreaming thus of love between the pages of the poets. These young dreams before love comes are more bewitching than love itself: a whole unknown world suddenly discovered and entered with a quivering joy of discovery at each step. The unused strength of illusion appears inexhaustible, space becomes deeper and the heart more strong...

A long time afterwards, when, recovered from all that, Augustine speaks to us of the Divine love, he will know fully the infinite value of it from having gone through all the painful entrancements of the other. And he will say to us, with the sureness of experience: "The pleasure of the human heart in the light of truth and the abundance of wisdom—yea, the pleasure of the human heart, of the faithful heart, and of the heart which is holy, stands alone. You will find nothing in any voluptuousness fit to be compared to it. I say not that this other pleasure is less, for that which is called less hath only to increase to become equal. No, I shall not say that all other pleasure is less. No comparison can be made. It is another kind, it is another reality."

Chapter 6
THE HOLIDAYS AT THAGASTE

In the city of Apuleius, the Christian Monnica's son became simply a pagan. He was near his sixteenth year: the awkward time of early virility was beginning for him. Prepared at Madaura, it suddenly burst out at Thagaste.

Augustine came back to his parents, no doubt during the vacation. But this vacation lasted perhaps a whole year. He had come to the end of his juvenile studies. The grammarians at Madaura could teach him nothing more. To round off his acquirements, it would be necessary to attend the lectures of some well-known rhetorician. Now there were very good rhetoricians only at Carthage. Besides, it was a fashion, and point of honour, for Numidian families to send their sons to finish their education in the provincial capital. Patricius was most eager to do this for his son, who at Madaura had shewn himself a very brilliant pupil and ought not therefore to be pulled up half-way down the course. But the life of a student cost a good deal, and Patricius had no money. His affairs were always muddled. He was obliged to wait for the rents from his farms, to grind down his tenants, and, ultimately, despairing of any other way out of it, to ask for an advance of money from a rich patron. That needed time and diplomacy.

Days and months went by, and Augustine, with nothing to do, joined in with easily-made friends and gave himself up to the pleasures of his time of life, like all the young townsmen of Thagaste—pleasures rather rough and little various, such as were to be got in a little free-town of those days, and as they have remained for the natives of to-day, whether they live a town or country life. To hunt, to ride horseback, to play at games of chance, to drink, eat, and make love—they wanted nothing beyond that. When Augustine in his *Confessions* accuses himself of his youthful escapades he uses the most scathing language. He speaks of them with horror and disgust. Once more we are tempted to believe that he exaggerates through an excess of Christian remorse. There are even some who, put on their guard by this vehement tone, have questioned the historical value of the *Confessions*. They argue that when the Bishop of Hippo wrote these things his views and feelings had altered. He could no longer judge with the same eye and in the same spirit the happenings of his youth. All this is only too certain: when he wrote, it was as a Christian he judged himself, and not as a cold historian who refuses to go beyond the brutal fact. He tried to unravel the origin and to trace the consequences of the humblest of his actions, because this is of the highest importance for salvation. But however severe his judgment may be, it does not impair the reality of the fact itself. Moreover, in natures like his, acts which others would hardly think of have a vibration out of all proportion with the act itself. The evil of sin depends upon the consciousness of the sin and the pleasure taken in it. Augustine was very intelligent and very sensual.

In any case, young Africans develop early, and the lechery of the race is proverbial. It must have been a good deal stronger at a time when Christianity still had to fight against pagan slackness in these matters, ere Islam had imposed its hypocritical austerity upon the general conduct. There is even room for wonder that in Augustine's case this crisis of development did not happen earlier than his sixteenth year. It seems that it was only more violent. In what language he describes it! "I dared to roam the woods and pursue my vagrant loves beneath the shade." But he was not yet in love—this he points out himself. In his case then it was simple lust. "From the quagmire of concupiscence, from the well of puberty, exhaled a mist which clouded and befogged my heart, so that I could not distinguish between the clear shining of affection and the darkness of lust... I could not keep within the kingdom of light, where friendship binds soul to soul... And so I polluted the brook of friendship with the sewage of lust." Let us not try to make it clearer than he has left it himself. When one thinks of all the African vices, one dare not dwell upon such avowals. "Lord," he says, "I was loathsome in Thy sight." And with pitiless justice he analyses the effect of the evil: "It stormed confusedly within me, whirling my thoughtless youth over the precipices of desire. And I wandered still further from Thee, and Thou didst leave me to myself; the torrent of my fornications tossed and swelled and boiled and ran over." And during this time: "Thou saidst nothing, O my God!" This silence of God is the terrible sign of hardened sin, of hopeless damnation. It meant utter depravity of the will; he did not even feel remorse any more.

Here he is, then, as if unfastened from his child's soul—separated from himself. The object of his youthful faith has no more meaning for him. He understands no longer, and it is all one to him that he does not. Thus, told by himself, does this first crisis of Augustine's life emerge from the autobiography; and it takes on a general significance. Once for all, under a definite form, and to a certain degree classic, he has diagnosed with his subtle experience of doctor of souls the pubescent crisis in all young men of his age, in all the young Christians who are to come after him. For the story of Augustine is the story of each of us. The loss of faith always occurs when the senses first awaken. At this critical moment, when nature claims us for her service, the consciousness of spiritual things is, in most cases, either eclipsed or totally destroyed. The gradual usage to the brutalities of the instinct ends by killing the sensitiveness of the inward feelings. It is not reason which turns the young man from God; it is the flesh. Scepticism but provides him with excuses for the new life he is leading.

Thus started, Augustine was not able to pull up half-way on the road of pleasure; he never did anything by halves. In these vulgar revels of the ordinary wild youth, he wanted again to be best, he wanted to be first as he was at school. He stirred up his companions and drew them after him. They in their turn drew him. Among them was found that Alypius, who was the friend of all his life, who shared his faults and mistakes, who followed him even in his conversion, and became Bishop of Thagaste. These two future shepherds of Christ roamed the streets with the lost sheep. They spent the nights in the open spaces of the town, playing, or wantonly dreaming before cups of cool drinks. They lounged there, stretched out on mats, with a crown of leaves on the head, a jasmine garland round the neck, a rose or marigold thrust above the ear.

They never knew what to do next to kill time. So one fine evening the reckless crew took it into their heads to rifle a pear tree of one of Patricius's neighbours. This pear tree was just beyond the vineyard belonging to Augustine's father. The rascals shook down the pears. They took a few bites to find out the taste, and having decided this to be rather disappointing, they chucked all the rest to the hogs.

In this theft, done merely for the pleasure of the thing, Augustine sees an evidence of diabolical mischief. Doubtless he committed many another misdeed where, like this, the whole attraction lay in the Satanic joy of breaking the law. His fury for dissolute courses knew no rest. Did Monnica observe anything of this change in Augustine? The boy, grown big, had escaped from the supervision of the women's apartments. If the mother guessed anything, she did not guess all. It fell to her husband to open her eyes. With the freedom of manners among the ancients, Augustine relates the fact quite plainly... That took place in the bath-buildings at Thagaste. He was bathing with his father, probably in the *piscina* of cold baths. The bathers who came out of the water with dripping limbs were printing wet marks of their feet upon the mosaic flooring, when Patricius, who was watching them, suddenly perceived that his son had about him the signs of manhood, that he was already bearing —as Augustine says himself in his picturesque language—the first signs of turbulent youth, like another *toga praetexta*. Patricius, as a good pagan, welcomed with jubilation this promise of grand-children, and rushed off joyously to brag of his discovery to Monnica. She took the news in quite another way. Frightened at the idea of the dangers to which her son's virtue was exposed, she lectured him in private. But Augustine, from the height of his sixteen years, laughed at her. "A lot of old-women's gossip! Why does she want to talk about things she can't understand!..." Tired out at last, Monnica tried to get a promise from her son that he would at least have some restraint in his dissipation—that he would avoid women of the town, and above all, that he would have nothing to do with married women. For the rest, she put him in God's hands.

It may be wondered—Augustine himself wonders—that she did not think of finding him a wife. They marry early in Africa. Even now any Arab labourer buys a wife for his son, hardly turned sixteen, so that the fires of a too warm youth may be quenched in marriage. But Monnica, who was not yet a saint, acted in this matter like a foreseeing and practical woman of the prosperous class. A wife would be a drag for a young man like Augustine, who seemed likely to have such a brilliant career. A too early marriage would jeopardize his future. Before all things, it was important that he should become an illustrious rhetorician, and raise the fortunes of the family. For her, all else yielded to this consideration. But she hoped at least that the headstrong student might consent to be good into the bargain.

This was also Patricius's way of looking at the matter. And so, says Augustine, "My father gave himself no concern how I grew towards Thee, or how chaste I was, provided only that I became a man of culture —however destitute of Thy culture, O God... My mother and he slackened the curb without regard to due severity, and I was suffered to enjoy myself according to my dissolute fancy." Meanwhile, Patricius was now become (very tardily) a catechumen. The entreaties of his wife had won him to the Catholic faith. But his sentiments were not much more Christian—"He hardly thought of Thee, my God," acknowledges his son, who nevertheless was pleased at this conversion. If Patricius decided to get converted, it was probably from political reasons. Since the death of Julian the Apostate, paganism appeared finally conquered. The Emperor Valentinianus had just proclaimed heavy penalties against night-sacrifices. In Africa, the Count Romanus persecuted the Donatists. All the Christians in Thagaste were Catholic. What was the good of keeping up a useless and dangerous resistance? Perhaps the end of Patricius—which was near—was as edifying as Monnica could wish. But at all events, at the present moment, he was not the man to interfere with Augustine's pleasures: he only thought of the eventual fortune of the young man. Alone, Monnica might have had some influence on him, and she herself was fascinated by his future career in the world. Perhaps, to quiet her conscience, she said to herself that this frivolous education would be more or less of a help to her son towards bringing him back to God, that a day would come when the famous rhetorician would plead the cause of Christ?...

Scandalized though she might be at his conduct, it is however apparent that it was about this time she began to get fonder of him, to worry over him as her favourite child. But it was not till much later that the union between mother and son became quite complete. Too many old customs still remained preventing close intercourse between the men and women of a family. And it will hardly do to picture such intimacy from the intimacy which may exist between a mother and son of our own time. There was none of the spoiling, or indulgence, or culpable weakness which enervates maternal tenderness and makes it injurious to the energy of a manly character. Monnica was severe and a little rough. If she let her feelings be seen, it was solely before God. And yet it is most certain that in the depth of her heart she loved Augustine, not only as a future member of Christ, but humanly, as a woman frustrated of love in a badly assorted marriage may spend her love on her child. The brutality of pagan ways revolted her, and she poured on this young head all her stored-up affection. In Augustine she loved the being she wished she could love in her husband.

A number of personal considerations were no doubt involved in the deep and unselfish attachment she had for her son: instinctively, she looked for him to protect her against the father's violence. She felt that he would be the support of her old age, and also, she foresaw dimly what one day he would be. All this aided to bring about the tie, the understanding, which grew more and more close between Augustine and Monnica. And so from this time they both appear to us as they were to appear to all posterity—the pattern of the Christian Mother and Son. Thanks to them, the hard law of the ancients has been abrogated. There shall be no more barriers between the mother and her child. No longer shall it be vain exterior rites which draw together the members of the same family: they shall communicate in spirit and truth. Heart speaketh to heart. The fellowship of souls is founded, and the ties of the domestic hearth are drawn close, as they never were in antiquity. No more shall they work in concert only for material things; they will join together to love—and to love each other more. The son will belong more to his mother.

At the time we have now come to, Monnica was already undertaking the conquest of Augustine's soul. She prayed for him fervently. The young man cared very little: gratitude came to him only after his conversion. At this time he was thinking of nothing but amusement. For this he even forgot his career. But Monnica and Patricius thought of it constantly—especially Patricius, who gave himself enormous trouble to enable this student on a holiday to finish his studies. Eventually he got together the necessary money, possibly borrowed enough to make up the sum from some rich landowner who was the patron of the people of small means in Thagaste—say, that gorgeous Romanianus, to whom

Augustine, in acknowledgment, dedicated one of his first books. The young man could now take the road for Carthage.

He left by himself, craving for knowledge and glory and pleasure, his heart full of longing for what he knew not, and melancholy without cause. What was going to become of him in the great, unknown city?

THE ENCHANTMENT OF CARTHAGE

Amare et amari
To love and to be loved.

— *Confessions*, III, 1.

Chapter 1
CARTHAGO VENERIS

"I went to Carthage, where shameful loves bubbled round me like boiling oil."

This cry of repentance, uttered by the converted Augustine twenty-five years later, does not altogether stifle his words of admiration for the old capital of his country. One can see this patriotic admiration stirring between the lines. Carthage made a very strong impression on him. He gave it his heart and remained faithful to the end. His enemies, the Donatists, called him "the Carthaginian arguer." After he became Bishop of Hippo, he was continually going to Carthage to preach, or dispute, or consult his colleagues, or to ask something from men in office. When he is not there, he is ever speaking of it in his treatises and plain sermons. He takes comparisons from it: "You who have been to Carthage—" he often says to his listeners. For the boy from little Thagaste to go to Carthage, was about the same as for our youths from the provinces to go to Paris. *Veni Carthaginem*—in these simple words there is a touch of naive emphasis which reveals the bewilderment of the Numidian student just landed in the great city.

And, in fact, it was one of the five great capitals of the Empire: there were Rome, Constantinople, Antioch, Alexandria—Carthage. Carthage was the sea-port capital of the whole western Mediterranean. With its large new streets, its villas, its temples, its palaces, its docks, its variously dressed cosmopolitan population, it astonished and delighted the schoolboy from Madaura. Whatever local marks were left about him, or signs of the rustic simpleton, it brushed off. At first, Augustine must have felt himself as good as lost there.

There he was, his own master, with nobody to counsel and direct him. He does indeed mention his fellow-countryman, that Romanianus, the patron of his father and of other people in Thagaste, as a high and generous friend who invited him to his house when he, a poor youth, came to finish his studies in a strange city, and helped him, not only with his purse, but with his friendship. Unfortunately the allusion is not very clear. Still, it does seem to shew that Augustine, in the first days after his arrival at Carthage, stayed with Romanianus. It is not in the least improbable that Romanianus had a house at Carthage and spent the winter there: during the rest of the year he would be in his country houses round about Thagaste. This opulent benefactor might not have been satisfied with giving Augustine a good "tip" for his journey when he was leaving his native town, but may also have put him up in his own house at Carthage. Such was the atonement for those enormous fortunes of antiquity: the rich had to give freely and constantly. With the parcelling out of wealth we have become much more egoistical.

In any case, Romanianus, taken up with his pleasures and business, could not have been much of a guide for Monnica's son. Augustine was therefore without control, or very nearly. No doubt he came to Carthage with a strong desire to increase his knowledge and get renown, but still more athirst for love and the emotions of sentiment. The love-prelude was deliriously prolonged for him. He was at that time so overwhelmed by it, that it is the first thing he thinks of when he relates his years at Carthage. "To love and be loved" seems to him, as to his dear Alexandrine poets, the single object of life. Yet he was not in love, "but he loved the idea of love." *Nondum amabam, et amare amabam ... amare amans...*

Truly, never a pagan poet had hitherto found such language to speak of love. These subtle phrases are not only the work of a marvellous wordsmith: through their almost imperceptible shades of meaning may be described an entirely new soul, the pleasure-loving soul of the old world awakening to spiritual life. Modern people have repeated the words more than enough, but by translating them too literally—"I loved to love" —they have perhaps distorted the sense. They have made Augustine a kind of Romantic like Alfred de Musset, a dilettante in love. Augustine is not so modern, although he often seems one of ourselves. When he wrote those words he was a bishop and a penitent. What strikes him above all in looking back upon his uneasy and feverish life as a youth and young man, is the great onrush of all his being which swept him towards love. Plainly, man is made for love, since he loves without object and without cause, since in itself alone the idea of love is already for him a beginning of love. Only he falls into error in giving to creatures a heart that the Creator alone can fill and satisfy. In this love for love's sake, Augustine discerned the sign of the predestined soul whose tenderness will find no rest but in God. That is why he repeats this word "Love" with a kind of intoxication. He knows that those who love like him cannot love long with a human love. Nor does he blush to acknowledge it:—he loved—he loved with all his soul—he loved to the point of loving the coming of love. Happy intimation for the Christian! A heart so afire is pledged to the eternal marriage.

With this heat of passion, this lively sensibility, Augustine was a prey for Carthage. The voluptuous city took complete hold on him by its charm and its beauty, by all the seductions of mind and sense, by its promises of easy enjoyment.

First of all, it softened this young provincial, used to the harder country life of his home; it relaxed the Numidian contracted by the roughness of his climate; it cooled his eyes burned by the sun in the full-flowing of its waters and the suavity of its horizons. It was a city of laziness, and above all, of pleasure, as well for those plunged in business as for the idlers. They called it *Carthago Veneris*—Carthage of Venus. And certainly the old Phoenician Tanit always reigned there. Since the rebuilding of her temple by the Romans, she had transformed herself into *Virgo Coelestis*. This Virgin of Heaven was the great Our Lady of unchastity, towards whom still mounted the adoration of the African land four hundred years after the birth of Christ. "Strange Virgin," Augustine was to say later, "who can only be honoured by the loss of virginity." Her dissolving influence seemed to overcome the whole region. There is no more feminine country than this Carthaginian peninsula, ravished on all sides by the caress of the waters. Stretched out between her lakes on the edge of the sea, Carthage lounged in the humid warmth of her mists, as if in the suffocating atmosphere of her vapour-baths.

She stole away the energies, but she was an enchantment for the eyes. From the top of the impressive flight of steps which led up to the temple of Æsculapius on the summit of the Acropolis, Augustine could see at his feet the huge, even-planned city, with its citadel walls which spread out indefinitely, its gardens, blue waters, flaxen plains, and the mountains. Did he pause on the steps at sunset, the two harbours, rounded cup-shape, shone, rimmed by the quays, like lenses of ruby. To the left, the Lake of Tunis, stirless, without a ripple, as rich in ethereal lights as a Venetian lagoon, radiated in ever-altering sheens, delicate and splendid. In front, across the bay, dotted with the sails of ships close-hauled to the wind, beyond the wind-swept and shimmering intervals, the mountains of Rhodes raised their aerial summit-lines against the sky. What an outlook on the world for a young man dreaming of fame! And what more exhilarating spot than this Mount Byrsa, where, in deep layers, so many heroic memories were gathered and superimposed. The great dusty plains which bury themselves far off in the sands of the desert, the mountains—yes, and isles and headlands, all bowed before the Hill that Virgil sang and seemed to do her reverence. She held in awe the innumerable tribes of the barbaric continent; she was mistress of the sea. Rome herself, from the height of her Palatine, surged less imperial.

More than any other of the young men seated with him on the benches of the school of rhetoric, Augustine hearkened to the dumb appeals which came from the ancient ruins and new palaces of Carthage. But the supple and treacherous city knew the secret of enchaining the will. She tempted him by the open display of her amusements. Under this sun which touches to beauty the plaster of a hut, the grossest pleasures have an attraction which men of the North cannot understand. The overflowing of lust surrounds you. This prolific swarming, all these bodies, close-pressed and soft with sweat, give forth as it were a breath of fornication which melts the will. Augustine breathed in with delight the heavy burning air, loaded with human odours, which filled the streets and squares of Carthage. To all the bold soliciting, to all the hands stretched out to detain him as he walked, he yielded.

But for a mind like his Carthage had more subtle allurements in reserve. He was taken by her theatres, by the verses of her poets and the melodies of her musicians. He shed tears at the plays of Menander and Terence; he lamented upon the misfortunes of separated lovers; he shared their quarrels, rejoiced and despaired with them. And still he awaited the epiphany of Love—that Love which the performance of the actors shewed him to be so touching and fine.

Such then was Augustine, given over to the irresponsibility of his eighteen years—a heart spoiled by romantic literature, a mind impatient to try every sort of intellectual adventure in the most corrupting and bewitching city known to the pagan centuries, set amidst one of the most entrancing landscapes in the world.

Chapter 2
THE AFRICAN ROME

Carthage did not offer only pleasures to Augustine; it was besides an extraordinary subject to think about for an understanding so alert and all-embracing as his.

At Carthage he understood the Roman grandeur as he could not at Madaura and the Numidian towns. Here, as elsewhere, the Romans made a point of impressing the minds of conquered races by the display of their strength and magnificence. Above all, they aimed at the immense. The towns built by them offered the same decorative and monumental character of the Greek cities of the Hellenistic period, which the Romans had further exaggerated—a character not without emphasis and over-elaboration, but which was bound to astonish, and that was the main thing in their view. In short, their ideal was not perceptibly different from that of our modern town councillors. To lay out streets which intersected at right angles; to create towns cut into even blocks like chessboards; to multiply prospects and huge architectural masses—all the Roman cities of this period revealed such an aim, with an almost identical plan.

Erected after this type, the new Carthage caused the old to be forgotten. Everybody agreed that it was second only to Rome. The African writers squandered the most hyperbolical praises upon it. For them it is "The splendid, the august, the sublime Carthage." Although there may well be a certain amount of triviality or of patriotic exaggeration in these praises, it is certain that the Roman capital of the Province of Africa was no less considerable than the old metropolis of the Hanno and Barcine factions. With a population almost as large as that of Rome, it had almost as great a circumference. It must further be recalled that as it had no ramparts till the Vandal invasion, the city overflowed into the country. With its gardens, villas, and burial-places of the dead, it covered nearly the entire peninsula, to-day depopulated.

Carthage, as well as Rome, had her Capitol and Palatine upon Mount Byrsa, where rose no doubt a temple consecrated to the Capitolean triune deities, Jupiter, Juno, and Minerva, not far from the great temple of Æsculapius, a modern transformation of the old Punic Eschmoum. Hard by these sanctuaries, the Proconsul's palace dominated Carthage from the height of the acclivity of the Acropolis. The Forum was at the foot of the hill, probably in the neighbourhood of the ports—a Forum built and arranged in the Roman way, with its shops of bankers and money-changers placed under the circular galleries, with the traditional image of Marsyas, and a number of statues of local celebrities. Apuleius no doubt had his there. Further off was the Harbour Square, where gathered foreigners recently landed and the idlers of the city in search of news, and where the booksellers offered the new books and pamphlets. There was to be seen one of the curiosities of Carthage—a mosaic representing fabulous monsters, men without heads, and men with only one leg and one foot—a huge foot under which, lying upon their backs, they sheltered from the sun, as under a parasol. On account of this feature they were called the *sciapodes*. Augustine, who like everybody else had paused before these grotesque figures, recalls them somewhere to his readers... Beside the sea, in the lower town and upon the two near hills of the Acropolis, were a number of detached buildings that the old authors have preserved the names of and briefly described. Thanks to the zeal of archæologists, it is now become impossible to tell where they stood.

The pagan sanctuaries were numerous. That of the goddess Coelestis, the great patroness of Carthage, occupied a space of five thousand feet. It comprised, besides the actual [Greek: hieron], where stood the image of the goddess, gardens, sacred groves, and courts surrounded with columns. The ancient Phoenician Moloch had also his temple under the name of Saturn. They called him *The Old One*, so Augustine tells us, and his worshippers were falling away. On the other hand,

Carthage had another sanctuary which was very fashionable, a *Serapeum* as at Alexandria, where were manifested the pomps of the Egyptian ritual, celebrated by Apuleius. Neighbouring the holy places, came the places of amusement: the theatre, the Odeum, circus, stadium, and amphitheatre—this last, of equal dimensions with the Colosseum at Rome, its gallery rising upon gallery, and its realistic sculptures of animals and artisans. Then there were the buildings for the public service: the immense cisterns of the East and the Malga, the great aqueduct, which, after being carried along a distance of fifty-five miles, emptied the water of the Zaghouan into the reservoirs at Carthage. Finally, there were the Baths, some of which we know—those of Antoninus and of Maximianus, and those of Gargilius, where one of the most important Councils known to the history of the African Church assembled. There were likewise many Christian basilicas at the time of Augustine. The authors mention seventeen: it is likely there were more. That of Damous-el-Karita, the only one of which considerable traces have been found, was vast and richly decorated, and was perhaps the cathedral of Carthage.

What other buildings there were are utterly lost to history. It may be conjectured, however, that Carthage, as well as Rome, had a *septizonium*—a decorative building with peristyles one above the other which surrounded a reservoir. In fact, it is claimed that the one at Rome was copied from Carthage. Straight streets paved with large flags intersected around these buildings, forming a network of long avenues, very bright and ventilated. Some of them were celebrated in the ancient world either for their beauty or the animation of their trade: the street of the Jewellers, the street of Health, of Saturn, of Coelestis, too, or of Juno. The fig and vegetable markets and the public granaries were also some of the main centres of Carthaginian life.

It is unquestionable that Carthage, with its buildings and statues, its squares, avenues and public gardens, looked like a large capital, and was a perfect example of that ideal of rather brutal magnificence and strength which the Romans obtruded everywhere.

And even while it dazzled the young provincial from Thagaste, the African Rome shewed him the virtue of order—social and political order. Carthage, the metropolis of Western Africa, maintained an army of officials who handled the government in its smallest details. First of all, there were the representatives of the central power, the imperial rulers—the Proconsul, a sort of vice-emperor, who was surrounded by a full court, a civil and military staff, a privy council, an *officium* which included a crowd of dignitaries and subaltern clerks. Then there was the Propraetor of Africa who, being in control of the government of the whole African province, had an *officium* still larger perhaps than the Proconsul's. After them came the city magistrates, who were aided in their functions by the Council of the Decurions—the Senate of Carthage. These Carthaginian senators cut a considerable figure: for them their colleagues at Rome were full of airs and graces, and the Emperors endeavoured to keep them in a good-humour. All the details of city government came under their supervision: the slaughter-houses, buildings, the gathering of municipal taxes, and the police, which comprised even the guardians of the Forum. Then there were the army and navy. The home port of a grain-carrying fleet which conveyed the African cereals to Ostia, Carthage could starve Rome if she liked. The grain and oil of all countries lay in her docks—the storehouses of the state provisions, which were in charge of a special prefect who had under his orders a whole corporation of overseers and clerks.

Augustine must have heard a good deal of grumbling at Carthage against this excess of officialism. But, all the same, so well-governed a city was a very good school for a young man who was to combine later the duties of bishop, judge, and governor. The blessings of order, of what was called "the Roman peace" no doubt impressed him the more, as he himself came from a turbulent district often turned upside down by the quarrels of religious sects and by the depredations of the nomads—a boundary-land of the Sahara regions where it was much harder to bring the central government into play than in Carthage and the coast-towns. To appreciate the beauty of government, there is nothing like living in a country where all is at the mercy of force or the first-comer's will. Such of the Barbarians who came in contact with Roman civilization were overcome with admiration for the good order that it established. But what astonished them more than anything else was that the Empire was everywhere.

No man, whatever his race or country, could help feeling proud to belong to the Roman city. He was at home in all the countries in the world subject to Rome. Our Europe, split into nationalities, can hardly understand now this feeling of pride, so different from our narrow patriotisms. The way to feel something of it is to go to the colonies: out there the least of us may believe himself a sovereign, simply from the fact that he is a subject of the governing country. This feeling was very strong in the old world. Carthage, where the striking effect of the Empire appeared in all its brilliancy, would increase it in Augustine. He had only to look around him to value the extent of the privilege conferred by Rome on her citizens. Men coming from all countries, without exception of race, were, so to speak, made partners of the Empire and collaborated in the grandeur of the Roman scheme. If the Proconsul who then occupied the Byrsa palace, the celebrated Symmachus, belonged to an old Italian family, he whom he represented, the Emperor Valentinian, was the son of a Pannonian soldier. The Count Theodosius, the general who suppressed the insurrection of Firmus in Mauretania, was a Spaniard, and the army he led into Africa was made up, for the most part, of Gauls. Later on, under Arcadius, another Gaul, Rufinus, shall be master of the whole of the East.

An active mind like Augustine's could not remain indifferent before this spectacle of the world thrown open by Rome to all men of talent. He had the soul of a poet, quick to enthusiasm; the sight of the Eagles planted on the Acropolis at Carthage moved him in a way he never forgot. He acquired the habit of seeing big, and began to cast off race prejudices and all the petty narrowness of a local spirit. When he became a Christian he did not close himself up, like the Donatists, within the African Church. His dream was that Christ's Empire upon earth should equal the Empire of the Cæsars.

Still, it is desirable not to fall into error upon this Roman unity. Behind the imposing front it shewed from one end to the other of the Mediterranean, the variety of peoples, with their manners, traditions, special religions, was always there, and in Africa more than elsewhere. The population of Carthage was astonishingly mixed. The hybrid character of this country without unity was illustrated by the streaks found in the Carthaginian crowds. All the specimens of African races elbowed one another in the streets, from the nigger, brought from his native Soudan by the slave-merchant, to the Romanized Numidian. The inflow, continually renewed, of traffickers and cosmopolitan adventurers increased this confusion. And so Carthage was a Babel of races, of costumes, of beliefs and ideas. Augustine, who was at heart a mystic, but also a dialectician extremely fond of showy discussions, found in Carthage a lively summary of the religions and philosophies of his day.

During these years of study and reflection he captured booty of knowledge and observation which he would know how to make use of in the future.

In the Carthage sanctuaries and schools, in the squares and the streets, he could see pass the disciples of all the systems, the props of all the superstitions, the devotees of all the religions. He heard the shrill clamour of disputes, the tumult of fights and riots. When a man was at the end of his arguments, he knocked down his opponent. The authorities had a good deal of trouble to keep order. Augustine, who was an intrepid logician, must have longed to take his share in these rows. But one cannot exactly improvise a faith between to-day and to-morrow. While he awaited the enlightenment of the truth, he studied the Carthaginian Babel.

First of all, there was the official religion, the most obvious and perhaps the most brilliant, that of the Divinity of the Emperors, which was still kept up even under the Christian Cæsars. Each year, at the end of October, the elected delegates of the entire province, having at their head the *Sacerdos province*, the provincial priest, arrived at Carthage. Their leader, clad in a robe broidered with palms, gold crown on head, made his solemn entry into the city. It was a perfect invasion, each member dragging in his wake a mob of clients and servants. The Africans, with their taste for pomp and colour, seized the chance to give themselves over to a display of ruinous sumptuosities: rich dresses, expensive horses splendidly caparisoned, processions, sacrifices, public banquets, games at the circus and amphitheatre. These strangers so overcrowded the city that the imperial Government had to forbid them, under severe penalties, to stay longer than five days. A very prudent measure! At these times, collisions were inevitable between pagans and Christians. It was desirable to scatter such crowds as soon as possible, for riots were always smouldering in their midst.

No less thronged were the festivals of the Virgin of Heaven. A survival of the national religion, these feasts were dear to the hearts of the Carthaginians. Augustine went to them with his fellow-students. "We trooped there from every quarter," he says. There was a great gathering of people in the interior court which led up to the temple. The statue, taken from its sanctuary, was placed before the peristyle upon a kind of repository. Wantons, arrayed with barbarous lavishness, danced around the holy image; actors performed and sang hymns. "Our eager eyes," Augustine adds maliciously, "rested in turn on the goddess, and on the girls, her adorers." The Great Mother of the Gods, the Goddess of Mount Berecyntus, was worshipped with similar license. Every year the people of Carthage went to wash her solemnly in the sea. Her statue, carried in a splendid litter, robed with precious stuffs, curled and farded, passed through the streets of the city, with its guard of mummers and Corybants. These last, "with hair greasy from pomade, pale faces, and a loose and effeminate walk, held out bowls for alms to the onlookers."

The devotion to Isis was yet another excuse for processions: the *Serapeum* was a rival attraction to the temple of the Heavenly Maiden. If we may trust Tertullian, the Africans swore only by Serapis. Possibly Mithras had also worshippers in Carthage. Anyhow, the occult religions were fully represented there. Miracle-working was becoming more and more the basis even of paganism. Never had the soothsayers been more flourishing. Everybody, in secret, pried into the entrails of the sacrificial victims, or used magic spells. As to the wizards and astrologers, they did business openly. Augustine himself consulted them, like all the Carthaginians. The public credulity had no limits.

On the opposite side from the pagan worship, the sects which had sprung from Christianity sprouted. True, Africa has given birth to but a small number of heresies: the Africans had not the subtle mind of the Orientals and they were not given to theorizing. But a good many of the Eastern heresies had got into Carthage. Augustine must have still met Arians there, although at this period Arianism was dying out in Africa. What is certain is that orthodox Catholicism was in a very critical state. The Donatists captured its congregations and churches; they were unquestionably in the majority. They raised altar against altar. If Genethlius was the Catholic bishop, the Donatist bishop was Parmenianus. And they claimed to be more Catholic than their opponents. They boasted that they were the Church, the single, the unique Church, the Church of Christ. But these schismatics themselves were already splitting up into many sects. At the time Augustine was studying at Carthage, Rogatus, Bishop of Tenes, had just broken publicly with Parmenian's party. Another Donatist, Tyconius, published books wherein he traversed many principles dear to his fellow-religionists. Doubt darkened consciences. Amid these controversies, where was the truth? Among whom did the Apostolic tradition dwell?

To put the finishing touch on this anarchy, a sect which likewise derived from Christianity—Manicheeism—began to have numerous adepts in Africa. Watched with suspicion by the Government, it concealed part of its doctrine, the most scandalous and subversive. But the very mystery which enveloped it, helped it to get adherents.

Among all these apostles preaching their gospel, these devotees beating the drum before their god, these theologians reciprocally insulting and excommunicating one another, Augustine brought the superficial scepticism of his eighteenth year. He wanted no more of the religion in which his mother had brought him up. He was a good talker, a clever dialectician; he was in a hurry to emancipate himself, to win freedom for his way of thinking as for his way of life; and he meant to enjoy his youth. With such gifts, and with such dispositions, he could only choose among all these doctrines that which would help most the qualities of his mind, at once flattering his intellectual pretensions, and leaving his pleasure-loving instincts a loose rein.

Chapter 3
THE CARTHAGE STUDENT

However strong were the attractions of the great city, Augustine well knew that he had not been sent there to amuse himself, or to trifle as an amateur with philosophy. He was poor, and he had to secure his future—make his fortune. His family counted on him. Neither was he ignorant of the difficult position of his parents and by what sacrifices they had supplied him with the means to finish his studies. Necessarily he was obliged to be a student who worked.

With his extraordinary facility, he stood out at once among his fellow-students. In the rhetoric school, where he attended lectures, he was, he tells us, not only at the top, but he was the leader of his companions. He led in everything. At that time, rhetoric was extremely far-reaching: it had come to take in all the divisions of education, including science and philosophy. Augustine claims to have learned all that the masters of his time had to teach: rhetoric, dialectic, geometry, music, mathematics. Having gone through the whole scholastic system, he thought of studying law, and aided by his gift of words, to become a barrister. For a gifted young man it was the shortest and surest road to money and honours.

Unhappily for him, hardly was he settled down at Carthage than his father died. This made his future again problematical. How was he to keep up his studies without the sums coming from his father? The affairs of Patricius must have been left in the most parlous condition. But Monnica, clinging to her ambitious plans for her son, knew how to triumph over all difficulties, and she continued to send Augustine money. Romanianus, the Mæcenas of Thagaste, who was doubtless applied to by her, came once more to the rescue of the hard-up student. The young man, set at ease about his expenses, resumed light-heartedly his studious and dissipated life.

As a matter of fact, this family bereavement does not seem to have caused him much grief. In the *Confessions* he mentions the death of his father in a few words, and, so to speak, in parenthesis, as an event long foreseen without much importance. And yet he owed him a great deal. Patricius was hard pressed, and he took immense trouble to provide the means for his son's education. But with the fine egotism of youth, Augustine perhaps thought it enough to have profited by his father's sacrifices, and dispensed himself from gratitude. In any case, his affection for his father must have been rather lukewarm; the natural differences between them ran too deep. In these years, Monnica filled all the heart of Augustine.

But the influence of Monnica herself was very slight upon this grown-up youth, eighteen years old. He had forgotten her lessons, and it did not trouble him much if his conduct added to the worries of the widow, who was now struggling with her husband's creditors. At heart he was a good son and he deeply loved his mother, but inevitably the pressure of the life around him swept him along.

He has pictured his companions for us, after his conversion, as terrible blackguards. No doubt he is too severe. Those young men were neither better nor worse than elsewhere. They were rowdy, as they were in the other cities of the Empire, and as one always is at that age. Imperial regulations enjoined the police to have an eye on the students, to note their conduct and what company they kept. They were not to become members of prohibited societies, not to go too often to the theatre, nor to waste their time in raking and feastings. If their conduct became too outrageous, they were to be beaten with rods and sent back to their parents. At Carthage there was a hard-living set of men who called themselves "The Wreckers." Their great pleasure was to go and make a row at a professor's lecture; they would burst noisily into the classroom and smash up anything they could lay hold of. They amused themselves also by "ragging" the freshmen, jeering at their simplicity, and playing them a thousand tricks. Things haven't much changed since then. The fellow-students of Augustine were so like students of to-day that the most modern terms suggest themselves to describe their performances.

Augustine, who was on the whole well conducted, and, as behoved a future professor, had a respect for discipline, disapproved of "The Wreckers" and their violence. This did not prevent him from enjoying himself in their society. He was overcome with shame because he could not keep pace with them—we must believe it at least, since he tells us so himself. With a certain lack of assurance, blended however with much juvenile vanity, he joined the band. He listened to that counsel of vulgar wisdom which is disastrous to souls like his: "Do as others do." He accordingly did do as the others; he knew all their debauchery, or he imagined he did, for however low he went, he was never able to do anything mean. He was then so far from the faith that he arranged love-trysts in the churches. "I was not afraid to think of my lust, and plan a scheme for securing the deadly fruit of sin, even within the walls of Thy church during the celebration of Thy mysteries." We might be reading the confession of a sensualist of to-day. One grows astonished at these morals, at once so old and so modern. What, already! These young Christian basilicas, but newly sprung out of the earth, where the men were strictly separated from the women—were they already become places of assignation, where love-letters were slipped into hands, and procuresses sold their furtive services!...

At length the great happiness for which Augustine had so long been sighing was granted him: he loved and he was loved.

He loved as he indeed was able to love, with all the impetuosity of his nature and all the fire of his temperament, with all his heart and all his senses. "I plunged headlong into love, whose fetters I longed to wear." But as he went at once to extremes, as he meant to give himself altogether, and expected all in return, he grew irritated at not receiving this same kind of love. It was never enough love for him. Yet he was loved, and the very certainty of this love, always too poor to his mind, exasperated the violence and pertinacity of his desire. "Because I was loved, I proudly riveted round myself the chain of woe, to be soon scourged with the red-hot iron rods of jealousy, torn by suspicions, fears, anger, and quarrels." This was passion with chorus and orchestra, a little theatrical, with its violences, its alternations between fury and ecstasy, such as an African, steeped in romantic literature, would conceive it. Deceived, he flung himself in desperate pursuit of the ever-flitting love. He had certainly more than one passion. Each one left him more hungry than the last.

He was sensual, and he felt each time how brief is pleasure, in what a limited circle all enjoyment turns. He was tender, eager to give himself; and he saw plainly that one never gives oneself quite altogether, that even in the maddest hours of surrender one always reserves oneself in secret, keeping for oneself something of oneself; and he felt that most of the time his tenderness got no answer. When the joyous heart brings the offering of its love, the heart of her he loves is absent. And when it is there, on the edge of the lips, decked and smiling to meet the loved one, it is the other who is absent. Almost never do they join together, and they never join together altogether. And so this Love, which claims to be constant and even eternal, ought to be, if it would prolong itself, a continual act of faith, and hope, and charity. To believe in it in spite of its darkening and falling away; to hope its return, often against all evidence; to pardon its injustices and sometimes its foul actions—how many are capable of such abnegation? Augustine went through all that. He was in despair about it. And then, the nostalgia of predestined souls took hold of him. He had an indistinct feeling that these human loves were unworthy of him, and that if he must have a master, he was born to serve another Master. He had a desire to shake off the platitude of here below, the melancholy fen where stagnated what he calls "the marsh of the flesh"; to escape, in a word, from the wretched huts wherein for a little he had sheltered his heart; to burn all behind him, and so prevent the weakness of a return; and to go and pitch his tent further, higher, he knew not where—upon some unapproachable mountain where the air is icy, but before the eyes, the vasty stretches of light and space...

These first loves of Augustine were really too fierce to last. They burned up themselves. Augustine did not keep them up long. There was in him, besides, an instinct which counteracted his exuberant, amorous sentimentality—the sense of beauty. That in itself was enough to make him pause on the downhill of riot. The anarchy and commotion of passion was repellent to a mind devoted to clearness and order. But there was still another thing—the son of the Thagaste freeholder had any amount of common sense. That at least was left to him of the paternal heritage. A youth of what we call the lower middle class, strictly brought up in the hard and frugal discipline of the provinces, he felt the effects of his training. The bohemianism in which his friends revelled could not hold him indefinitely. Besides this, the career he desired, that of a barrister or professor, had a preliminary obligation to maintain a certain outward decorum. He himself tells us so; in the midst of his most disreputable performances he aspired to be known for his fashion and wit—*elegans atque urbanus*. Politeness of speech and manners, the courteous mutual deference of the best society—such, was the ideal of this budding professor of rhetoric.

Anxiety about his future, joined to his rapid disenchantments, ere long sobered the student: he just took his fling and then settled down. Love turned for him into sensual habit. His head became clear for study and meditation. The apprentice to rhetoric liked his business. Up to his last breath, despite his efforts to change, he continued, like all his contemporaries, to love rhetoric. He handled words like a worker in verbals who is aware of their price and knows all their resources. Even after his conversion, if he condemns profane literature as a poisoner of souls, he absolves the beauty of language. "I accuse not words," he says. "Words are choice and precious vessels. I accuse the wine of error that drunken doctors pour out for us into these fair goblets." At the Rhetoric School he took extreme pleasure in declaiming. He was applauded; the professor gave him as an example to the others. These scholastic triumphs foretold others more celebrated and reverberating. And so, in his heart, literary vanity and ambition disputed the ever-lively illusions of love. And then, above all! he had to live; Monnica's remittances were necessarily small; the generosity of Romanianus had its limit. So he beat about to enlarge his small student's purse. He wrote verses for poetic competitions. Perhaps already he was able to act as tutor to certain of his fellow-students, less advanced.

If the need of loving tormented his sentimental heart, he tried to assuage it in friendship. He loved friendship as he loved love. He was a passionate and faithful friend up to his death. At this time of his life, he was riveting friendships which were never to be broken. He had beside him his fellow-countryman, Alypius, the future Bishop of Thagaste, who had followed him to Carthage and would, later on, follow him to Milan;

Nebridius, a not less dear companion, fated to die early; Honoratus, whom he drew into his errors and later did his best to enlighten; and, finally, that mysterious young man, whose name he does not tell us, and whose loss he mourned as never any one has mourned the death of a friend.

They lived in daily and hourly intimacy, in continual fervour and enthusiasm. They were great theatre-goers, where Augustine was able to satisfy his desire for tender emotions and romantic adventures. They had musical parties; they tried over again the popular airs heard at the Odeum or some other of the innumerable theatres at Carthage. All the Carthaginians, even the populace, were mad about music. The Bishop of Hippo, in his sermons, recalls a mason upon his scaffolding, or a shoemaker in his stall, singing away the tunes of well-known musicians. Then our students strolled on the quays or in the Harbour Square, contemplating the many-coloured sea, this splendour of waters at the setting sun, which Augustine will extol one day with an inspiration unknown to the ancient poets. Above all, they fell into discussions, commented what they had lately read, or built up astonishing plans for the future. So flowed by a happy and charming life, abruptly interpolated with superb anticipations. With what a full heart the Christian penitent calls it back for us!—"What delighted me in the intercourse of my friends, was the talk, the laughter, the good turns we did each other, the common study of the masters of eloquence, the comradeship, now grave now gay, the differences that left no sting, as of a man differing with himself, the spice of disagreement which seasoned the monotony of consent. Each by turns would instruct or listen; impatiently we missed the absent friend, and savoured the joy of his return. We loved each other with all our hearts, and such tokens of friendship springing from the heart and displayed by a word, a glance, an expression, by a thousand pretty complaisances, supply the heat which welds souls together, and of many make one."

It is easily understood that such ties as these had given Augustine a permanent disgust for his rowdy comrades of a former time: he went no more with "The Wreckers." The small circle he took pleasure in was quiet and cheerful. Its merriment was controlled by the African gravity. He and his friends come before my eyes, a little like those students of theology, or those cultivated young Arabs, who discuss poetry, lolling indolently upon the cushions of a divan, while they roll between their fingers the amber beads of their rosary, or walking slowly under the arcades of a mosque, draped in their white-silk simars, with a serious and meditative air, gestures elegant and measured, courteous and harmonious speech, and something discreet, polite, and already clerical in their tone and manners.

In fact, the life which Augustine was at that time relishing was the pagan life on its best and gentlest side. The subtle network of habits and daily occupations enveloped him little by little. There was some risk of his growing torpid in this soft kind of life, when suddenly a rude shock roused him... It was a chance, but in his eyes a providential chance, which put the *Hortensius* of Cicero between his hands. Augustine was about nineteen, still a student; according to the order which prevailed in the schools, the time had come for him to read and explain this philosophical dialogue. He had no curiosity about the book. He took it from his sense of duty as a student, because it figured on the schedule. He unrolled the book, and began it, doubtless with calm indifference. All of a sudden, a great unexpected light shone between the lines. His heart throbbed. His whole soul sprang towards these phrases, so dazzling and revealing. He awoke from his long drowsiness. Before him shone a marvellous vision... As this dialogue is lost, we can hardly to-day account for such enthusiasm, and we hold that the Roman orator was a very middling philosopher. We know, however, through Augustine himself, that the book contained an eloquent praise of wisdom. And then, words are naught without the soul of the reader; all this, falling into Augustine's soul, rendered a prolonged and magnificent sound. It is evident, too, that just at the moment when he unrolled the book he was in a condition to receive this uplifting summons. In such minutes, when the heart, ignorant of itself, swells like the sea before a storm, when all the inner riches of the being overflow, the slightest glimmer is enough to reveal all these imprisoned forces, and the least shock to set them free.

He has at least preserved for us, in pious and faithful gratitude, some phrases of this dialogue which moved him so deeply. Especially does he admire this passage, wherein the author, after a long discussion, ends in these terms: "If, as pretend the philosophers of old time, who are also the greatest and most illustrious, we have a soul immortal and divine, it behoves us to think, that the more it has persevered in its way, that is to say, in reason, love, and the pursuit of truth, and the less it has been intermingled and stained in human error and passion, the easier will it be for it to raise itself and soar again to the skies."

Such phrases, read in a certain state of mind, might well overwhelm this young man, who was ere long to yearn for the cloister and was destined to be the founder of African monasticism. To give his whole life to the study of wisdom, to compel himself towards the contemplation of God, to live here below an almost divine life—this ideal, impossible to pagan wisdom, Augustine was called to realize in the name of Christ. That had dawned on him, all at once, while he was reading the *Hortensius*. And this ideal appeared to him so beautiful, so well worth the sacrifice of all he had hitherto loved, that nothing else counted for him any more. He despised rhetoric, the vain studies it compelled him to pursue, the honour and glory it promised him. What was all that to the prize of wisdom? For wisdom he felt himself ready to give up the world... But these heroic outbursts do not, as a rule, keep up very long in natures so changeable and impressionable as Augustine's. Yet they are not entirely thrown away. Thus, in early youth, come dim revelations of the future. There comes a presentiment of the port to which one will some day be sailing; a glimpse of the task to fulfil, the work to build up; and all this rises before the eyes in an entrancement of the whole being. Though the bright image be eclipsed, perhaps for years, the remembrance of it persists amid the worst degradations or the worst mediocrities. He who one single time has seen it pass, can never afterwards live quite like other people.

This fever calmed, Augustine set himself to reflect. The ancient philosophers promised him wisdom. But Christ also promised it! Was it not possible to reconcile them? And was not the Gospel ideal essentially more human than that of the pagan philosophers? Suppose he tried to submit to that, to bring the faith of his childhood into line with his ambitions as a young man of intellect? To be good after the manner of his mother, of his grandparents, of the good Thagaste servants, of all the humble Christian souls whose virtues he had been taught to respect, and at the same time to rival a Plato by the strength of thought—what a dream! Was it possible?... He tells us himself that the illusion was brief, and that he grew cool about the *Hortensius* because he did not find the name of Christ in it. He deceives himself, probably. At this time he was not so Christian. He yields to the temptation of a fine phrase: when he wrote his *Confessions* he had not yet entirely lost this habit.

But what remains true is, that feeling the inadequateness of pagan philosophy, he returned for a moment towards Christianity. The Ciceronian dialogue, by disappointing his thirst for the truth, gave him the idea of knocking at the door of the Church and trying to find out if on that side there might not be a practicable road for him. This is why the reading of *Hortensius* is in Augustine's eyes one of the great dates of his life. Although he fell back in his errors, he takes credit for his effort. He recognizes in it the first sign, and, as it were, a promise of his conversion. "Thenceforth, my God, began my upward way, and my return towards Thee."

He began then to study the Holy Scriptures with a more or less serious intention to instruct himself in them. But to go to the Bible by way of Cicero was to take the worst road. Augustine got lost there. This direct popular style, which only cares about saying things, and not about how they are said, could only repel the pupil of Carthage rhetoricians, the imitator of the harmonious Ciceronian sentences. Not only had he much too spoiled a taste in literature, but there was also too much literature in this pose of a young man who starts off one fine morning to conquer wisdom. He was punished for his lack of sincerity, and especially of humility. He understood nothing of the Scripture, and "I found it," he says, "a thing not known to the proud, nor yet laid open to children, but poor in appearance, lofty in operation, and veiled in mysteries. At that time, I was not the man to bow my head so as to pass in at its door."...

He grew tired very quickly. He turned his back on the Bible, as he had thrown aside *Hortensius*, and he went to find pasture elsewhere. Nevertheless, his mind had been set in motion. Nevermore was he to know repose, till he had found truth. He demanded this truth from all the sects and all the churches. So it was, that in despair he flung himself into Manicheeism.

Some have professed amazement that this honest and practical mind should have stuck fast in a doctrine so tortuous, so equivocal, contaminated by fancies so grossly absurd. But perhaps it is forgotten that there was everything in Manicheeism. The leaders of the sect did not deliver the bulk of the doctrine all at once to their catechumens; the entire initiation was a matter of several degrees. Now Augustine never went higher than a simple *auditor* in the Manichean Church. What attracted specially fine minds to the Manichees, was that they began by declaring themselves rationalists. To reconcile faith with natural science and philosophy has been the fad of heresiarchs and free-thinkers in all ages. The Manicheans bragged that they had succeeded. They went everywhere, crying out: "Truth, Truth!" That suited Augustine very well: it was just what he was looking for. He hastened to the preachings of these humbugs, impatient to receive at last this "truth," so noisily announced. From what they said, it was contained in several large books written by their prophet under the guidance of the Holy Ghost. There was quite a library of them. By way of bamboozling the crowd, they produced some of them which looked very important, ponderous as Tables of the Law, richly bound in vellum, and embellished with striking illuminations. How was it possible to doubt that the entire revelation was contained in such beautiful books? One felt at once full of respect for a religion which was able to produce in its favour the testimony of such a mass of writings.

However, the priests did not open them. To allay the impatience of their hearers, they amused them by criticizing the books and dogmas of the Catholics. This preliminary criticism was the first lesson of their instruction. They pointed out any number of incoherences, absurdities, and interpolations in the Bible: according to them, a great part of the Scriptures had been foisted on the world by the Jews. But they triumphed especially in detecting the contradictions of the Gospel narratives. They sapped them with syllogisms. It is easy to understand that these exercises in logic should have at once attracted the youthful Augustine. With his extraordinary dialectical subtilty, he soon became very good at it himself—much better even than his masters. He made speeches in their assemblies, fenced against a text, peremptorily refuted it, and reduced his adversaries to silence. He was applauded, covered with praise. A religion which brought him such successes must be the true one.

After he became a bishop, he tried to explain to himself how it was that he fell into Manicheeism, and could find only two reasons. "The first," he says, "was a friendship which took hold of me under I know not what appearance of kindness, and was like a cord about my neck... The second was those unhappy victories that I almost always won in our disputes."

But there is still another which he mentions elsewhere, and it had perhaps the most weight. This was the loose moral code which

Manicheeism authorized. This doctrine taught that we are not responsible for the evil we do. Our sins and vices are the work of the evil Principle—the God of Darkness, enemy of the God of Light. Now at the moment when Augustine was received as *auditor* by the Manichees, he had a special need of excusing his conduct by a moral system so convenient and indulgent. He had just formed his connection with her who was to become the mother of his child.

Chapter 4
THE SWEETNESS OF TEARS

Augustine was nearly twenty. He had finished his studies in rhetoric within the required time. According to the notions of that age, a young man ought to have concluded his course by his twentieth year. If not, he was considered past mending and sent back there and then to his family.

It may appear surprising that a gifted student like Augustine did not finish his rhetoric course sooner. But after his terms at Madaura, he had lost nearly a year at Thagaste. Besides, the life of Carthage had so many charms for him that doubtless he was in no hurry to leave. However that may be, the moment was now come for him to make up his mind about his career. The wishes of his parents, the advice of his masters, as well as his own ambitions and qualities, urged him, as we know, to become a barrister. But now, suddenly, all his projects for the future changed. Not only did he give up the law, but at the very moment when all appeared to smile on him, at the opening of his youth, he left Carthage to go and bury himself as a teacher of grammar in the little free-town his birthplace.

As he has neglected to give any explanation of this sudden determination, we are reduced to conjectures. It is likely that his mother was bothered about household expenses and could no longer afford to keep him at Carthage. Besides, she had other children, a son and daughter, to start in life. Augustine was on the point of being, if not poor, at least very hard up. He must do something to earn his living, and as quickly as possible. In these conditions, the quickest way out of the difficulty was to sell to others what he had bought from his masters. To live, he would open a word-shop, as he calls it disdainfully. But as he had only just ceased to be a student, he could not dream of becoming a professor in a great city such as Carthage, and setting himself up in rivalry to so many celebrated masters. The best thing he could do, if he did not want to vegetate, was to fall back on some more modest post. Now his protector, Romanianus, wanted him to go to Thagaste. This rich man had a son almost grown up, whom it was necessary to put as soon as possible in the hands of a tutor. Augustine, so often helped by the father, was naturally thought of to look after the youth. Furthermore, Romanianus, who appreciated Augustine's talent, must have been anxious to attract him to Thagaste and keep him there. With an eye to the interests of his freetown, he desired to have such a shining light in the place. So he asked this young man, whom he patronized, to return to his native district and open a grammar school. He promised him pupils, and, above all, the support of his influence, which was considerable, Monnica, as we may conjecture, added her entreaties to those of the great head of the Thagaste municipality. Augustine yielded.

Did it grieve him very much to make up his mind to this exile? It must have been extremely hard for a young man of twenty to give up Carthage and its pleasures. Moreover, it is pretty nearly certain that at this time he had already started that connection which was to last so long. To leave a mistress whom he loved, and that in all the freshness of a passion just beginning—one wonders how he was able to make up his mind to it. And yet he did leave, and spent nearly a year at Thagaste.

One peculiar mark of the youth, and even of the whole life of Augustine, is the ease with which he unlearns and breaks off his habits—the sentimental as well as the intellectual. He used up a good many doctrines before resting in the Catholic truth; and even afterwards, in the course of a long life, he contradicted and corrected himself more than once in his controversies and theological writings. His *Retractations* prove this. One might say that the accustomed weighs on him as a hindrance to his liberty; that the look of the places where he lives becomes hateful to him as a threat of servitude. He feels dimly that his true country is elsewhere, and that if he must settle anywhere it is in the house of his Heavenly Father. *Inquietum est cor nostrum, donec requi-*

escat in te... "Restless are our hearts, O my God, until they rest in Thee." Long before St. Francis of Assisi, he practised the mystic rule: "As a stranger and a pilgrim." It is true that in his twentieth year he was very far from being a mystic. But he already felt that restlessness which made him cross the sea and roam Italy from Rome to Milan. He is an impulsive. He cannot resist the mirages of his heart or his imagination. He is always ready to leave. The road and its chances tempt him. He is eager for the unknown. He lets himself be carried in delight by the blowing wind. God calls him; he obeys without knowing where he goes. This unsettled young man, halting between contrary passions, who feels at home nowhere, has already the soul of an apostle.

This changeableness of mood was probably the true cause of his departure for Thagaste. But other more apparent reasons, reasons more patent to a juvenile consciousness, guided him also. No doubt he was not sorry to reappear in his little town, although he was so young, with the importance and authority of a master. His former companions were going to become his pupils. And then the Manichees had fanaticized him. Carried away by the neophyte's bubbling zeal, elevated by his triumphs at the public meetings in Carthage, he meant to shine before his fellow-countrymen, and perhaps convert them. He departed with his mind made up to proselytize. Let us believe also, that in spite of his dissolute life, and the new passion that filled his heart, he did not come back to Thagaste without an affectionate thought at the back of his head for his mother.

The reception that Monnica had in reserve for him was going to surprise him considerably. Since her widowhood, the wife of Patricius had singularly advanced in the way of Christian perfection. The early Church not only offered widows the moral help of its sacraments and consolations, it also granted a special dignity with certain privileges to those who made a vow to refrain from sex-intercourse. They had in the basilicas, even as the consecrated virgins, a place of honour, divided from that of the other matrons by a balustrade. They wore a special dress. They were obliged to a conduct which would shew them worthy of all the outer marks of respect which surrounded them. The austerity of Monnica had increased with the zeal of her faith. She set an example to the Church people at Thagaste. Docile to the teachings of her priests, eager to serve her brethren, multiplying alms as much as she could with her straitened means, she was unfailing at the services of the Church.

Twice daily, morning and evening, she might be seen, exact to the hour of prayer and sermon. She did not go there, her son assures us, to mingle in cabals and the gossip of pious females, but to hear God's word in homily, and that God might hear her in prayer.

The widow compelled all who were about her to the same severe rule which she herself observed. In this rigid atmosphere of his home, the student from Carthage, with his free, fashionable airs, must have caused a painful astonishment. Monnica felt at once that she and her son understood each other no longer. She began by remonstrating with him. Augustine rebelled. Things got worse when, with his presumption of the young professor new-enamelled by the schools, the harsh and aggressive assurance of the heresiarch, he boasted as loud as he could of being a Manichee. Monnica, deeply wounded in her piety and motherly tenderness, ordered him to give up his errors. He refused, and only replied by sarcasms to the poor woman's complaints. Then she must have believed that the separation was final, that Augustine had committed an irreparable crime. Being an African Christian, absolute in her faith and passionate for its defence, she regarded her son as a public danger. She was filled with horror at his treason. It is possible, too, that guided by the second-sight of her affection, she saw clearer into Augustine's heart than he did himself. She was plunged in sorrow that he mistook himself to this extent, and refused the Grace which desired to win him to the Catholic unity. And as he was not content with losing himself, but also drew others into peril—disputing, speech-making before his friends, abusing his power of language to throw trouble into consciences—Monnica finally made up her mind. She forbade her son to eat at her table, or to sleep under her roof. She drove him from the house.

This must have been a big scandal in Thagaste. It does not appear, however, that Augustine cared much. In all the conceit of his false knowledge, he had that kind of inhumanity which drives the intellectual to make litter of the sweetest and deepest feelings as a sacrifice to his abstract idol. Not only did he not mind very much if his apostasy made his mother weep, but he did not trouble, either, to reconcile the chimeras of his brain with the living reality of his soul and the things of life. Whatever he found inconvenient, he tranquilly denied, content if he had talked well and entangled his adversary in the net of his syllogisms.

Put in interdict by Monnica, he simply went and quartered himself on Romanianus. The sumptuous hospitality he received there very soon consoled him for his exile from his home. And if his self-esteem had been affronted, the pride of living familiarly with so important a personage was, for a vain young man, a very full compensation.

In fact, this Romanianus roused the admiration of the whole country by his luxury and lavish expenditure. He was bound to ruin himself in the long run, or, at any rate, to raise up envious people bent upon his ruin. Being at the head of the Decurions, he was the protector, not only of Thagaste, but of the neighbouring towns. He was the great patron, the influential man, who had nearly the whole country for his dependents. The town council, through gratitude and flattery, had had his name engraved upon tables of brass, and had put up statues to him. It had even conferred powers on him wider than municipal powers. The truth is that Romanianus did not dole out his benefactions to his fellow-citizens. He gave them bear-fights and other spectacles till then unknown at Thagaste. He did not grudge public banquets, and every day a free meal was to be got at his house. The guests were served plentifully. After having eaten his dinner, they dipped in the purse of the host. Romanianus knew the art of doing an obliging thing discreetly, and even how to anticipate requests which might be painful. So he was proclaimed unanimously, "the most humane, the most liberal, the most polite and happiest of men."

Generous to his dependents, he did not forget himself. He built a villa which, by the space it occupied, was a real palace, with *thermæ* walled in precious marbles. He passed his time in the baths, or gaming, or hunting—in short, he led the life of a great landed proprietor of those days.

No doubt these villas had neither the beauty nor the art-value of the great Italian villas, which were a kind of museums in a pretty, or grand, natural frame; but they did not lack charm. Some of them, like that of Romanianus, were built and decorated at lavish expense. Immensely large, they took in sometimes an entire village; and sometimes, also, the villa, properly speaking, the part of the building where the master dwelt, was fortified, closed in by walls and towers like a feudal castle. Upon the outer gates and the entrance door might be read in big letters: "The Property of So-and-so." Often, the inscription was repeated upon the walls of an enclosure or of a farm, which really belonged to a dependent of the great man. Under the shelter of the lord's name, these smallholders defended themselves better against fiscal tyranny, or were included in the immunities of their patrons. So was formed, under the cover of patronage, a sort of African feudalism. Augustine's father, who owned vineyards, was certainly a vassal of Romanianus.

As the African villa was a centre of agricultural activity, it maintained on the estate a whole population of slaves, workmen, and smallholders. The chief herdsman's house neighboured that of the forester. Through deer-parks, enclosed by latticed fences, wandered gazelles. Oil factories, vats and cellars for wine, ran on from the bath-buildings and the offices. Then there was the main building with its immense doorway, its belvedere of many stories, as in the Roman villas, its interior galleries, and wings to the right and left of the *atrium*. In front lay the terraces, the gardens with straight walks formed by closely-clipped hedges of box which led to pools and jets of water, to arbours covered with ivy, to nymph-fountains ornamented with columns and statues. In these gardens was a particular place called the "philosopher's corner." The mistress of the house used to go there to read or dream. Her chair, or folding-seat, was placed under the shade of a palm tree. Her "philosopher" followed her, holding her parasol and leading her little favourite dog.

It is easy to realize that Augustine managed to stand his mother's severity without overmuch distress in one of these fine country houses. To be comfortable there, he had only to follow his natural inclination, which was, he tells us, epicureanism. It is most certain that at this period the only thing he cared about and sought after was pleasure. Staying with Romanianus, he took his share in all the pleasant things of life, *suavitates illius vitæ*—shared the amusements of his host, and only bothered about his pupils when he had nothing better to do. He must have been as little of a grammarian as possible—he hadn't the time. With the tyrannical friendship of rich people, who are hard put to it to find occupation, Romanianus doubtless monopolized him from morning till night. They hunted together, or dined, or read poetry, or discussed in the evergreen alleys of the garden or "the philosopher's corner." And naturally, the recent convert to Manicheeism did his best to indoctrinate and convert his patron—so far at least as a careless man like Romanianus could be converted. Augustine accuses himself of having "flung" Romanianus into his own errors. Augustine probably was not so guilty. His wealthy friend does not seem to have had any very firm convictions. In all likelihood, he was a pagan, a sceptical or hesitating pagan, such as existed in numbers at that time. Led by Augustine, he drew near to Manicheeism. Then, when Augustine gave up Manicheeism for Platonic philosophy, we see Romanianus take the airs of a philosopher. Later, when Augustine came back to Catholicism, he drew Romanianus in his wake towards that religion. This man of fashion was one of those frivolous people who never go deep into things, for whom ideas are only a pastime, and who consider philosophers or men of letters as amusers. But it is certain that he liked to listen to Augustine, and let himself be influenced. If he trifled with Manicheeism, the reason was that Augustine dazzled him with his arguments and fine phrases. This orator of twenty had already extraordinary charm.

So Augustine led a delightful life with Romanianus. Everything pleased him—his talking triumphs, the admiration of his hearers, the flattery and luxury which surrounded him. Meanwhile, Monnica was plunged in grief at his conduct, and implored God to draw him from his errors. She began to be sorry that she had sent him away, and with the clear-sightedness of the Christian, she perceived that Romanianus' house was not good for the prodigal. It would be better to have him back. Near her he would run less risk of being corrupted. Through intense praying, came to her a dream which quickened her determination. "She dreamed that she was weeping and lamenting, with her feet planted on a wooden rule, when she saw coming towards her a radiant youth who smiled upon her cheerfully. He asked the reason of her sorrow and her daily tears ... and when she told him she was bewailing my perdition, he bade her be of good comfort, look and see, for where she was, there was I also. She looked, and saw me standing by her side on the same rule."

Filled with joy by this promise from on high, Monnica asked her son to come home. He did come back, but with the quibbles of the Sophist, the rhetorician cavilled against his mother. He tried to upset her happiness. He said to her:

"Since, according to your dream, we are to be both standing on the same rule, that means that you are going to be a Manichean."

"No," answered Monnica. "*He* did not say, where he is you will be, but where you are he will be."

Augustine confesses that this strong good sense made a certain impression on him. Nevertheless he did not change. For still nine years he remained a Manichee.

As a last resource, Monnica begged a bishop she knew, a man deeply read in the Scriptures, to speak with her son and refute his errors. But so great was the reputation of Augustine as an orator and dialectician that the holy man dared not try a fall with such a vigorous jouster. He answered the mother very wisely, that a mind so subtle and acute could not long continue in such gross sophisms. And he offered his own example, for he, too, had been a Manichee. But Monnica pressed him with entreaties and tears. At last the bishop, annoyed by her persistence, but at the same time moved by her tears, answered with a roughness mingled with kindness and compassion:

"Go, go! Leave me alone. Live on as you are living. It cannot be that the son of such tears should be lost."

Filius istarum lacrymarum: the son of such tears!... Was it indeed the country bishop, or rather the rhetorician Augustine who, in a burst of gratitude, hit upon this sublime sentence? Certain it is that later on Augustine saw in his mother's tears as it were a first baptism whence he came forth regenerate. After having borne him according to the flesh, Monnica, by her tears and moans, gave him birth into the spiritual life. Monnica wept because of Augustine. Monnica wept for Augustine. This is rather astonishing in the case of so severe a mother—this African a trifle rough. The expressions—tears and moans and weeping—occur so often in her son's writings, that we are at first tempted to take them for pious metaphors—figures of a sacred rhetoric. We suspect that Monnica's tears must come from the Bible, an imitation of King David's penitential tears. But it would be quite an error to believe that. Monnica wept real tears. In her whole-hearted prayers she bedewed the pavement of the basilica; she moistened the balustrade against which she leant her forehead. This austere woman, this widow whose face nobody saw any more, whose body was shapeless by reason of the mass of stuffs, grey and black, which wrapped her from head to foot—this rigid Christian concealed a heart full of love. Love such as this was then a perfectly new thing.

That an African woman should carry her piety to the point of fanaticism; that she should work to conquer her son to her faith; that, if he strayed from it, she should hate him and drive him out with curses—this has been seen in Africa at all times. But that a mother should mourn at the thought that her child is lost for another life; that she grows terror-stricken and despairing when she thinks that she may possess a happiness in which he will have no part, and walk in the gardens of Heaven while her child will not be there—no, this had never been seen before. "Where I am you will be," near me, against my heart, our two hearts meeting in the one same love—in this union of souls, continued beyond the grave, lies all the Christian sweetness and hope.

Augustine was no longer, or not yet, a Christian. But in his tears he is the true son of his mother. This gift of tears that Saint Lewis of France begged God with so much earnestness and contrition to grant him, Monnica's son had to the full. "For him to weep was a pleasure."* He inebriated himself with his tears. Now, just while he was at Thagaste, he lost a friend whom he loved intensely. This death set free the fountain of tears. They are not yet the holy tears which he will shed later before God, but only poor human tears, more pathetic perhaps to our own weakness.

Who was this friend? He tells us in very vague terms. We only know that they had grown up as boys together and had gone to the same schools; that they had just passed a year together, probably at Carthage; that this young man, persuaded by him, was become a Manichee; and that, in a word, they loved passionately. Augustine, while speaking of him, recalls in a deeper sense what Horace said of his friend Virgil: *dimidium animæ*—"O thou half of my soul!"

Well, this young man fell gravely sick of a fever. As all hope was at an end, they baptized him, according to the custom. He grew better, was almost cured, "As soon as I was able to talk to him," says Augustine—"and that was as soon as he could bear it, for I never left his side, and we were bound up in one another—I ventured a jest, thinking that he would jest too, about the baptism which he had received, when he could neither think nor feel. But by this time he had been told of his baptism. He shrank from me as from an enemy, and with a wonderful new-found courage, warned me never to speak so to him again, if I wished to remain his friend. I was so astounded and confused that I said no more, resolving to wait till he should regain his strength, *when I would tell him frankly what I thought.*"

So, at this serious moment, he whom they called "the Carthaginian disputer" was sorry not to be able to measure himself in a bout of dialectics with his half-dead friend. The intellectual poison had so perverted

---

* Sainte-Beuve.

his mind, that it almost destroyed in him the feelings of common decency. But if his head, as he acknowledges, was very much spoiled, his heart remained intact. His friend died a few days after, and Augustine was not there. He was stunned by it.

His grief wrought itself up to wildness and despair. "This sorrow fell like darkness on my heart, and wherever I looked I saw nothing but death. My country became a torture, my father's house a misery. All the pleasures that I had shared with him, turned into hideous anguish now that he was gone. My eyes sought for him everywhere, and found him not. I hated the familiar scenes because he was not there, and they could no more cry to me, 'Lo! he will come.' as they used when he was absent but alive..." Then Augustine began to weep louder, he prolonged his weeping, finding consolation only in tears. Monnica's tenderness was restrained; in him it was given full vent and exaggerated. At that time, the Christian moderation was unknown to him, as well as the measure which the good taste of the ancients prompted. He has often been compared to the most touching geniuses, to Virgil, to Racine, who had also the gift of tears. But Augustine's tenderness is more abandoned, and, so to speak, more romantic. It even works up, sometimes, into an unhealthy excitement.

To be full of feeling, as Augustine was then, is not only to feel with excessive sensitiveness the least wounds, the slightest touches of love or hate, nor is it only to give oneself with transport; but it is especially to take delight in the gift of oneself, to feel at the moment of full abandonment that one is communicating with something infinitely sweet, which already has ceased to be the creature loved. It is love for love, it is to weep for the pleasure of tears, it is to mix with tenderness a kind of egoism avid of experiences. Having lost his friend, Augustine loathes all the world. He repeats: "Tears were my only comfort. I was wretched, and my wretchedness was dear to me." And accordingly, he did not want to be consoled. But as, little by little, the terrors of that parting subsided, he perceived himself that he played with grief and made a joy of his tears. "My tears," he says, "were dearer to me than my friend had been." By degrees the friend is almost forgotten. Though Augustine may hate life because his friend has gone, he confesses naively that he would not have sacrificed his existence for the sake of the dead. He surmises that what is told of Orestes and Pylades contending to die for each other is but a fable. Ultimately, he comes to write: "Perhaps I feared to die, *lest the other half of him whom I had loved so dearly, should perish.*" He himself, in his *Retractations*, condemns this phrase as pure rhetoric. It remains true that what was perhaps the deepest sorrow of his life—this sorrow so sincere and painful which had "rent and bloodied his soul"—ended with a striking phrase.

It should be added, that in a stormy nature like his, grief, like love, wears itself out quickly. It burns up passion and sentiment as it does ideas. When at length he regained his calm, everything appeared drab. Thagaste became intolerable. With his impulsive temperament, his changeable humour, he all at once hit upon a plan: To go back to Carthage and open a rhetoric school. Perhaps, too, the woman he loved and had abandoned there was pressing him to return. Perhaps she told him that she was about to become a mother. Always ready to go away, Augustine scarcely hesitated. It is more than likely that he did not consult Monnica. He only told Romanianus, who, as he had all kinds of reasons for wanting to keep Augustine at Thagaste, at first strongly objected. But the young man pointed to his future, his ambition to win fame. Was he going to bury all that in a little town?

Romanianus yielded, and with a generosity that is no longer seen, he paid the expenses this time too.

Chapter 5
THE SILENCE OF GOD

Augustine was going to live nine years at Carthage—nine years that he squandered in obscure tasks, in disputes sterile or unfortunate for himself and others—briefly, in an utter forgetfulness of his true vocation. "And during this time Thou wert silent, O my God!" he cries, in recalling only the faults of his early youth. Now, the silence of God lay heavy. And yet even in those years his tormented soul had not ceased to appeal. "Where wert Thou then, O my God, while I looked for Thee? Thou wert before me. But I had drawn away from myself and I could not find myself. How much less, then, could I find Thee."

This was certainly the most uneasy, and, at moments, the most painful time of his life. Hardly was he got back to Carthage than he had to struggle against ever-increasing money difficulties. Not only had he to get his own living, but the living of others—possibly his mother's and that of his brother and sister—at all events, he had to support his mistress and the child. It is possible that the infant was born before its father left Thagaste; if not, the birth must have occurred shortly after.

The child was called Adeodatus. There is a kind of irony in this name, which was then usual, of Adeodatus—"Gift of God." This son of his sin, as Augustine calls him, this son whom he did not want, and the news of whose birth must have been a painful shock—this poor child was a gift of Heaven which the father could have well done without.

And then, when he saw him, he was filled with joy, and he cherished him as a real gift from God.

He accepted his fatherhood courageously, and, as it happens in such cases, he was drawn closer to his mistress, their association taking on something of conjugal dignity. Did the mother of Adeodatus justify such attachment—an attachment which was to last more than ten years? The mystery in which Augustine intended that the woman he had loved the most should remain enveloped for all time, is nearly impenetrable to us. No doubt she was of a very humble, not to say low class, since Monnica judged it impossible to bring about a marriage between the ill-assorted pair. There must have been an extreme inequality between the birth and education of the lovers. This did not prevent Augustine from loving his mistress passionately, for her beauty perhaps, or perhaps for her goodness of heart, or both. Nevertheless, it is surprising, that in view of his changing humour, and his prompt and impressionable soul, he remained faithful to her so long. What was to prevent his taking his son and going off? Ancient custom authorized such an act. But Augustine was tender-hearted. He was afraid to cause pain; he dreaded for others the wounds that caused him so much suffering himself. So he stayed on from kindness, from pity, habit too, and also because, in spite of everything, he loved the mother of his child. Up to the time of his conversion, they lived like husband and wife.

So now, to keep his family, he really turns "a dealer in words." In spite of his youth (he was barely twenty) the terms he had kept at Thagaste as a teacher of grammar allowed him to take his place among the rhetoricians at Carthage. Thanks to Romanianus, he got pupils at once. His protector at Thagaste sent his son, that young Licentius whose education Augustine had already begun, with one of his brothers, doubtless younger. It seems likely that the two youths lived in Augustine's house. A small fact which their master has preserved, looks like a proof of this. A spoon having been lost in the house, Augustine, to find out where it was, told Licentius to go and consult a wizard, one Albicerius, who had, just then, a great name in Carthage. This message is scarcely to be explained unless we suppose the lad was lodging in his professor's house. Another of the pupils is known to us. This is Eulogius, who was later on a rhetorician at Carthage, and of whom Augustine relates an extraordinary dream. Finally, there was Alypius, a little younger than himself, his friend—"the brother of his heart," as he calls him. Alypius had been attending his lessons at Thagaste. When the schoolmaster abruptly threw up his employment, the father of the pupil was angry, and in sending his son to Carthage, he forbade him to go near Augustine's class. But it was difficult to keep such eager friends apart. Little by little, Alypius overcame his father's objections, and became a pupil of his friend.

Augustine's knowledge, when he began to lecture, could not have been very deep, for he had only lately quitted the student's bench himself. His duties forced him to learn what he did not know. In teaching he taught himself. It was at this time that he did most of the reading which afterwards added substance to his polemics and treatises. He tells us himself that he read in those days all that he could lay hands on. He is very proud of having read by himself and understood without any assistance from a master, the *Ten Categories* of Aristotle, which was considered one of the most abstruse works of the Stagirite. In an age when instruction was principally by word of mouth, and books comparatively rare, it is obvious that Augustine was not what we call an "all-devouring reader." We do not know if Carthage had many libraries, or what the libraries were worth. It is no less true that the author of *The City of God* is the last of the Latin writers who had a really all-round knowledge. It is he who is the link between modern times and pagan antiquity. The Middle Age hardly knew classical literature, save by the allusions and quotations of Augustine.

So in spite of family and professional cares, he did not lose his intellectual proclivities. The conquest of truth remained always his great ambition. He still hoped to find it in Manicheeism, but he began to think that it was a long time coming. The leaders of the sect could not have trusted him thoroughly. They feared his acute and subtle mind, so quick to detect the flaw in a thesis or argument. That is why they postponed his initiation into their secret doctrines. Augustine remained a simple *auditor* in their Church. By way of appeasing the enormous activity of his intelligence, they turned him on to controversy, and the critical discussion of the Scriptures. Giving themselves out for Christians, they adopted a part of them, and flung aside as interpolated or forged all that was not in tune with their theology. Augustine, as we know, triumphed in disputes of this kind, and was vain because he excelled in them.

And when he grew tired of this negative criticism and asked his evangelists to give him more substantial food, they put him on some exoteric doctrine calculated to appeal to a young imagination by its poetic or philosophical colouring. The catechumen was not satisfied, but he put up with it for lack of anything better. Very prettily he compares these enemies of the Scriptures to the snarers of birds, who defile or fill with earth all the water-places where the birds use to drink, save one mere; and about this they set their snares. The birds all fly there, not because the water is better, but because there is no other water, and they know not where else to go and drink. So Augustine, not knowing where to quench his thirst for truth, was fain to make the best of the confused pantheism of the Manichees.

What remains noteworthy is, that however unstable his own convictions were, he yet converted everybody about him. It was through him that his friends became Manichees: Alypius one of the first; then Nebridius, the son of a great landowner near Carthage; Honoratius, Marcianus; perhaps, too, the youngest of his pupils, Licentius and his brother—all victims of his persuasive tongue, which he exerted later on to draw them back from their errors. So great was his charm—so deep, especially, was public credulity!

This fourth century was no longer a century of strong Christian faith. On the other hand, the last agony of paganism was marked by a new attack of the lowest credulity and superstition. As the Church energetically combated both one and the other, it is not surprising that it was chiefly the pagans who were contaminated. The old religion was to end by foundering in magic. The greatest minds of the period, the neo-Platonists, the Emperor Julian himself, were miracle-workers, or at any rate, adepts in the occult sciences. Augustine, who was then separated from Christianity, followed the general impulse, together with the young men he knew. Just now we saw him sending to consult the soothsayer, Albicerius, about the loss of a spoon. And this man of intellect believed also in astrologers and nigromancers.

Strips of lead have been found at Carthage upon which are written magic spells against horses entered for races in the circus. Just like the Carthaginian jockeys, Augustine had recourse to these hidden and fraudulent practices, to make sure of success. On the eve of a verse competition in the theatre, he fell in with a wizard who offered, if they could agree about the price, to sacrifice a certain number of animals to buy the victory. Upon this, Augustine, very much annoyed, declared that if the prize were a crown of immortal gold, not a fly should be sacrificed to help him win it. Really, magic was repellent to the honesty of his mind, as well as to his nerves, by reason of the suspicious and brutal part of its operations. As a rule, it was involved with haruspicy, and had a side of sacred anatomy and the kitchen which revolted the sensitive—dissection of flesh, inspection of entrails, not to mention the slaughtering and strangling of victims. Fanatics, such as Julian, gave themselves up with delight to these disgusting manipulations. What we know of Augustine's soul makes it quite clear why he recoiled with horror.

Astrology, on the contrary, attracted him by its apparent science. Its adepts called themselves "mathematicians," and thus seemed to borrow from the exact sciences something of their solidity. Augustine often discussed astrology with a Carthage physician, Vindicianus, a man of great sense and wide learning, who even reached Proconsular honours. In vain did he point out to the young rhetorician that the pretended prophecies of the mathematicians were the effect of chance; in vain did Nebridius, less credulous than his friend, join his arguments to those of the crafty physician; Augustine clung obstinately to his chimera. His dialectical mind discovered ingenious justifications for what the astrologers claimed.

Thus, dazzled by all the intellectual phantasms, he strayed from one science to another, repeating meanwhile in his heart the motto of his Manichean masters: "The Truth, the Truth!". But whatever might be the attractions of the speculative life, he had first to face the needs of actual life. The sight of his child called him back to a sense of his position. To get money, and for that purpose to push himself forward, put himself in evidence, increase his reputation—Augustine worked at that as hard as he could. It led him to enter for the prize of dramatic poetry. He was declared the winner. His old friend, the physician Vindicianus, who was then Proconsul, placed the crown, as he says, upon his "disordered head." The future Father of the Church writing for the theatre—and what a theatre it was then!—is not the least extraordinary thing in this life so disturbed and, at first sight, so contradictory.

It was also from literary ambition that about the same time he wrote a book on æsthetics called *Upon the Beautiful and the Fit*, which he dedicated to a famous colleague, the Syrian Hierius, "orator to the City of Rome," one of the professors of the official education appointed either by the Roman municipality or the Imperial treasury. This Levantine rhetorician had an immense success in the capital of the Empire. His renown had got beyond academical and fashionable circles and crossed the sea. Augustine admired him on trust, like everybody else. It is clear that, at this time he could not imagine a more glorious fortune for himself than to become, like Hierius, orator to the City of Rome. Later in life, the Bishop of Hippo, while condemning the vanity of his youthful ambitions, must have made some extremely ironical reflections as to their modesty. How mistaken he was about himself! An Augustine had dreamed of equalling one day this obscure pedagogue, of whom nobody, save for him, would ever have spoken again. Men of instinct, like Augustine, continually go wrong in this way about their object and the means to employ. But their mistakes are only in appearance. A will stronger than their own leads them, by mysterious ways, whither they ought to go.

This first book of Augustine's is lost, and we are unable to say whether there be any reason to regret it. He himself recalls it to us in a very indifferent tone and rather vague terms. It would seem, however, that his æsthetic had a basis of Manichean metaphysics. But what is significant for us, in this youthful essay, is that the first time Augustine wrote as an author it was to define and to praise Beauty. He did not yet know, at least not directly from the text, the dialogues of Plato, and he is already inclined to Platonism. He was this by nature. His Christianity will be a religion all of light and beauty. For him, the supreme Beauty is identical with the supreme Love. "Do we love anything," he used to say to his friends, "except what is beautiful?" *Num amamus aliquid, nisi pulchrum?* Again, at the end of his life, when he strives in *The City of God* to make clear for us the dogma of the resurrection of the body, he thinks our bodies shall rise free from all earthly flaws, in all the splendour of the perfect human type. Nothing of the body will be lost. It will keep all its limbs and all its organs *because they are beautiful.* One recognizes in this passage, not only the Platonist, but the traveller and art-lover, who had gazed upon some of the finest specimens of ancient statuary.

This first book had hardly any success. Augustine does not even say whether the celebrated Hierius paid him a compliment about it, and he has an air of giving us to understand that he had no other admirer but himself. New disappointments, more serious mortifications, changed little by little his state of mind and his plans for the future. He was obliged to acknowledge that after years of effort he was scarcely more advanced than at the start. There was no chance to delude himself with vain pretences: it was quite plain to everybody that the rhetorician Augustine was not a success. Now, why was this? Was it that he lacked the gift of teaching? Perhaps he had not the knack of keeping order, which is the most indispensable of all for a schoolmaster. What suited him best no doubt was a small and select audience which he charmed rather than ruled. Large and noisy classes he could not manage. At Carthage, these rhetoric classes were particularly difficult to keep in order, because the students were more rowdy than elsewhere. At any moment "The Wreckers" might burst in and make a row. Augustine, who had not joined in these "rags" when he was a student, saw himself obliged to endure them as a professor. He had nothing worse to complain of than his fellow-professors, in whose classes the same kind of disturbance took place. That was the custom and, in a manner of speaking, the rule in the Carthage schools. For all that, a little more authoritative bearing would not have harmed him in the eyes of these disorderly boys. But he had still graver defects for a professor who wants to get on: he was not a schemer, and he could not make the most of himself.

It is quite possible that he did not possess the qualities which just then pleased the pagan public in a rhetorician. The importance that the ancients attached to physical advantages in an orator is well known. Now, according to an old tradition, Augustine was a little man and not strong: till the end of his life he complained of his health. He had a weak voice, a delicate chest, and was often hoarse. Surely this injured him before audiences used to all the outward emphasis and all the studied graces of Roman eloquence. Finally, his written and spoken language had none of those brilliant and ingenious curiosities of phrase which pleased in literary and fashionable circles. This inexhaustibly prolific writer is not in the least a stylist. In this respect he is inferior to Apuleius, or Tertullian, though he leaves them far behind in the qualities of sincere and deep sentiment, poetic flow, colour, the vividness of metaphor, and, besides, the emotion, the suavity of the tone. With all that, no matter how hard he tried, he could never grasp what the rhetoricians of his time understood by style. This is why his writings, as well as his addresses, were not very much liked.

Nevertheless, good judges recognized his value, and guessed the powers, lying still unformed within him, which he was misusing ere they were mature. He was received at the house of the Proconsul Vindicianus, who liked to talk with him, and treated him with quite fatherly kindness. Augustine knew people in the best society. He did all his life. His charm and captivating manners made him welcome in the most exclusive circles. But just because he was valued by fashionable society, it came home to him more painfully that he had not the position he deserved with the public at large. Little by little his humour grew bitter. In this angry state of mind he was no longer able to consider things with the same confidence and serenity. His mental disquietudes took hold of him again.

His ideas were affected, first of all. He began to have doubts, more and more definite, about Manicheeism. He began by suspecting the rather theatrical austerity which the initiated of the sect made such a great parade of. Among other turpitudes, he saw one day in one of the busiest parts of Carthage "three of the Elect whinny after some women or other who were passing, and begin making such obscene signs that they surpassed the coarsest people for impudence and shamelessness." He was scandalized at that; but, after all, it was a small thing. He himself was not so very virtuous then. Generally your intellectual worries very little about squaring his conduct with his principles, and does not bother about the practical part. No; what was much worse in his eyes is that the Manichean physical science, a congeries of fables more or less symbolical, suddenly struck him as ruinous. He had just been studying astronomy, and he found that the cosmology of the Manichees—of these men who called themselves materialists—did not agree with scientific facts. Therefore Manicheeism must be wrong universally, since it ran counter to reason confirmed by experience.

Augustine spoke about his doubts, not only to his friends, but to the priests of his sect. These got out of the difficulty by evasions and the most dazzling promises. A Manichee bishop, a certain Faustus, was coming to Carthage. He was a man of immense learning. Most certainly he would refute every objection without the least trouble. He would confirm the young *auditors* in their faith... So Augustine and his friends waited for Faustus as for a Messiah. Their disappointment was immense. The supposed doctor turned out to be an ignorant man, who possessed no tincture of science or philosophy, and whose intellectual baggage consisted of nothing but a little grammar. A delightful talker and a wit, the most he could do was to discourse pleasantly on literature.

This disappointment, joined to the set-backs in his profession, brought about a crisis of soul and conscience in Augustine. So this Truth which he had sighed after so long, which had been so much promised to him, was only a decoy! One must be content not to know!... Then what was left to do since truth was unapproachable? Possibly fortune and honours would console him for it. But he was far enough from them too. He felt that he was on the wrong road, that he was getting into a rut at Carthage, as he had got into a rut at Thagaste. He must succeed, whatever the cost!... And then he gave way to one of those moments of weariness, when a man has no further hope of saving himself save by some desperate step. He was sick of where he was and of those about him. His friends, whom he knew too well, had nothing more to teach him, and could not help him in the only search which passionately interested him. And his entanglement became irksome. Here was nine years that this sharing of bed and board had lasted. His son was at that unattractive age which rather bores a young father than it revives an affection already old. No doubt he did not want to abandon him. He did not intend to break altogether with his mistress. But he felt the need of a change of air, to take himself off somewhere else, where he could breathe more freely and get fresh courage for his task.

Then it dawned on him to try his fortune at Rome. It was there that literary reputations were made. He would find there, no doubt, better judges than at Carthage. He would very likely end by getting a post in the public instruction, with a steady salary—this would relieve him of present worries, at all events. Probably he had already this plan in his head when he sent his treatise *On the Beautiful* to Hierius, orator to the City of Rome; he thought that by this politeness he might depend, later, on the backing of the well-known rhetorician. Lastly, his friends, Honoratius, Marcianus, and the others, earnestly persuaded him to go and find a stage worthy of him at Rome. Alypius, who was at this time finishing his law studies there, and must have felt their separation, pressed him to come to Rome and promised him success.

Once more, Augustine was ready to go away. He was not long in making up his mind. He was going to leave all belonging to him, his mistress, his child, till the time when his new position would enable him to send for them. He himself tells us that the chief motive which led him to decide on this journey was that the Roman students were said to be better disciplined and less noisy than the students at Carthage. Evidently, that is a reason which would weigh with a professor who objected to act the policeman in his class. But besides the reasons we have given, there were others which must have influenced his decision. Theodosius had lately ordered very heavy penalties against the Manichees. Not only did he condemn them to death, but he had instituted a perfect Inquisition, with the special duty of spying upon and prosecuting these heretics. Did it occur to Augustine that he might hide better in Rome, where he was unknown, than in a city where he was a marked man on account of his proselytizing zeal? In any case, his departure gave rise to calumnies which his adversaries, the Donatists, did not fail many years later to bring up again and make worse. They accused him of having run away from prosecution; he fled the country, so they said, on account of a judgment which was out against him, pronounced by the Proconsul Messianus. Augustine had no trouble in refuting these false insinuations. But all these facts seem to prove that the most ordinary prudence warned him to cross the sea as soon as possible.

Accordingly, he prepared to set sail. Let us hope that in spite of his lofty indifference to material things, he made some provision for the existence of the woman and child he left behind. As for her, she appeared to agree without over-many violent scenes to this parting, which, he said, was temporary. It was not the same with his mother. The very idea of Rome, which seemed to her another Babylon, terrified this austere African woman. What spiritual dangers lay in wait for her son there! She wanted to keep him near her, both to bring him to the faith and also to love him—this Augustine who had been her only human love. And then he was doubtless the chief support of the widow. Without him, what was going to become of her?

The fugitive was forced to put a trick on Monnica so as to carry out his plan. She would not leave him a moment, folded him in her arms, implored him with tears not to go. The night he was to sail she followed him down to the dock, although Augustine, to allay her suspicions, had told her a lie. He pretended that he was only going down to the ship with a friend to see him off. But Monnica, only half believing, followed. Night fell. Meanwhile, the ship, anchored in a little bay to the north of the city, did not move. The sailors were waiting till a wind rose to slip their moorings. The weather was moist and oppressive, as it usually is in the Mediterranean in August and September. There was not a breath of air. The hours passed on. Monnica, overcome by heat and fatigue, could hardly stand. Then Augustine cunningly persuaded her to go and pass the night in a chapel hard by, since it was plain that the ship would not weigh anchor till dawn. After many remonstrances, she at length agreed to rest in this chapel—a *memoria* consecrated to St. Cyprian, the great martyr and patron of Carthage.

Like most of the African sanctuaries of those days, and the *marabouts* of to-day, this one must have been either surrounded, or approached, by a court with a portico in arcades, where it was possible to sleep. Monnica sat down on the ground under her heap of veils among other poor people and travellers, who were come like her to try to find a little cool air on this stifling night near the relics of the blessed Cyprian. She prayed for her child, offering to God "the blood of her heart," begging God not to let him go, "for she loved to keep me with her" says Augustine, "as mothers are wont, yes, far more than most mothers." And like a true daughter of Eve, "weeping and crying, she sought again with groans the son she had brought forth with groans." She prayed for a long time; then, worn out with sorrow, she slept. The porter of the chapel, without knowing it, watched that night not only the mother of the rhetorician Augustine, but the ancestor of an innumerable line of souls; this humble woman, who slept there on the ground, on the flags of the courtyard, carried in her heart all the yearning of all the mothers of the future.

While she slept, Augustine went stealthily on board. The silence and the tempered splendour of the night weighed him down. Sometimes the cry of the sailors on watch took a strange note in the lustrous vaporous spaces. The Gulf of Carthage gleamed far off under the scintillation of the stars, under the palpitating of a milky way all white like the flowers of the garden of Heaven. But Augustine's heart was heavy, heavier than the air weighted by the heat and sea-damp—heavy from the lie and the cruelty he had just committed. He saw already the awakening and sorrow of his mother. His conscience was troubled, overcome by remorse and forebodings... Meanwhile, his friends tried to cheer him, and urged him to have courage and hope. Marcianus, while embracing him, reminded him of the verses of Terence:

"This day which brings to thee another life
Demands that thou another man shalt be."

Augustine smiled sadly. At last the ship began to move. The wind had risen, the wind of the grand voyage which was bearing him to the unknown... Suddenly, at the keen freshness of the open sea, he thrilled. His strength and confidence rushed back. To go away! What enchantment for all those who cannot fasten themselves to a corner of the earth, who know by instinct that they belong *elsewhere*, who always pass "as strangers and as pilgrims," and who go away with relief, as if they cast a burthen behind them. Augustine was of those people—of those who, among the fairest attractions of the Road, never cease to think of the Return. But he knew not where God was leading him. Marcianus was right: a new life was really beginning for him; only it was not the life that either of them hoped for.

He who departed as a rhetorician, to sell words, was to come back as an apostle, to conquer souls.

THE RETURN

Et ecce ibi es in corde eorum, in corde confitentium tibi, et projicientium se in te, et plorantium in sinu tuo, post vias suas difficiles...
And behold! Thou art there in their hearts, in the hearts of that confess to Thee, and cast themselves upon Thee, and sob upon Thy breast, after their weary ways...

— *Confessions*, V, 2.

Chapter 1
THE CITY OF GOLD

Augustine fell ill just after he got to Rome. It would seem that he arrived there towards the end of August or beginning of September, before the students reassembled, just at the time of heat and fevers, when all Romans who could leave the city fled to the summer resorts on the coast.

Like all the great cosmopolitan centres at that time, Rome was unhealthy. The diseases of the whole earth, brought by the continual inflow of foreigners, flourished there. Accordingly, the inhabitants had a panic fear of infection, like our own contemporaries. People withdrew prudently from those suffering from infectious disorders, who were left to their unhappy fate. If, from a sense of shame, they sent a slave to the patient's bedside, he was ordered to the sweating-rooms, and there disinfected from head to foot, before he could enter the house again.

Augustine must have had at least the good luck to be well looked after, since he recovered. He had gone to the dwelling of one of his Manichee brethren, an *auditor* like himself, and an excellent kind of man, whom he stayed with all the time he was in Rome. Still, he had such a bad attack of fever that he very nearly died. "I was perishing," he says; "and I was all but lost." He is frightened at the idea of having seen death so near, at a moment when he was so far from God—so far, in fact, that it never occurred to him to ask for baptism, as he had done, in like case, when he was little. What a desperate blow would that have been for Monnica! He still shudders when he recalls the danger: "Had my mother's heart been smitten with that wound, it never could have been healed. *For I cannot express her tender love towards me,* or with how far greater anguish she travailed of me now in the spirit, than when she bore me in the flesh." But Monnica prayed. Augustine was saved. He ascribes his recovery to the fervent prayers of his mother, who, in begging of God the welfare of his soul, obtained, without knowing it, the welfare of his body.

As soon as he was convalescent, he had to set to work to get pupils. He was obliged to ask the favours of many an important personage, to knock at many an inhospitable door. This unfortunate beginning, the almost mortal illness which he was only just recovering from, this forced drudgery—all that did not make him very fond of Rome. It seems quite plain that he never liked it, and till the end of his life he kept a grudge against it for the sorry reception it gave him. In the whole body of his writings it is impossible to find a word of praise for the beauty of the Eternal City, while, on the contrary, one can make out through his invectives against the vices of Carthage, his secret partiality for the African Rome. The old rivalry between the two cities was not yet dead after so many centuries. In his heart, Augustine, like a good Carthaginian—and because he was a Carthaginian—did not like Rome.

The most annoying things joined together as if on purpose to disgust him with it. The bad season of the year was nigh when he began to reside there. Autumn rains had started, and the mornings and evenings were cold. What with his delicate chest, and his African constitution sensitive to cold, he must have suffered from this damp cold climate. Rome seemed to him a northern city. With his eyes still full of the warm light of his country, and the joyous whiteness of the Carthage streets, he wandered as one exiled between the gloomy Roman palaces, saddened by the grey walls and muddy pavements. Comparisons, involuntary and continual, between Carthage and Rome, made him unjust to Rome. In his eyes it had a hard, self-conscious, declamatory look, and gazing at the barren Roman *campagna*, he remembered the laughing Carthage suburbs, with gardens, villas, vineyards, olivets, circled everywhere by the brilliance of the sea and the lagoons.

And then, besides, Rome could not be a very delightful place to live in for a poor rhetoric master come there to better his fortune. Other strangers before him had complained of it. Always to be going up and down the flights of steps and the ascents, often very steep, of the city of the Seven Hills; to be rushing between the Aventine and Sallust's garden, and thence to the Esquiline and Janiculum! To bruise the feet on the pointed cobbles of sloping alley-ways! These walks were exhausting, and there seemed to be no end to this city. Carthage was also large—as large almost as Rome. But there Augustine was not seeking employment. When he went for a walk there, he strolled. Here, the bustle of the crowds, and the number of equipages, disturbed and exasperated the southerner with his lounging habits. Any moment there was a risk of being run over by cars tearing at full gallop through the narrow streets: men of fashion just then had a craze for driving fast. Or again, the passenger was obliged to step aside so that some lady might go by in her litter, escorted by her household, from the handicraft slaves and the kitchen staff, to the eunuchs and house-servants—all this army manoeuvring under the orders of a leader who held a rod in his hand, the sign of his office. When the street became clear once more, and at last the palace of the influential personage to whom a visit had to be paid was reached, there was no admittance without greasing the knocker. In order to be presented to the master, it was necessary to buy the good graces of the slave who took the name (*nomenclator*), and who not only introduced the suppliant, but might, with a word, recommend or injure. Even after all these precautions, one was not yet sure of the goodwill of the patron. Some of these great lords, who were not always themselves sprung from old Roman families, prided themselves upon their uncompromising nationalism, and made a point of treating foreigners with considerable haughtiness. The Africans were regarded unfavourably in Rome, especially in Catholic circles. Augustine must have had an unpleasant experience of this.

Through the long streets, brilliantly lighted at evening (it would seem that the artificial lighting of Rome almost equalled the daylight), he would return tired out to the dwelling of his host, the Manichee. This dwelling, according to an old tradition, was in the Velabrum district, in a street which is still to-day called *Via Greca*, and skirts the very old church of Santa Maria-in-Cosmedina—a poor quarter where swarmed a filthy mass of Orientals, and where the immigrants from the Levantine countries, Greeks, Syrians, Armenians, Egyptians, lodged. The warehouses on the Tiber were not very far off, and no doubt there were numbers of labourers, porters, and watermen living in this neighbourhood. What a place for him who had been at Thagaste the guest of the magnificent Romanianus, and intimate with the Proconsul at Carthage! When he had climbed up the six flights of stairs to his lodging, and crouched shivering over the ill-burning movable hearth, in the parsimonious light of a small bronze or earthenware lamp, while the raw damp sweated through the walls, he felt more and more his poverty and loneliness. He hated Rome and the stupid ambition which had brought him there. And yet Rome should have made a vivid appeal to this cultured man, this æsthete so alive to beauty. Although the transfer of the Court to Milan had drawn away some of its liveliness and glitter, it was still all illuminated by its grand memories, and never had it been more beautiful. It seems impossible that Augustine should not have been struck by it, despite his African prejudices. However well built the new Carthage might be, it could not pretend to compare with a city more than a thousand years old, which at all periods of its history had maintained the princely taste for building, and which a long line of emperors had never ceased to embellish.

When Augustine landed at Ostia, he saw rise before him, closing the perspective of the *Via Appia*, the Septizonium of Septimus Severus—an imitation, doubtless, on a far larger scale, of the one at Carthage. This huge construction, water-works probably of enormous size, with its ordered columns placed line above line, was, so to speak, the portico whence opened the most wonderful and colossal architectural mass known to the ancient world. Modern Rome has nothing at all to shew which comes anywhere near it. Dominating the Roman Forum, and the Fora of various Emperors—labyrinths of temples, basilicas, porticoes, and libraries—the Capitol and the Palatine rose up like two stone mountains, fashioned and sculptured, under the heap of their palaces and sanctuaries. All these blocks rooted in the soil, suspended, and towering up from the flanks of the hills, these interminable regiments of columns and pilasters, this profusion of precious marbles, metals, mosaics, statues, obelisks—in all that there was something enormous, a lack of restraint which disturbed the taste and floored the imagination. But it was, above all, the excessive use of gold and gilding that astonished the visitor. Originally indigent, Rome became noted for its greed of gold. When the gold of conquered nations began to come into its hands, it spread it all over with the rather indiscreet display of the upstart. When Nero built the Golden House he realized its dream. The Capitol had golden doors.

Statues, bronzes, the roofs of temples, were all gilded. All this gold, spread over the brilliant surfaces and angles of the architecture, dazzled and tired the eyes: *Acies stupet igne metalli*, said Claudian. For the poets who have celebrated it, Rome is the city of gold—*aurata Roma*.

A Greek, such as Lucian, had perhaps a right to be shocked by this architectural debauch, this beauty too crushing and too rich. A Carthage rhetorician, like Augustine, could feel at the sight of it nothing but the same irritated admiration and secret jealousy as the Emperor Constans felt when he visited his capital for the first time.

Even as the Byzantine Cæsar, and all the provincials, Augustine, no doubt, examined the curiosities and celebrated works which were pointed out to strangers: the temple of Jupiter Capitolinus; the baths of Caracalla and Diocletian; the Pantheon; the temple of Roma and of Venus; the Place of Concord; the theatre of Pompey; the Odeum, and the Stadium. Though he might be stupefied by all this, he would remember, too, all that the Republic had taken from the provinces to construct these wonders, and would say to himself: "Tis we who have paid for them." In truth, all the world had been ransacked to make Rome beautiful. For some time a muffled hostility had been brewing in provincial hearts against the tyranny of the central power, especially since it had shewn itself incapable of maintaining peace, and the Barbarians were threatening the frontiers. Worn out by so many insurrections, wars, massacres, and pillages, the provinces had come to ask if the great complicated machine of the Empire was worth all the blood and money that it cost.

For Augustine, moreover, the crisis was drawing near which was to end in his return to the Catholic faith. He had been a Christian, and as such brought up in principles of humility. With these sentiments, he would perhaps decide that the pride and vanity of the creature at Rome claimed far too much attention, and was even sacrilegious. It was not only the emperors who disputed the privileges of immortality with the gods, but anybody who took it into his head, provided that he was rich or had any kind of notoriety. Amid the harsh and blinding gilt of palaces and temples, how many statues, how many inscriptions endeavoured to keep an obscure memory green, or the features of some unknown man! Of course, at Carthage too, where they copied Rome, as in all the big cities, there were statues and inscriptions in abundance upon the Forum, the squares, and in the public baths. But what had not shocked Augustine in his native land, did shock him in a strange city. His home-sick eyes opened to faults which till then had been veiled by usage. In any case, this craze for statues and inscriptions prevailed at Rome more than anywhere else. The number of statues on the Forum became so inconvenient, that on many occasions certain ones were marked for felling, and the more insignificant shifted. The men of stone drove out the living men, and forced the gods into their temples. And the inscriptions on the walls bewildered the mind with such a noise of human praise, that ambition could dream of nothing beyond. It was all a kind of idolatry which revolted the strict Christians; and in Augustine, even at this time, it must have offended the candour of a soul which detested exaggeration and bombast.

The vices of the Roman people, with whom he was obliged to live cheek by jowl, galled him still more painfully. And to begin with, the natives hated strangers. At the theatres they used to shout: "Down with the foreign residents!" Acute attacks of xenophobia often caused riots in the city. Some years before Augustine arrived, a panic about the food supply led to the expulsion, as useless mouths, of all foreigners domiciled in Rome, even the professors. Famine was an endemic disease there. And then, these lazy people were always hungry. The gluttony and drunkenness of the Romans roused the wonder and also the disgust of the sober races of the Empire—of the Greeks as well as the Africans. They ate everywhere—in the streets, at the theatre, at the circus, around the temples. The sight was so ignoble, and the public intemperance so scandalous, that the Prefect, Ampelius, was obliged to issue an order prohibiting people who had any self-respect from eating in the street, the keepers of wine-shops from opening their places before ten o'clock in the morning, and the hawkers from selling cooked meat in the streets earlier than a certain hour of the day. But he might as well have saved himself the trouble. Religion itself encouraged this greediness. The pagan sacrifices were scarcely more than pretexts for stuffing. Under Julian, who carried the great public sacrifices of oxen to an abusive extent, the soldiers got drunk and gorged themselves with meat in the temples, and came out staggering. Then they would seize hold of any passers-by, whom they forced to carry them shoulder-high to their barracks.

All this must be kept in mind so as to understand the strictness and unyielding attitude of the Christian reaction. This Roman people, like the pagans in general, was frightfully material and sensual. The difficulty of shaking himself free from matter and the senses is going to be the great obstacle which delays Augustine's conversion; and if it was so with him, a fastidious and intellectual man, what about the crowd? Those people thought of nothing but eating and drinking and lewdness. When they left the tavern or their squalid rooms, they had only the obscenities of mimes, or the tumbles of the drivers in the circus, or the butcheries in the amphitheatre to elevate them. They passed the night there under the awnings provided by the municipality. Their passion for horse-races and actors and actresses, curbed though it was by the Christian emperors, continued even after the sack of Rome by the Barbarians. At the time of the famine, when the strangers were expelled, they excepted from this wholesale banishment three thousand female dancers with the members of their choirs, and their leaders of orchestra.

The aristocracy did not manifest tastes much superior. Save a few cultivated minds, sincerely fond of literature, the greatest number only saw in the literary pose an easy way of being fashionable. These became infatuated about an unknown author, or an ancient author whose books were not to be had. They had these books sought for and beautifully copied. They, "who hated study like poison," spoke only of their favourite author: the others did not exist for them. As a matter of fact, music had ousted literature: "the libraries were closed like sepulchres." But fashionable people were interested in an hydraulic organ, and they ordered from the lute-makers "lyres the size of chariots." Of course, this musical craze was sheer affectation. Actually, they were only interested in sports: to race, to arrange races, to breed horses, to train athletes and gladiators. As a pastime, they collected Oriental stuffs. Silk was then fashionable, and so were precious stones, enamels, heavy goldsmiths' work. Rows of rings were worn on each finger. People took the air in silk robes, held together by brooches carved in the figures of animals, a parasol in one hand, and a fan with gold fringes in the other. The costumes and fashions of Constantinople encroached upon the old Rome and the rest of the Western world.

Immense fortunes, which had gathered in the hands of certain people, either through inheritance or swindling, enabled them to keep up a senseless expenditure. Like the American millionaires of to-day, who have their houses and properties in both hemispheres, these great Roman lords possessed them in every country in the Empire. Symmachus, who was Prefect of the City when Augustine was in Rome, had considerable estates not only in Italy and in Sicily, but even in Mauretania. And yet, in spite of all their wealth and all the privileges they enjoyed, these rich people were neither happy nor at ease. At the least suspicion of a despotic power, their lives and property were threatened. Accusations of magic, of disrespect to the Cæsar, of plots against the Emperor—any pretext was good to plunder them. During the preceding reign, that of the pitiless Valentinian, the Roman nobility had been literally decimated by the executioner. A certain vice-Prefect, Maximinus, had gained a sinister reputation for cleverness in the art of manufacturing suspects. By his orders, a basket at the end of a string was hung out from one of the windows of the Prætorium, into which denunciations might be cast. The basket was in use day and night.

It is clear that at the time that Augustine settled in Rome this abominable system was a little moderated. But accusation by detectives was always in the air. And living in this atmosphere of mistrust, hypocrisy, bribery, and cruelty—small wonder if the Carthaginian fell into bitter reflections upon Roman corruption. However impressive from the front, the Empire was not nice to look at close at hand.

But Augustine was, above all, home-sick. When he strolled tinder the shady trees of the Janiculum or Sallust's gardens, he already said to himself what he would repeat later to his listeners at Hippo: "Take an African, put him in a place cool and green, and he won't stay there. He will feel he must go away and come back to his blazing desert." As for himself, he had something better to regret than a blazing desert. In front of the City of Gold, stretched out at his feet, and the horizon of the Sabine Hills, he remembered the feminine softness of the twilights upon the Lake of Tunis, the enchantment of moonlit nights upon the Gulf of Carthage, and that astonishing landscape to be discovered from the height of the terrace of Byrsa, which all the grandeur of the Roman *campagna* could not make him forget.

Chapter 2
THE FINAL DISILLUSION

The new professor had managed to secure a certain number of pupils whom he gathered together in his rooms. He could make enough to live at Rome by himself, if he could not support there the woman and child he had left behind at Carthage. In this matter of finding work, his host and his Manichee friends had done him some very good turns. Although forced to conceal their beliefs since the edict of Theodosius, there were a good many Manichees in the city. They formed an occult Church, strongly organized, and its adepts had relations with all classes of Roman society. Possibly Augustine presented himself as one driven out of Africa by the persecution. Some compensation would be owing to this young man who had suffered for the good cause.

It was his friend Alypius, "the brother of his heart," who, having preceded him to Rome to study law at his parents' wishes, now was the most useful in helping Augustine to make himself known and find pupils. Himself a Manichee, converted by Augustine, and a member of one of the leading families in Thagaste, he had not long to wait for an important appointment in the Imperial administration. He was assessor to the Treasurer-General, or "Count of the Italian Bounty Office," and decided fiscal questions. Thanks to his influence, as well as to his acquaintances among the Manichees, he was a valuable friend for the new arrival, a friend who could aid him, not only with his purse, but with advice. Without much capacity for theorizing, this Alypius was a practical spirit, a straight and essentially honest soul, whose influence was excellent for his impetuous friend. Of very chaste habits, he urged Augustine to restraint. And even in abstract studies, the religious controversies which Augustine dragged him into, his strong good sense moderated the imaginative dashes, the overmuch subtilty which sometimes led the other beyond healthy reason.

Unhappily they were both very busy—the judge and the rhetorician —and although their friendship became still greater during this stay in Rome, they were not able to see each other as much as they desired. Their pleasures, too, were perhaps not the same. Augustine did not in the least care about being chaste, and Alypius had a passion for the amphitheatre—a passion which his friend disapproved of. Some time earlier, at Carthage, Augustine had filled him with disgust of the circus. But hardly was Alypius arrived in Rome, than he became mad about the gladiatorial shows. Some fellow-students took him to the amphitheatre, almost by force. Thereupon, he said that he would stay, since they had dragged him there; but he bet that he would keep his eyes shut all through the fight, and that nothing could make him open them. He sat down on the benches with those who had brought him, his eyelids pressed down, refusing to look. Suddenly there was a roar of shouting, the shout of the crowd hailing the fall of the first wounded. His lids parted of themselves; he saw the flow of blood. "At the sight of the blood" says Augustine, "he drank in ruthlessness; no longer did he turn away, but fixed his gaze, and he became mad—and he knew no more... He was fascinated by the criminal atrocity of this battle, and drunk with the pleasure of blood."

These breathless phrases of the *Confessions* seem to throb still with the wild frenzy of the crowd. They convey to us directly the kind of Sadic excitement which people went to find about the arena. Really, a wholesome sight for future Christians, for all the souls that the brutality of pagan customs revolted! The very year that Augustine was at Rome, certain prisoners of war, Sarmatian soldiers, condemned to kill each other in the amphitheatre, chose suicide rather than this shameful death. There was in this something to make him reflect—him and his friends. The fundamental injustices whereon the ancient world rested—the crushing of the slave and the conquered, the contempt for human life—these things they touched with the finger when they looked on at the butcheries in the amphitheatre. All those whose hearts sickened with disgust and horror before these slaughter-house scenes, all those who longed for a little more mildness, a little more justice, were all recruits marked out for the peaceful army of the Christ.

For Alypius, especially, it was not a bad thing to have known this blood-drunkenness at first hand: he shall be only the more ashamed when he falls at the feet of the merciful God. Equally useful was it for him to have personal experience of the harshness of men's justice; and in the fulfilment of his duties as a judge to observe its errors and flaws. While he was a student at Carthage he just escaped being condemned to death upon a false accusation of theft—the theft of a piece of lead! Already they were dragging him, if not to the place of capital punishment, at least to prison, when a chance meeting with a friend of his who was a senator saved him from the threatening mob. At Rome, while Assessor to the Count of the Italian Bounty Office, he had to resist an attempt to bribe him, and by doing so risked losing his appointment, and, no doubt, something worse too. Official venality and dishonesty were evils so deeply rooted, that he himself nearly succumbed. He wanted some books copied, and he had the temptation to get this done at the charge of the Treasury. This peculation had, in his eyes, a good enough excuse, and it was certain to go undetected. Nevertheless, when he thought it over he changed his mind, and virtuously refrained from giving himself a library at the expense of the State.

Augustine, who relates these anecdotes, draws the same moral from them as we do, to wit—that for a man who was going to be a bishop and, as such, administrator and judge, this time spent in the Government service was a good preparatory school. Most of the other great leaders of this generation of Christians had also been officials; before ordination, they had been mixed up in business and politics, and had lived freely the life of their century. So it was with St. Ambrose, with St. Paulinus of Nola, with Augustine himself, and Evodius and Alypius, his friends.

And yet, however absorbed in their work the two Africans might be, it is pretty near certain that intellectual questions took the lead of all others. This is manifest in Augustine's case at least. He must have astonished the good Alypius when he got to Rome by acknowledging that he hardly believed in Manicheeism any longer. And he set forth his doubts about their masters' cosmogony and physical science, his suspicions touching the hidden immorality of the sect. As for himself, the controversies, which were the Manichees' strong point, did not dazzle him any longer. At Carthage, but lately, he had heard a Catholic, a certain Helpidius, oppose to them arguments from Scripture, which they were unable to refute. To make matters worse, the Manichee Bishop of Rome made a bad impression on him from the very outset. This man, he tells us, was of rough appearance, without culture or polite manners. Doubtless this unmannerly peasant, in his reception of the young professor, had not shewn himself sufficiently alive to his merits, and the professor felt aggrieved.

From then, his keen dialectic and his satirical spirit (Augustine had formidable powers of ridicule all through his life) were exercised upon the backs of his fellow-religionists. Provisionally, he had admitted as indisputable the basic principles of Manicheeism: first of all, the primordial antagonism of the two substances, the God of Light and the God of Darkness; then, this other dogma, that particles of that Divine Light, which had been carried away in a temporary victory of the army of Darkness, were immersed in certain plants and liquors. Hence, the distinction they made between clean and unclean food. All those foods were pure which contained some part of the Divine Light; impure, those which did not. The purity of food became evident by certain qualities of taste, smell, and appearance. But now Augustine found a good deal of arbitrariness in these distinctions, and a good deal of simplicity in the belief that the Divine Light dwelt in a vegetable. "Are they not ashamed," he said, "to search God with their palates or with their nose? And if His presence is revealed by a special brilliancy, by the goodness of the taste or the smell, why allow that dish and condemn this, which is of equal savour, light, and perfume?

"Yea, why do they look upon the golden melon as come out of God's treasure-house, and yet will have none of the golden fat of the ham or the yellow of an egg? Why does the whiteness of lettuce proclaim to them the Divinity, and the whiteness of cream nothing at all? And why this horror of meat? For, look you, roast sucking-pig offers us a brilliant colour, an agreeable smell, and an appetizing taste—sure signs, according to them, of the Divine Presence."... Once started on this topic, Augustine's vivacity has no limits. He even drops into jokes which would offend modern shamefacedness by their Aristophanic breadth.

These arguments, to say the truth, did not shake the foundations of the doctrine, and if a doctrine must be judged according to its works, the Manichees might entrench themselves behind their rigid moral rules, and their conduct. Contrary to the more accommodating Catholicism, they paraded a puritan intolerance. But Augustine had found out at Carthage that this austerity was for the most part hypocrisy. At Rome he was thoroughly enlightened.

The Elect of the religion made a great impression by their fasts and their abstinence from meat. Now it became clear that these devout personages, under pious pretexts, literally destroyed themselves by overeating and indigestion. They held, in fact, that the chief work of piety consisted in setting free particles of the Divine Light, imprisoned in matter by the wiles of the God of Darkness. They being the Pure, they purified matter by absorbing it into their bodies. The faithful brought them stores of fruit and vegetables, served them with real feasts, so that by eating these things they might liberate a little of the Divine Substance. Of course, they abstained from all flesh, flesh being the dwelling-place of the Dark God, and also from fermented wine, which they called "the devil's gall." But how they made up for it over the rest! Augustine makes great fun of these people who would think it a sin if they took as a full meal a small bit of bacon and cabbage, with two or three mouthfuls of undiluted wine, and yet ordered to be served up, from three o'clock in the afternoon, all kinds of fruit and vegetables, the most exquisite too, rendered piquant by spices, the Manichees holding that spices were very full of fiery and luminous principles. Then, their palates titillating from pepper, they swallowed large draughts of mulled wine or wine and honey, and the juice of oranges, lemons, and grapes. And these junketings began over again at nightfall. They had a preference for certain cakes, and especially for truffles and mushrooms—vegetables more particularly mystic.

Such a diet put human gluttony to a heavy test. Many a scandal came to light in the Roman community. The Elect made themselves sick by devouring the prodigious quantity of good cheer brought to them with a view to purification. As it was a sacrilege to let any be lost, the unhappy people forced themselves to get down the lot. There were even victims: children, gorged with delicacies, died of stuffing. For children, being innocent things, were deemed to have quite special purifying virtues.

Augustine was beginning to get indignant at all this nonsense. Still, except for these extravagances, he continued to believe in the asceticism of the Elect—asceticism of such severity that the main part of the faithful found it impossible to practise. And see! just at this moment, whom should he discover very strange things about but Bishop Faustus, that Faustus whom he had looked for at Carthage as a Messiah. The holy man, while he preached renunciation, granted himself a good many indulgences: he lay, for one thing, on feathers, or upon soft goatskin rugs. And these puritans were not even honest. The Manichee Bishop of Rome, that man of rough manners who had so offended Augustine, was on the point of being convicted of stealing the general cash-box. Lastly, there were rumours in the air, accusing the Elect of giving themselves over to reprehensible practices in their private meetings. They condemned marriage and child-bearing as works of the devil, but they authorized fornication, and even, it is said, certain acts against nature. That, for Augustine, was the final disillusion.

In spite of it, he did not separate openly from the sect. He kept his rank of *auditor* in the Manichee Church. What held him to it, were some plausible considerations on the intellectual side. Manicheeism, with its distinction of two Principles, accounted conveniently for the problem of evil and human responsibility. Neither God nor man was answerable for sin and pain, since it was the other, the Dark Principle, who distributed them through the world among men. Augustine, who continued to sin, continued likewise to be very comfortable with such a system of morals and metaphysics. Besides, he was not one of those convinced, downright minds who feel the need to quarrel noisily with what they take to be error. No one has opposed heresies more powerfully, and with a more tireless patience, than he has. But he always put some consideration into the business. He knew by experience how easy it is to fall into error, and he said this charitably to those whom he wished to persuade. There was nothing about him like St. Jerome.

Personal reasons, moreover, obliged him not to break with his fellow-religionists who had supported him, nursed him even, on his arrival at Rome, and who, as we shall see in a moment, might still do him services. Augustine was not, like his friend Alypius, a practical mind, but he had tact, and in spite of all the impulsiveness and mettle of his nature, a certain suppleness which enabled him to manoeuvre without too many collisions in the midst of the most embarrassing conjunctures. Through instinctive prudence he prolonged his indecision. Little by little, he who had formerly flung himself so enthusiastically in pursuit of Truth, glided into scepticism—the scepticism of the Academics in its usual form.

And at the same time that he lost his taste for speculative thinking, new annoyances in his profession put the finishing touch on his discouragement. If the Roman students were less noisy than those of Carthage, they had a deplorable habit of walking off and leaving their masters unpaid. Augustine was ere long victimized in this way: he lost his time and his words. As at Carthage, so at Rome, he had to face the fact that he could not live by his profession. What was he to do? Would he have to go back home? He had fallen into despair, when an unforeseen chance turned up for him.

The town council of Milan threw open a professorship of Rhetoric to public competition. It would be salvation for him if he could get appointed. For a long time he had wanted a post in the State education. In receipt of a fixed salary, he would no longer have to worry about beating up a class, or to guard against the dishonesty of his pupils. He put his name down immediately among the candidates. But no more in those days than in ours was simple merit by itself enough. It was necessary to pull strings. His friends the Manichees undertook to do this for him. They urged his claims warmly on the Prefect Symmachus, who doubtless presided at the competitive trials. By an amusing irony of fate, Augustine owed his place to people he was getting ready to separate from, whom even he was soon going to attack, and also to a man who was in a way the official enemy of Christianity. The pagan Symmachus appointing to an important post a future Catholic bishop—there is matter for surprise in that! But Symmachus, who had been Proconsul at Carthage, protected the Africans in Rome. Furthermore, it is likely that the Manichees represented their candidate to him as a man hostile to Catholics. Now in this year, A.D. 384, the Prefect had just begun an open struggle with the Catholics. He believed, therefore, that he made a good choice in appointing Augustine.

So a chain of events, with which his will had hardly anything to do, was going to draw the young rhetorician to Milan—yes, and how much farther!—to where he did not want to go, to where the prayers of Monnica summoned him unceasingly: "Where I am, there shall you be also." When he was leaving Rome, he did not much expect that. What he chiefly thought of was that he had at last won an independent financial position, and that he was become an official of some importance. He had a flattering evidence of this at once: It was at the expense of the city of Milan and in the Imperial carriages that he travelled through Italy to take up his new post.

Chapter 3
THE MEETING BETWEEN AMBROSE AND AUGUSTINE

Before he left Rome, and during his journey to Milan, Augustine must have recalled more than once the verses of Terence which his friend Marcianus had quoted by way of encouragement and advice the night he set sail for Italy:

"This day which brings to thee another life
Demands that thou another man shalt be."

He was thirty years old. The time of youthful wilfulness was over. Age, disappointments, the difficulties of life, had developed his character. He was now become a man of position, an eminent official, in a very large city which was the second capital of the Western Empire and the principal residence of the Court. If he wished to avoid further set-backs in his career, it behoved him to choose a line of conduct carefully thought out.

And first of all, it was time to get rid of Manicheeism. A Manichee would have made a scandal in a city where the greatest part of the population was Christian, and the Court was Catholic, although it did not conceal its sympathy with Arianism. It was a long time now since Augustine had been a Manichee in his heart. Accordingly, he was not obliged to feign in order to re-enter a Church which already included him formally among its catechumens. Doubtless he was a very lukewarm catechumen, since at intervals he inclined to scepticism. But he thought it decent to remain, at least for the time being, in the Catholic body, in which his mother had brought him up, until the day when some sure light should arise to direct his path. Now St. Ambrose was at that time the Catholic Bishop of Milan. Augustine was very eager to gain his goodwill. Ambrose was an undoubted political power, an important personage, a celebrated orator whose renown was shed all across the Roman world. He belonged to an illustrious family. His father had been Prætorian prefect of Gaul. He himself, with the title of Consul, was governing the provinces of Emilia and Liguria when the Milanese forced him, much against his will, to become their bishop. Baptized, ordained priest, and consecrated, one on top of the other, it was only apparently that he gave up his civil functions. From the height of his episcopal throne he always personified the highest authority in the country.

As soon as he arrived at Milan, Augustine hurried to call upon his bishop. Knowing him as we do, he must have approached Ambrose in a great transport of enthusiasm. His imagination, too, was kindled. In his thought this was a man of letters, an orator, a famous writer, almost a fellow-worker, that he was going to see. The young professor admired in Bishop Ambrose all the glory that he was ambitious of, and all that he already believed himself to be. He fancied, that however great might be the difference in their positions, he would find himself at once on an equal footing with this high personage, and would have a familiar talk with him, as he used to have at Carthage with the Proconsul Vindicianus. He told himself also that Ambrose was a priest, that is to say, a doctor of souls: he meant to open to him all his spiritual wretchedness, the anguish of his mind and heart. He expected consolation from him, if not cure.

Well, he was mistaken. Although in all his writings he speaks of "the holy Bishop of Milan" with feelings of sincere respect and admiration, he lets it be understood that his expectations were not realized. If the Manichean bishop of Rome had offended him by his rough manners, Ambrose disconcerted him alike by his politeness, his kindliness, and by the reserve, perhaps involuntarily haughty, of his reception. "He received me," says Augustine, "like a father, and as a bishop he was pleased enough at my coming:"—*peregrinationem meam satis episcopaliter dilexit*. This *satis episcopaliter* looks very like a sly banter at the expense of the saint. It is infinitely probable that St. Ambrose received

Augustine, not exactly as a man of no account, but still, as a sheep of his flock, and not as a gifted orator, and that, in short, he shewed him the same "episcopal" benevolence as he had from a sense of duty for all his hearers. It is possible too that Ambrose was on his guard from the outset with this African, appointed a municipal professor through the good offices of the pagan Symmachus, his personal enemy. In the opinion of the Italian Catholics, nothing good came from Carthage: these Carthaginians were generally Manichees or Donatists—sectaries the more dangerous because they claimed to be orthodox, and, mingling with the faithful, hypocritically contaminated them. And then Ambrose, the great lord, the former Governor of Liguria, the counsellor of the Emperors, may not have quite concealed a certain ironic commiseration for this "dealer in words," this young rhetorician who was still puffed up with his own importance.

Be this as it will, it was a lesson in humility that St. Ambrose, without intending it, gave to Augustine. The lesson was not understood. The rhetoric professor gathered only one thing from the visit, which was, that the Bishop of Milan had received him well. And as human vanity immediately lends vast significance to the least advances of distinguished or powerful persons, Augustine felt thankful for it. He began to love Ambrose almost as much as he admired him, and he admired him for reasons altogether worldly. "Ambrose I counted one of the happy ones of this world, because he was held in such honour by the great." The qualification which immediately follows shews naively enough the sensual Augustine's state of mind at that time: "Only it seemed to me that celibacy must be a heavy burthen upon him."

In those years the Bishop of Milan might, indeed, pass for a happy man in the eyes of the world. He was the friend of the very glorious and very victorious Theodosius; he had been the adviser of the young Emperor Gratian, but lately assassinated; and although the Empress Justina, devoted to the Arians, plotted against him, he had still great influence in the council of Valentinian II—a little Emperor thirteen years old, whom a Court of pagans and Arians endeavoured to draw into an anti-Catholic reaction.

Almost as soon as Augustine arrived in Milan, he was able to see for himself the great authority and esteem which Ambrose possessed, the occasion being a dispute which made a great noise.

Two years earlier, Gratian had had the statue and altar of *Victory* removed from the *Curia*, declaring that this pagan emblem and its accompaniments no longer served any purpose in an assembly of which the majority was Christian. By the same stroke, he suppressed the incomes of the sacerdotal colleges with all their privileges, particularly those of the Vestals; confiscated for the revenue the sums granted for the exercise of religion; seized the property of the temples; and forbade the priests to receive bequests of real estate. This meant the complete separation of the State and the ancient religion. The pagan minority in the Senate, with Symmachus, the Prefect, at its head, protested against this edict. A deputation was sent to Milan to place the pagan grievances before the Emperor. Gratian refused to receive them. It was thought that his successor, Valentinian II, being feebler, would be more obliging. A new senatorial committee presented themselves with a petition drawn up by Symmachus—a genuine piece of oratory which Ambrose himself admired, or pretended to admire. This speech made a deep impression when it was read in the Imperial Council. But Ambrose intervened with all his eloquence. He demanded that the common law should be applied equally to pagans as to Christians, and it was he who won the day. *Victory* was not replaced in the Roman *Curia*, neither were the goods of the temples returned.

Augustine must have been very much struck by this advantage which Catholicism had gained. It became clear that henceforth this was to be the State religion. And he who envied so much the fortunate of the world, might take note, besides, that the new religion brought, along with the faith, riches and honours to its adepts. At Rome he had listened to the disparaging by pagans and his Manichee friends of the popes and their clergy. They made fun of the fashionable clerics and legacy hunters. It was related that the Roman Pontiff, servant of the God of the poor, maintained a gorgeous establishment, and that his table rivalled the Imperial table in luxury. The prefect Prætextatus, a resolute pagan, said scoffingly to Pope Damasus: "Make me Bishop of Rome, and I'll become a Christian at once."

Certainly, commonplace human reasons can neither bring about nor account for a sincere conversion. Conversion is a divine work. But human reasons, arranged by a mysterious Will with regard to this work, may at least prepare a soul for it. Anyhow, it cannot be neglected that Augustine, coming to Milan full of ambitious plans, there saw Catholicism treated with so much importance in the person of Ambrose. This religion, which till then he had despised, now appeared to him as a triumphant religion worth serving.

But though such considerations might attract Augustine's attention, they took no hold on his conscience. It was well enough for an intriguer about the Court to get converted from self-interest. As for him, he wanted all or nothing; the chief good in his eyes was certainty and truth. He scarcely believed in this any longer, and surely had no hope of finding it among the Catholics; but still he went to hear Ambrose's sermons. He went in the first place as a critic of language, with the rather jealous curiosity of the trained man who watches how another man does it. He wanted to judge himself if the sacred orator was as good as his reputation. The firm and substantial eloquence of this former official, this statesman who was more than anything a man of action, immediately got control of the frivolous rhetorician. To be sure, he did not find in Ambrose's sermons the exhilaration or the verbal caress which had captivated him in those of Faustus the Manichean; but yet they had a persuasive grace which held him. Augustine heard the bishop with pleasure. Still, if he liked to hear him talk, he remained contemptuous of the doctrine he preached.

Then, little by little, this doctrine forced itself on his meditations: he perceived that it was more serious than he had thought hitherto, or, at least, that it could be defended. Ambrose had started in Italy the exegetical methods of the Orientals. He discovered in Scripture allegorical meanings, sometimes edifying, sometimes deep, always satisfying for a reasonable mind. Augustine, who was inclined to subtilty, much relished these explanations which, if ingenious, were often forced. The Bible no longer seemed to him so absurd. Finally, the immoralities which the Manichees made such a great point of against the Holy Writ, were justified, according to Ambrose, by historical considerations: what God did not allow to-day, He allowed formerly by reason of the conditions of existence. However, though the Bible might be neither absurd nor contrary to morals, this did not prove that it was true. Augustine found no outlet for his doubts.

He would have been glad to have Ambrose help him to get rid of them. Many a time he tried to have a talk with him about these things. But the Bishop of Milan was so very busy a personage! "I could not ask him," says Augustine, "what I wanted as I wanted, because the shoals of busy people who consulted him about their affairs, and to whose infirmities he ministered, came between me and his ear and lips. And in the few moments when he was not thus surrounded, he was refreshing either his body with needful food, or his mind with reading. While he read his eye wandered along the page and his heart searched out the meaning, but his voice and his tongue were at rest. Often when we attended (for the door was open to all, and no one was announced), we saw him reading silently, but never otherwise, and after sitting for some time without speaking (*for who would presume to trouble one so occupied?*) we went away again. We divined that, for the little space of time which was all that he could secure for the refreshment of his mind, he allowed himself a holiday from the distraction of other people's business, and did not wish to be interrupted; *and perhaps he was afraid lest eager listeners should invite him to explain the harder passages of his author, or to enter upon the discussion of difficult topics,* and hinder him from perusing as many volumes as he wished... *Of course the reason that guided a man of such remarkable virtue must have been good...*"

Nobody could comment more subtly—nor, be it said also, more maliciously—the attitude of St. Ambrose towards Augustine, than Augustine himself does it here. At the time he wrote this page, the events he was relating had happened a long time ago. But he is a Christian, and, in his turn, he is a bishop: he understands now what he could not understand then. He feels thoroughly at heart that if Ambrose withdrew himself, it was because the professor of rhetoric was not in a state of mind to have a profitable discussion with a believer: he lacked the necessary humility of heart and intellect. But at the moment, he must have taken things in quite another way, and have felt rather hurt, not to say more, at the bishop's apparent indifference.

Just picture a young writer of to-day, pretty well convinced of his value, but uneasy about his future, coming to ask advice of an older man already famous—well, Augustine's advances to Ambrose were not unlike that, save that they had a much more serious character, since it was not a question of literature, but of the salvation of a soul. At this period, what Augustine saw in Ambrose, even when he consulted him on sacred matters, was chiefly the orator, that is to say, a rather older rival... He enters. He is shewn into the private room of the great man, without being announced, *like any ordinary person*. The great man does not lay aside his book to greet him, does not even speak a word to him... What would the official professor of Rhetoric to the City of Milan think of such a reception? One can make out clearly enough through the lines of the *Confessions*. He said to himself that Ambrose, being a bishop, had charge of souls, and he was surprised that the bishop, no matter how great a lord he might be, made no attempt whatever to offer him spiritual aid. And as he was still devoid of Christian charity, no doubt he thought too that Ambrose was conscious that he had not the ability to wrestle with a dialectician of Augustine's strength, and that, into the bargain, the prelate was to seek in knowledge of the Scriptures. And, in truth, Ambrose had been made a bishop so suddenly that he must have found himself obliged to improvise a hasty knowledge. Anyhow, Augustine concluded that if he refused to discuss, it was because he was afraid of being at a disadvantage.

Very surely St. Ambrose had no notion of what the catechumen was thinking. He soared too high to trouble about miserable stings to self-respect. In his ministry he was for all alike, and he would have thought it against Christian equality to shew any special favour to Augustine. If, in the brief talks he had with the young rhetorician, he was able to gather anything of his character, he could not have formed a very favourable opinion of it. The high-strung temperament of the African, these vague yearnings of the spirit, these sterile melancholies, this continual temporizing before the faith—all that could only displease Ambrose, the practical Roman, the official used all his life to command.

However that was, Augustine, in following years, never allowed himself the least reproach towards Ambrose. On the contrary, everywhere he loads him with praise, quotes him repeatedly in his treatises, and takes refuge on his authority. He calls him his "father." But once, when he is speaking of the spiritual desolation in which he was plunged at Milan, there does escape him something like a veiled complaint which appears to be aimed at Ambrose. After recalling the eagerness with which he sought truth in those days, he adds: "If any one could have been found then to trouble about instructing me, he would have had a most willing and docile pupil."

This phrase, in such marked contrast with so many laudatory passages in the *Confessions* about St. Ambrose, seems to be indeed a statement of the plain truth. If God made use of Ambrose to convert Augustine, it is nevertheless likely that Ambrose personally did nothing, or very little, to bring about this conversion.

Chapter 4
PLANS OF MARRIAGE

But even as he draws nearer the goal, Augustine would appear, on the contrary, to get farther away from it. Such are God's secret paces, Who snatches souls like a thief: He drops on them without warning. Till the very eve of the day when Christ shall come to take him, Augustine will be all taken up with the world and the care of making a good figure in it.

Although Ambrose's sermons stimulated him to reflect upon the great historical reality which Christianity is, he had as yet but dim glimpses of it. He had given up his superficial unbelief, and yet did not believe in anything definite. He drifted into a sort of agnosticism compounded of mental indolence and discouragement. When he scrutinized his conscience to the depths, the most he could find was a belief in the existence of God and His providence—quite abstract ideas which he was incapable of enlivening. But whatever was the use of speculating upon Truth and the Sovereign Good! The main thing to do was to live.

Now that his future was certain, Augustine endeavoured to arrange his life with a view to his tranquillity. He had no longer very large ambitions. What he principally wanted to do was to create for himself a nice little existence, peaceful and agreeable, one might almost say, middle-class. His present fortune, although small, was still enough for that, and he was in a hurry to enjoy it.

Accordingly, he had not been long in Milan ere he sent for his mistress and his son. He had rented an apartment in a house which gave on a garden. The owner, who did not live there, allowed him the use of the whole house. A house, the dream of the sage! And a garden in Virgil's country! Augustine, the professor, should have been wonderfully happy. His mother soon joined him. Gradually a whole tribe of Africans came down on him, and took advantage of his hospitality. Here was his brother, Navigius, his two cousins, Rusticus and Lastidianus, his friend Alypius, who could not make up his mind to part from him, and probably Nebridius, another of his Carthage friends. Nothing could be more in harmony with the customs of the time. The Rhetorician to the City of Milan had a post which would pass for superb in the eyes of his poor relations. He was acquainted with very important people, and had access to the Imperial Court, whence favours and bounties came. Immediately, the family ran to put themselves under his protection and be enrolled beneficiaries, to get what they could out of his new fortune and credit. And then these immigrations of Africans and Orientals into the northern countries always come about in the same way. It is enough if one of them gets on there: he becomes immediately the drop of ink on the blotting-paper.

The most important person in this little African phalanstery was unquestionably Monnica, who had taken in hand the moral and material control of the house. She was not very old—not quite fifty-four—but she wanted to be in her own country. That she should have left it, and faced the weariness of a long journey over sea and land, she must have had very serious reasons. The poverty into which she had fallen since the death of her husband would not be an adequate explanation of her departure from her native land. She had still some small property at Thagaste; she could have lived there. The true motives of her departure were of an altogether different order. First of all, she passionately loved her son, to the point that she was not able to live away from him. Let us recall Augustine's touching words: "For she loved to keep me with her, as mothers are wont, yes, far more than most mothers." Besides that, she wanted to save him. She completely believed that this was her work in the world.

Beginning from now, she is no longer the widow of Patricius: she is already Saint Monnica. Living like a nun, she fasted, prayed, mortified her body. By long meditating on the Scriptures, she had developed within her the sense of spiritual realities, so that before long she astonished Augustine himself. She had visions; perhaps she had trances. As she came over the sea from Carthage to Ostia, the ship which carried her ran into a wild gale. The danger became extreme, and the sailors themselves could no longer hide their fear. But Monnica intrepidly encouraged them. "Never you fear, we shall arrive in port safe and sound!" God, she declared, had promised her this.

If, in her Christian life, she knew other minutes more divine, that was truly the most heroic. Across Augustine's calm narrative, we witness the scene. This woman lying on the deck among passengers half dead from fatigue and terror, suddenly flings back her veils, stands up before the maddened sea, and with a sudden flame gleaming over her pale face, she cries to the sailors: "What do you fear? We shall get to port. *I am sure of it!*" The glorious act of faith!

At this solemn moment, when she saw death so near, she had a clear revelation of her destiny; she knew with absolute certainty that she was entrusted with a message for her son, and that her son would receive this message, in spite of all, in spite of the wildness of the sea—aye, in spite of his own heart.

When this sublime emotion had subsided, it left with her the conviction that sooner or later Augustine would change his ways. He had lost himself, he was mistaken about himself. This business of rhetorician was unworthy of him. The Master of the field had chosen him to be one of the great reapers in the time of harvest. For a long while Monnica had foreseen the exceptional place that Augustine was to take in the Church. Why fritter away his talent and intelligence in selling vain words, when there were heresies to combat, the Truth to make shine forth, when the Donatists were capturing the African basilicas from the Catholics? What, in fact, was the most celebrated rhetorician compared to a bishop —protector of cities, counsellor of emperors, representative of God on earth? All this might Augustine be. And he remained stubborn in his error! Prayers and efforts must be redoubled to draw him from that. It was also for herself that she struggled, for the dearest of her hopes as a mother. To bear a soul to Jesus Christ—and a chosen soul who would save in his turn souls without number—for this only had she lived. And so it was that on the deck, tired by the rolling of the ship, drenched by the seas that were breaking on board, and hardly able to stand in the teeth of the wind, she cried out to the sailors: "What do you fear? We shall get to port. I am sure of it..."

At Milan she was regarded by Bishop Ambrose as a model parishioner. She never missed his sermons and "hung upon his lips as a fountain of water springing up to eternal life." And yet it does not appear that the great bishop understood the mother any better than he did the son: he had not the time. For him Monnica was a worthy African woman, perhaps a little odd in her devotion, and given to many a superstitious practice. Thus, she continued to carry baskets of bread and wine and pulse to the tombs of the martyrs, according to the use at Carthage and Thagaste. When, carrying her basket, she came to the door of one of the Milanese basilicas, the doorkeeper forbade her to enter, saying that it was against the bishop's orders, who had solemnly condemned such practices because they smacked of idolatry. The moment she learned that this custom was prohibited by Ambrose, Monnica, very much mortified, submitted to take away her basket, for in her eyes Ambrose was the providential apostle who would lead her son to salvation. And yet it must have grieved her to give up this old custom of her country. Save for the fear of displeasing the bishop, she would have kept it up. Ambrose was gratified by her obedience, her fervour and charity. When by chance he met the son, he congratulated him on having such a mother. Augustine, who did not yet despise human praise, no doubt expected that Ambrose would in turn pay some compliments to himself. But Ambrose did not praise him at all, and perhaps he felt rather vexed.

He himself, however, was always very busy; he had hardly any time to profit by the pious exhortations of the bishop. His day was filled by his work and his social duties. In the morning he lectured. The afternoon went in friendly visits, or in looking up men of position whom he applied to for himself or his relations. In the evening, he prepared tomorrow's lecture. In spite of this very full and stirring life, which would seem to satisfy all his ambitions, he could not manage to stifle the cry of his heart in distress. He did not feel really happy. In the first place, it is doubtful whether he liked Milan any better than Rome. He felt the cold there very much. The Milanese winters are very trying, especially for a southerner. Thick fogs rise from the canals and the marsh lands which surround the city. The Alpine snows are very near. This climate, damper and frostier even than at Rome, did no good to his chest. He suffered continually from hoarseness; he was obliged to interrupt his lectures—a most disastrous necessity for a man whose business it is to talk. These attacks became so frequent that he was forced to wonder if he could keep on long in this state. Already he felt that he might be obliged to give up his profession. Then, in those hours when he lost heart, he flung to the winds all his youthful ambitions. As a last resort, the voiceless rhetorician would take a post in one of the administrative departments of the Empire. The idea of being one day a provincial governor did not rouse any special repugnance. What a fall for him! "Yes, but it is the wisest, the wisest thing," retorted the ill-advising voice, the one we are tempted to listen to when we doubt ourselves.

Friendship, as always with Augustine, consoled him for his hopeless thoughts. Near him was "the brother of his heart," the faithful Alypius, and also Nebridius, that young man so fond of metaphysical discussions. Nebridius had left his rich estate in the Carthaginian suburbs, and a mother who loved him, simply to live with Augustine in the pursuit of truth. Romanianus was also there, but for a less disinterested reason. The Mæcenas of Thagaste, after his ostentatious expenditure, found that his fortune was threatened. A powerful enemy, who had started a law-suit against him, worked to bring about his downfall. Romanianus had come to Milan to defend himself before the Emperor, and to win the support of influential personages about the Court. And so it came about that he saw a great deal of Augustine.

Besides this little band of fellow-countrymen, the professor of rhetoric had some very distinguished friends among the aristocracy. He was especially intimate with that Manlius Theodorus whom the poet Claudian celebrates, and to whom he himself later on was to dedicate one of his books. This rich man, who had been Proconsul at Carthage, where no doubt he had met Augustine, lived at this time retired in the country, dividing his leisure hours between the study of the Greek philosophers, especially of the Platonists, and the cultivation of his vineyards and olive trees.

Here, as at Thagaste, in these beautiful villas on the shores of the Italian lakes, the son of Monnica gave himself up once more to the sweetness of life. "I liked an easy life," he avows in all simplicity. He felt himself to be more Epicurean than ever. He might have chosen Epicureanism altogether, if he had not always kept a fear of what is beyond life. But when he was the guest of Manlius Theodoras, fronting the dim blue mountains of lake Como, framed in the high windows of the *triclinium*, he did not think much about what is beyond life. He said to himself: "Why desire the impossible? So very little is needed to satisfy a human soul." The enervating contact of luxury and comfort imperceptibly corrupted him. He became like those fashionable people whom he knew so well how to charm with his talk. Like the fashionable people of all times, these designated victims of the Barbarians built, with their small daily pleasures, a rampart against all offensive or saddening realities, leaving the important questions without answer, no longer even asking them. And they said: "I have beautiful books, a well-heated house, well-trained slaves, a delightfully arranged bathroom, a comfortable vehicle: life is sweet. I don't wish for a better. What's the use? This one is good enough for me." At the moment when his tired intellect gave up everything, Augustine was taken in the snare of easy enjoyment, and desired to resemble these people at all points, to be one of them. But to be one of them he must have a higher post than a rhetorician's, and chiefly it would be necessary to put all the outside forms and exterior respectability into his life that the world of fashion shews. Thus, little by little, he began to think seriously of marriage.

His mistress was the only obstacle in the way of this plan. He got rid of her.

That was a real domestic drama, which he has tried to hide; but it must have been extremely painful for him, to judge by the laments which he gives vent to, despite himself, in some phrases, very brief and, as it were, ashamed. In this drama Monnica was certainly the leader, though it is likely that Augustine's friends also played their parts. No doubt, they objected to the professor of rhetoric, that he was injuring his reputation as well as his future by living thus publicly with a concubine. But Monnica's reasons were more forcible and of quite another value.

To begin with, it is very natural that she should have suffered in her maternal dignity, as well as in her conscience as a Christian, by having to put up with the company of a stranger who was her son's mistress. However large we may suppose the house where the African tribe dwelt, a certain clashing between the guests was unavoidable. Generally, disputes as to who shall direct the domestic arrangements divide mother-in-law and daughter-in-law who live under one roof. What could be Monnica's feelings towards a woman who was not even a daughter-in-law and was regarded by her as an intruder? She did not consider it worth while to make any attempt at regulating the entanglement of her son by marrying them: this person was of far too low a class. It is all very well to be a saint, but one does not forget that one is the widow of a man of curial rank, and that a middle-class family with self-respect does not lower itself by admitting the first-comer into its ranks by marriage. But these were secondary considerations in her eyes. The only one which could have really preyed on her mind is that this woman delayed Augustine's conversion. On account of her, as Monnica saw plainly, he put off his baptism indefinitely. She was the chain of sin, the unclean past under whose weight he stifled. He must be freed from her as soon as possible.

Convinced therefore that such was her bounden duty, she worked continually to make him break off. By way of putting him in some sort face to face with a deed impossible to undo, she searched to find him a wife, with the fine eagerness that mothers usually put into this kind of hunt. She discovered a girl who filled, as they say, all the requirements, and who realized all the hopes of Augustine. She had a fortune considerable enough not to be a burthen on her husband. Her money, added to the professor's salary, would allow the pair to live in ease and comfort. So they were betrothed. In the uncertainty about all things which was Augustine's state just then, he allowed his mother to work at this marriage. No doubt he approved, and like a good official he thought it was time for him to settle down.

From that moment, the separation became inevitable. How did the poor creature who had been faithful to him during so many years feel at this ignominious dismissal? What must have been the parting between the child Adeodatus and his mother? How, indeed, could Augustine consent to take him from her? Here, again, he has decided to keep silent on this painful drama, from a feeling of shame easy to understand. Of course, he was no longer strongly in love with his mistress, but he was attached to her by some remains of tenderness, and by that very strong tie of pleasure shared. He has said it in words burning with regret. "When they took from my side, as an obstacle to my marriage, her with whom I had been used for such a long time to sleep, my heart was torn at the place where it was stuck to hers, and the wound was bleeding." The phrase casts light while it burns. "At the place where my heart stuck to hers"—*cor ubi adhærebat*. He acknowledges then that the union was no longer complete, since at many points he had drawn apart. If the soul of his mistress had remained the same, his had changed: however much he might still love her, he was already far from her.

Be that as it will, she behaved splendidly in the affair—this forsaken woman, this poor creature whom they deemed unworthy of Augustine. She was a Christian; perhaps she perceived (for a loving woman might well have this kind of second-sight) that it was a question not only of the salvation of a loved being, but of a divine mission to which he was predestined. She sacrificed herself that Augustine might be an apostle and a saint—a great servant of God. So she went back to her Africa, and to shew that she pardoned, if she could not forget, she vowed that she would never know any other man. "She who had slept" with Augustine could never be the wife of any one else.

However low she may have been to begin with, the unhappy woman was great at this crisis. Her nobility of soul humiliated Augustine, and Monnica herself, and punishment was not slow in falling on them both —on him, for letting himself be carried away by sordid plans for success in life, and upon her, the saint, for having been too accommodating. As soon as his mistress was gone, Augustine suffered from being alone. "I thought that I should be miserable," says he, "without the embraces of a woman." Now his promised bride was too young: two years must pass before he could marry her. How could he control himself till then? Augustine did not hesitate: he found another mistress.

There was Monnica's punishment, cruelly deceived in her pious intentions. In vain did she hope a great deal of good from this approaching marriage: the silence of God shewed her that she was on the wrong track. She begged for a vision, some sign which would reveal to her how this new-planned marriage would turn out. Her prayer was not heard.

"Meanwhile," says Augustine, "my sins were being multiplied." But he did not limit himself to his own sins: he led others into temptation. Even in matrimonial matters, he felt the need of making proselytes. So he fell upon the worthy Alypius. He, to be sure, guarded himself chastely from women, although in the outset of his youth, to be like everybody else, he had tried pleasure with women; but he had found that it did not suit his taste. However, Augustine put conjugal delights before him with so much heat, that he too began to turn his thoughts that way, "not that he was overcome by the desire of pleasure, *but out of curiosity.*" For Alypius, marriage would be a sort of philosophic and sentimental experience.

Here are quite modern expressions to translate very old conditions of soul. The fact is, that these young men, Augustine's friends and

Augustine himself, were startlingly like those of a generation already left behind, alas! who will probably keep in history the presumptuous name they gave themselves: *The Intellectuals.*

Like us, these young Latins of Africa, pupils of the rhetoricians and the pagan philosophers, believed in hardly anything but ideas. All but ready to affirm that Truth is not to be come at, they thought, just the same, that a vain hunt after it was a glorious risk to run, or, at the very least, an exciting game. For them this game made the whole dignity and value of life. Although they had spasms of worldly ambition, they really despised whatever was not pure speculation. In their eyes, the world was ugly; action degrading. They barred themselves within the ideal garden of the sage, "the philosopher's corner," as they called it, and jealously they stopped up all the holes through which the painful reality might have crept through to them. But where they differed from us, is that they had much less dryness of soul, with every bit as much pedantry—but such ingenuous pedantry! That's what saved them—their generosity of soul, the youth of their hearts. They loved each other, and they ended by growing fond of life and getting in contact with it again. Nebridius journeyed from Carthage to Milan, abandoning his mother and family, neglecting considerable interests, not only to talk philosophy with Augustine, but to live with him as a friend. From this moment they might have been putting in practice those words of the Psalm, which Augustine ere long will be explaining to his monks with such tender eloquence: "Behold, how good and how pleasant it is for brethren to dwell together in unity!"

This is not baseless hypothesis: they had really a plan for establishing a kind of lay monastery, where the sole rule would be the search after Truth and the happy life. There would be about a dozen solitaries. They would make a common stock of what means they possessed. The richest, and among these Romanianus, promised to devote their whole fortune to the community. But the recollection of their wives brought this naive plan to nothing. They had neglected to ask the opinions of their wives, and if these, as was likely, should refuse to enter the convents with their husbands, the married men could not face the scheme of living without them. Augustine especially, who was on the point of starting a new connection, declared that he would never find the courage for it. He had also forgotten that he had many dependents: his whole family lived on him. Could he leave his mother, his son, his brother, and his cousins?

In company with Alypius and Nebridius, he sincerely lamented that this fair dream of coenobite life was impracticable. "We were three famishing mouths," he says, "complaining of our distress one to another, and waiting upon Thee that Thou mightest give us our meat in due season. And in all the bitterness that Thy mercy put into our worldly pursuits, we sought the reason why we suffered; and all was darkness. Then we turned to each other shuddering, and asked: 'How much longer can this last?'..."

One day, a slight commonplace fact which they happened upon brought home to them still more cruelly their intellectual poverty. Augustine, in his official position as municipal orator, had just delivered the official panegyric of the Emperor. The new year was opening: the whole city was given over to mirth. And yet he was cast down, knowing well that he had just uttered many an untruth, and chiefly because he despaired of ever being happy. His friends were walking with him. Suddenly, as they crossed the street, they came upon a beggar, quite drunk, who was indulging in the jolliest pranks. So there was a happy man! A few pence had been enough to give him perfect felicity, whereas they, the philosophers, despite the greatest efforts and all their knowledge, could not manage to win happiness. No doubt, as soon as the drunkard grew sober, he would be more wretched than before. What matters that, if this poor joy—yes, though it be an illusion—can so much cheer a poor creature, thus raise him so far above himself! That minute, at least, he shall have lived in full bliss. And to Augustine came the temptation to do as the beggar-man, to throw overboard his philosophical lumber and set himself simply to live without afterthoughts, since life is sometimes good.

But an instinct, stronger than the instinct of pleasure, said to him: "*There is something else!*—Suppose that were true?—Perhaps you might be able to find out." This thought tormented him unceasingly. Now eager, now disheartened, he set about trying to find the "something else."

Chapter 5
THE CHRIST IN THE GARDEN

"I was tired of devouring time and of being devoured by it." The whole moral crisis that Augustine is about to undergo might be summed up in these few words so concentrated and so strong. No more to scatter himself among the multitude of vain things, no more to let himself flow along with the minutes as they flowed; but to pull himself together, to escape from the rout so as to establish himself upon the incorruptible and eternal, to break the chains of the old slave he continues to be so as to blossom forth in liberty, in thought, in love—that is the salvation he longs for. If it be not yet the Christian salvation, he is on the road which leads to that.

One might amuse oneself by drawing a kind of ideal map-route of his conversion, and fastening into one solid chain the reasons which made him emerge at the act of faith: he himself perhaps, in his *Confessions*, has given way too much to this inclination. In reality, conversion is an interior fact, and (let us repeat it) a divine fact, which is independent of all control by the reason. Before it breaks into light, there is a long preparation in that dark region of the soul which to-day is called the subconscious. Now nobody has more *lived* his ideas than did Augustine at this time of his life. He took them, left them, took them up again, persisted in his desperate effort. They reflect in their disorder his variable soul, and the misgivings which troubled it to its depths. And yet it cannot be that this interior fact should be in violent contradiction with logic. The head ought not to hinder the heart. With the future believer, a parallel work goes on in the feelings and in the thought. If we are not able to reproduce the marches and counter-marches, or follow their repeatedly broken line, we can at least shew the main halting-places.

Let us recall Augustine's state of mind when he came to Milan. He was a sceptic, the kind of sceptic who regards as useless all speculation upon the origin of things, and for whom cognition is but an approximation of the true. Vaguely deist, he saw in Jesus Christ only a wise man among the wise. He believed in God and the providences of God, which amounts to this: That although materialist by tendency, he admitted the divine interference in human affairs—the miracle. This is an important point which differentiates him from modern materialists.

Next, he listened to the preaching of Ambrose. The Bible no longer seemed to him absurd or at variance with a moral scheme. Ambrose's exegesis, half allegorical, half historic, might be accepted, taken altogether, by self-respecting minds. But what, above all, struck Augustine in the Scriptures, was the wisdom, the practical efficiency. Those who lived by the Christian rule were not only happy people, but, as Pascal would say, good sons, good husbands, good fathers, good citizens. He began to suspect that this life here below is bearable and has a meaning only when it is fastened to the life on high. Even as for nations glory is daily bread, so for the individual the sacrifice to something which is beyond the world is the only way of living in the world.

So, little by little, Augustine corrected the false notions that the Manichees had filled him with about Catholicism. He acknowledged that in attacking it he had "been barking against the vain imaginations of carnal thoughts." Still, he found great difficulty in getting free of all his Manichean prejudices. The problem of Evil remained inexplicable for him, apart from Manichee teachings. God could not be the author of evil. This truth admitted, he went on from it to think, against his former masters, that nothing is bad in itself—bad because it has within it a corrupting principle. On the contrary, all things are good, though in varying degrees. The apparent defects of creation, perceived by our senses, blend into the harmony of the whole. The toad and the viper have their place in the operation of a perfectly arranged world. But physical ill is not the only ill; there is also the evil that we do and the evil that others do us. Crime and pain are terrible arguments against God. Now the Christians hold that the first is the product solely of the human will, of liberty corrupted by original sin, and that the other is permitted by God as a means of purifying souls. Of course, this was a solution, but it implied a belief in the dogmas of the Fall and of the Redemption. Augustine did not accept them yet. He was too proud to recognize an impaired will and the need of a Saviour. "My puffed-out face," he says, "closed up my eyes."

Nevertheless he had taken a great step in rejecting the fundamental dogma of Manicheeism—the double Principle of good and evil. Henceforth for Augustine there exists only one Principle, unique and incorruptible—the Good, which is God. But his view of this divine substance is still quite materialistic, to such an extent is he governed by his senses. In his thought, it is corporeal, spatial, and infinite. He pictures it as a kind of limitless sea, wherein is a huge sponge bathing the world that it pervades throughout... He was at this point, when one of his acquaintances, "a man puffed up with immense vanity," gave him some of the Dialogues of Plato, translated into Latin by the famous rhetorician Victorinus Afer. It is worth noting, as we pass, that Augustine, now thirty-two years old, a rhetorician by profession and a philosopher by taste, had not yet read Plato. This is yet another proof to what extent the instruction of the ancients was oral, resembling in this the Mussulmans' instruction of to-day. Up to now, he had only known Plato by hearsay. He read him, and it was as a revelation. He learned that a reality could exist without diffusion through space. He saw God as unextended and yet infinite. The sense of the divine Soul was given to him. Then the primordial necessity of the Mediator or Word was borne in upon his mind. It is the Word which has created the world. It is through the Word that the world, and God, and all things, including ourselves, become comprehensible to us. What an astonishment! Plato corresponded with St. John! "In the beginning was the Word"—*in principio erat verbum*—said the fourth Gospel. But it was not only an Evangelist that Augustine discovered in the Platonist dialogues, it was almost all the essential part of the doctrine of Christ. He saw plainly the profound differences, but for the moment he was struck by the resemblances, and they carried him away. What delighted him, first of all, is the beauty of the world, constructed after His own likeness by the Demiurgus. God is Beauty; the world is fair as He who made it. This metaphysical vision entranced Augustine; his whole heart leaped towards this ineffably beautiful Divinity. Carried away by enthusiasm he cries: "I marvelled to find that now I loved Thee, O my God, and not a phantasm in Thy stead. If I was not yet in a state to enjoy Thee, *I was swept up to Thee by Thy beauty."*

But such an abandonment could not endure: "I was not yet in a state to enjoy Thee." There is Augustine's main objection to Platonism. He felt that instead of touching God, of enjoying Him, he would be held by purely mental conceptions, that he would be always losing his way among the phantasmagoria of idealism. What was the use of giving up the illusory realities of the senses, if it were not to get hold of more *solid* realities? Though his intelligence, his poet's imagination, might be attracted by the glamour of Platonism, his heart was not satisfied. "It is one thing," he says, "from some wooded height to behold the land of peace, another thing to march thither along the high road."

St. Paul it was who shewed him this road. He began to read the *Epistles* carefully, and the more he read of them the more he became aware of the abyss which separates philosophy from wisdom—the one which marshals the ideas of things, the other which, ignoring ideas, leads right up to the divine realities whereon the others are suspended. The Apostle taught Augustine that it was not enough to get a glimpse of God through the crystal of concepts, but that it is necessary to be united to Him in spirit and in truth—to possess and enjoy Him. And to unite itself to this Good, the soul must get itself into a fit state for such a union, purify and cure itself of all its fleshly maladies, descry its place in the world and hold to it. Necessity of repentance, of humility, of the contrite and humble heart. Only the contrite and humble heart shall see God. "The broken heart shall be cured," says the Scripture, "but the heart of the proud man shall be shattered." So Augustine, the intellectual, had to change his methods, and he felt that this change was right. If the writer who wants to write beautiful things ought to put himself beforehand into some sort of a state of grace, wherein not only vile actions, but unworthy thoughts become impossible, the Christian, in like manner, must cleanse and prepare his inward eye to perceive the divine verities. Augustine grasped this thought in reading St. Paul. But what, above all, appealed to him in the *Epistles*, was their paternal voice, the mildness and graciousness hidden beneath the uncultivated roughness of the phrases. He was charmed by this. How different from the philosophers! "Those celebrated pages have no trace of the pious soul, the tears of repentance, nor of Thy sacrifice, O my God, nor of the troubled spirit... No one there hearkened to the Christ that calleth, 'Come unto Me, all ye that labour!' They think it scorn to learn from Him, because He is meek and lowly of heart. For Thou hast hidden these things from the wise and prudent, and hast revealed them unto babes."

But it is not much to bend: what is, above all, requisite for him is to get rid of his passions. Now Augustine's passions were old friends. How could he part with them? He lacked courage for this heroic treatment. Just think of what a young man of thirty-two is. He is always thinking of women. Lust holds him by the entanglements of habit, and he takes pleasure in the impurity of his heart. When, yielding to the exhortations of the Apostle, he tried to shape his conduct to his new way of thinking, the old friends trooped to beg of him not to do anything of the kind. "They pulled me," he says, "by the coat of my flesh, and they murmured in my ear—What, are you leaving us? Shall we be no more with you, for ever? *Non erimus tecum ultra in aeternum?*... And from that instant, the thing you well know, and still another thing, will be forbidden you for ever—for eternity..."

Eternity! Dread word. Augustine shook with fear. Then, calming himself, he said to them: "I know you; I know you too well! You are Desire without hope, the Gulf without soundings that nothing can fill up. I have suffered enough because of you." And the anguished dialogue continued: "What matters that! If the only possible happiness for you is to suffer on our account, to fling your body into the voracious gulf, without end, without hope!"—"Let cowards act so!... For me there is another happiness than yours. There is *something else*: I am certain." Then the friends, put a little out of countenance by this convinced tone, muttered in a lower voice: "Still, just suppose you are losing this wretched pleasure for a phantasm still more empty... Besides, you are mistaken about your strength. You cannot—no, you never can exist without us." They had touched the galling spot: Augustine knew his weakness only too well. And his burning imagination presented to him with extraordinary lucidity these pleasures which he could not do without. They were not only embracements, but also those trifles, those superfluous nothings, "those light pleasantnesses which make us fond of life." The perfidious old friends continued to whisper: "Wait a bit yet! The things you despise have a charm of their own; they bring even no small sweetness. You ought not to cut yourself off light-heartedly, for it would be shameful to return to them afterwards." He passed in review all the things he was going to give up; he saw them shine before him tinted in the most alluring colours: gaming, elaborate entertainments, music, song, perfumes, books, poetry, flowers, the coolness of forests (he remembered the woods about Thagaste, and his hunting days with Romanianus)—in a word, all that he had ever cared about, even to "that freshness of the light, so kind to human eyes."

Augustine was not able to decide in this conflict between temptation and the decree of his conscience, and he became desperate. His will, enfeebled by sin, was unable to struggle against itself. And so he continued to endure life and to be "devoured by time."

The life of that particular period, if it was endurable for quiet folk who were careful to have nothing to do with politics—this life of the Empire near its end, could be nothing but a scandalous spectacle for an honest-minded and high-souled man such as Augustine. It ought to have disgusted him at once with remaining in the world. At Milan, connected as he was with the Court, he was in a good position to see how much baseness and ferocity may spring from human avarice and ambition. If the present was hideous, the future promised to be sinister. The Roman Empire no longer existed save in name. Foreigners, come from all the countries of the Mediterranean, plundered the provinces under its authority. The army was almost altogether in the hands of the Barbarians. They were Gothic tribunes who kept order outside the basilica where Ambrose had closed himself in with his people to withstand the order of the Empress Justina, who wished to hand over this church to the Arians. Levantine eunuchs domineered over the exchequer-clerks in the palace, and officials of all ranks. All these people plundered where they could. The Empire, even grown feeble, was always an excellent machine to rule men and extract gold from nations. Accordingly, ambitious men and adventurers, wherever they came from, tried for the Purple: it was still worth risking one's skin for. Even more than the patriots (and there were still some very energetic men of this sort who were overcome with grief at the state of things), the men of rapine and violence were interested in maintaining the Empire. The Barbarians themselves desired to be included, so that they might pillage it with more impunity.

As for the emperors, even sincere Christians, they were obliged to become abominable tyrants to defend their constantly threatened lives. Never were executions more frequent or more cruel than at this time. At Milan they might have shewn Augustine, hard by the Imperial sleeping apartments, the cave where the preceding Emperor, choleric Valentinian, kept two bears, "Bit of Gold" and "Innocence," who were his rapid executioners. He fed them with the flesh of those condemned to die. Possibly "Bit of Gold" was still living. "Innocence"—observe the atrocious irony of this name—had been restored to the liberty of her native forests, as a reward for her good and loyal services.

Was Augustine, who still thought of becoming an official, going to mix in with this lot of swindlers, assassins, and brute beasts? As he studied them near at hand, he felt his goodwill grow weak. Like all those who belong to worn-out generations, he must have been disgusted with action and the villainies it involves. Just before great catastrophes, or just after, there is an epidemic of black pessimism which freezes delicate souls. Besides, he was ill—a favourable circumstance for a disappointed man if he entertains thoughts of giving up the world. In the fogs of Milan his chest and throat became worse and worse. And then it is likely enough that he was not succeeding better as rhetorician than he had at Rome. It was a kind of fatality for all Africans. However great their reputation in their own country, that was the end of it as soon as they crossed the sea. Apuleius, the great man of Carthage, had tried the experiment to his cost. They had made fun of his guttural Carthaginian pronunciation. The same kind of thing happened to Augustine. The Milanese turned his African accent into ridicule. He even found among them certain purists who discovered solecisms in his phrases.

But these scratches at his self-respect, this increasing disgust of men and things, were small matters compared to what was going on within him. Augustine had a sick soul. The forebodings he had always been subject to were now become the suffering of every moment. At certain times he was assailed by those great waves of sadness which unfurl all of a sudden from the depths of the unknown. In such minutes we believe that the whole world is hurling itself against us. The great wave rolled him over; he got up again all wounded. And he felt stretch forth in him a new will which was not his own, under which the other, the will to sin, struggled. It was like the approach of an invisible being whose contact overcame him with an anguish which was full of pleasure. This being wanted to open out within him, but the weight of his old sins prevented. Then his soul cried out in pain.

In those moments, what a relief it was to let himself float on the canticles of the Church! The liturgical chants were then something new in the West. It was in the very year we are dealing with that St. Ambrose started the custom in the Milanese basilicas.

The childhood of our hymns! One cannot think about that without being moved. One envies Augustine for having heard them in their spring freshness. These lovely musics, which were to sound during so many centuries, and still soar against the vaults of cathedrals, were leaving the nest for the first time. We cannot think that a day will come when they will fold their wings and fall silent. Since human bodies, temples of the Holy Ghost, will live again in glory, one would like to believe with Dante that the hymns, temples of the Word, are likewise immortal, and that they will still be heard in the everlasting. Doubtless in the twilight glens of Purgatory the bewailing souls continue to sing the *Te lucis ante terminum*, even as in the star-circles, where the Blessed move ever, will always leap up the triumphant notes of the *Magnificat*...

Even on those who have lost the faith, the power of these hymns is irresistible. "If you knew," said Renan, "the charm that the Barbarian magicians knew how to put into their canticles. When I remember them, my heart melts." The heart of Augustine, who had not yet the faith, melted too in hearing them: "How I have cried, my God, over the hymns and canticles when the sweet sound of the music of Thy Church thrilled my soul! As the music flowed into my ears, and Thy truth trickled into my heart, the tide of devotion swelled high within me, and the tears ran down, and there was gladness in those tears." His heart cast off its heaviness, while his mind was shaken by the heavenly music. Augustine loved music passionately. At this time he conceived God as the Great Musician of the spheres; and soon he will write that "we are a strophe in a poem." At the same time, the vivid and lightning figures of the Psalms, sweeping over the insipid metaphors of the rhetoric which encumbered his memory, awoke in the depths of him his wild African imagination and sent him soaring. And then the affectionate note, the plaint in those sacred songs: *Deus, Deus meus!*—"O God! O my God!" The Divinity was no longer a cold abstraction, a phantom that withdrew into an unapproachable infinite; He became the actual possession of the loving soul. He leant over His poor scarred creature, took him in His arms, and comforted him like a kind father.

Augustine wept with tenderness and ecstasy, but also with despair. He wept upon himself. He saw that he had not the courage to be happy with the only possible happiness. What, indeed, was he seeking, unless it were to capture this "blessed life" which he had pursued so long? What he had tried to get out of all his loves was the complete gift of his soul—to realize himself completely. Now, this completeness of self is only in God—*in Deo salutari meo.* The souls we have wounded are in unison with us, and with themselves, only in God... And the sweet Christian symbolism invited him with its most enticing images: the Shades of Paradise; the Fountain of Living Water; the Repose in the Lord God; the green Branch of the Dove, harbinger of peace... But the passions still resisted. "To-morrow! Wait a little yet! Shall we be no more with you, for ever? *Non erimus tecum ultra in aeternum?*..." What a dismal sound in these syllables, and how terrifying for a timid soul! They fell, heavy as bronze, on the soul of Augustine.

An end had to be put to it somehow. What was needed was some one who would force him out of his indecision. Instinctively, led by that mysterious will which he felt had arisen within him, he went to see, and consult in his distress, an old priest named Simplicianus, who had converted or directed Bishop Ambrose in his young days. No doubt Augustine spoke to him of what he had lately been reading, and particularly of his Platonist studies, and of all the efforts he made to enter the communion of Christ. He acknowledged that he was convinced, but he could not bend to the practice of the Christian life. Then, very skilfully, as one artful in differentiating souls, perceiving that vanity was not yet dead in Augustine, Simplicianus offered him as an example the very translator of those Platonic books which he had just been reading so enthusiastically—that famous Victorinus Afer, that orator so learned and admired, who had his statue in the Roman Forum. Because of some remains of philosophical pride, and also from fear of offending his friends among the Roman aristocracy, who were still almost altogether pagan, Victorinus was a Christian only in his head. In vain Simplicianus pointed out to him how illogical his conduct was. But suddenly and unexpectedly he decided. The day of the baptism of the catechumens, this celebrated man mounted the platform set up in the basilica for the profession of faith of the newly converted, and there, like the meanest of the faithful, he delivered his profession before all the assembled people. That was a dramatic stroke. The crowd, jubilant over this fine performance, cheered the neophyte. And on all sides they shouted: "Victorinus! Victorinus!"

Augustine listened to this little story, whereof all the details were so happily chosen to act on an imagination like his:—the statue in the Roman Forum; the platform from the height of which the orator had spoken a language so new and unexpected; the exulting shouts of the crowd: "Victorinus! Victorinus!" Already he saw himself in the same position. There he was in the basilica, on the platform, in presence of Bishop Ambrose; he too repeated his profession of faith, and the people of Milan clapped their hands—"Augustine! Augustine!" But can a humble and contrite heart thus take pleasure in human adulation? If Augustine did become a convert, it would be entirely for God and before God. Very quickly he put aside the temptation... Nevertheless, this example, coming from so exalted a man, made a very deep and beneficial impression. He looked upon it as a providential sign, a lesson in courage which concerned him personally.

Some time after that, he received a visit from a fellow-countryman, a certain Pontitianus, who had a high position in the Imperial household. Augustine happened to be alone in the house with his friend Alypius. They sat down to talk, and by chance the visitor noticed the Epistles of St. Paul lying on a table for playing games. This started the conversation. Pontitianus, who was a Christian, praised the ascetic life, and especially the wonders of holiness wrought by Antony and his companions in the Egyptian deserts. This subject was in the air. In Catholic circles at Rome, they spoke of little else than these Egyptian solitaries, and of the number, growing larger and larger, of those who stripped themselves of their worldly goods to live in utter renunciation. What was the good of keeping these worldly goods, that the avarice of Government taxation confiscated so easily, and that the Barbarians watched covetously from afar! The brutes who came down from Germany would get hold of them sooner or later. And even supposing one might save them, retain an ever-uncertain enjoyment of them, was the life of the time really worth the trouble of living? There was nothing more to hope for the Empire. The hour of the great desolation was at hand...

Pontitianus, observing the effect of his words on his hearers, was led to tell them a quite private adventure of his own. He was at Trèves, in attendance on the Court. Well, one afternoon while the Emperor was at the circus, he and three of his friends, like himself attached to the household, went for a stroll beyond the city walls. Two of them parted from the others and went off into the country, and there they came upon a hut where dwelt certain hermits. They went in, and found a book—*The Life of St. Antony.* They read in it; and for them that was a conversion thunder-striking, instantaneous. The two courtiers resolved to join the solitaries there and then, and they never went back to the Palace. And they were betrothed!...

The tone of Pontitianus as he recalled this conscience-drama which he had witnessed, betrayed a strange emotion which gradually took hold of Augustine. His guest's words resounded in him like the blows of a clapper in a bell. He saw himself in the two courtiers of Trèves. He too was tired of the world, he too was betrothed. Was he going to do as the Emperor—remain in the circus taken up with idle pleasures, while others took the road to the sole happiness?

When Pontitianus was gone, Augustine was in a desperate state. The repentant soul of the two courtiers had passed into his. His will uprose in grievous conflict and tortured itself. He seized Alypius roughly by the arm and cried out to him in extraordinary excitement:

"What are we about? Yes, I say, what are we about? Did you not hear? Simple men arise and take Heaven by violence, and we with all our heartless learning—look how we are wallowing in flesh and blood!"

Alypius stared at him, stupefied. "The truth is," adds Augustine, "that I scarcely knew what I said. My face, my eyes, my colour, and the change in my voice expressed my meaning much better than my words." If he guessed from this upheaval of his whole frame how close at hand was the heavenly visitation, all he felt at the moment was a great need to weep, and he wanted solitude to weep freely. He went down into the garden. Alypius, feeling uneasy, followed at a distance, and in silence sat down beside him on the bench where he had paused. Augustine did not even notice that his friend was there. His agony of spirit began again. All his faults, all his old stains came once more to his mind, and he grew furious against his cowardly feebleness as he felt how much he still clung to them. Oh, to tear himself free from all these miseries—to finish with them once for all!... Suddenly he sprang up. It was as if a gust of the tempest had struck him. He rushed to the end of the garden, flung himself on his knees under a fig-tree, and with his forehead pressed against the earth he burst into tears. Even as the olive-tree at Jerusalem which sheltered the last watch of the Divine Master, the fig-tree of Milan saw fall upon its roots a sweat of blood. Augustine, breathless in the victorious embrace of Grace, panted: "How long, how long?... To-morrow and to-morrow?... Why not now? Why not this hour make an end of my vileness?..."

Now, at this very moment a child's voice from the neighbouring house began repeating in a kind of chant: *"Take and read, take and read."* Augustine shuddered. What was this refrain? Was it a nursery-rhyme that the little children of the countryside used to sing? He could not recollect it; he had never heard it before... Immediately, as upon a divine command, he rose to his feet and ran back to the place where Alypius was sitting, for he had left St. Paul's Epistles lying there. He opened the book, and the passage on which his eyes first fell was this: *Put ye on the Lord Jesus Christ, and make not provision for the flesh to fulfil the lusts thereof...* The flesh!... The sacred text aimed at him directly—at him, Augustine, still so full of lust! This command was the answer from on high...

He put his finger between the leaves, closed the volume. His frenzy had passed away. A great peace was shed upon him—it was all over. With a calm face he told Alypius what had happened, and without lingering he went into Monnica's room to tell her also. The Saint was not surprised. It was long now since she had been told, "Where I am, there shalt thou be also." But she gave way to an outburst of joy. Her mission was done. Now she might sing her canticle of thanksgiving and enter into God's peace.

Meanwhile, the good Alypius, always circumspect and practical, had opened the book again and shewn his friend what followed the verse, for Augustine, in his excitement, had neglected to read further. The Apostle said, *"Him that is weak in the faith receive ye."* This also applied to Augustine. That was only too certain: his new faith was still very unsteady. Let not presumption blind him! Yes, no doubt with all his soul he desired to be a Christian. It now remained for him to become one.

THE HIDDEN LIFE

Fac me, Pater, quærere te !
Cause me to seek Thee, O my Father.

— *Soliloques*, I, 1.

Chapter 1
THE LAST SMILE OF THE MUSE

Now that Augustine had been at last touched by grace, was he after all going to make a sensational conversion like his professional brother, the celebrated Victorinus?

He knew well enough that there is a good example set by these noisy conversions which works on a vast number of people. And however "contrite and humble" his heart might be, he was quite aware that in Milan he was an important personage. What excitement, if he were to resign his professorship on the ground that he wished to spend the rest of his life in the ascetic way of the Christians!... But he preferred to avoid the scandal on one side, and the loud praise on the other. God alone and some very dear friends should witness his repentance.

There were now hardly twenty days before the vacation. He would be patient till then. Thus, the parents of his pupils would not have any ground to reproach him for leaving them before the end of term, and as his health was getting worse, he would have a good excuse to give up his post. The dampness of the climate had given him a sort of chronic bronchitis which the summer had not cured. He had difficulty in breathing; his voice was muffled and thin—so much so, that he began to think his lungs were attacked. Augustine's health really needed care. This was a quite good enough reason to interrupt his lectures. Having fulfilled his professional duties to the very end—and he assures us that it took some courage—he left the professorial chair with the declared intention of never occupying it again.

Here, then, he is free from all worldly ties. From now on he can prepare himself for baptism in silence and retreat. But still he must live somehow! Augustine had more souls depending on him than ever: his son, his mother, his brother, his cousins—a heavy burthen which he had been struggling under for a long time. It is probable that once more Romanianus, who was still in Milan, came to his assistance. It will be remembered that the Mæcenas of Thagaste had taken up warmly the plan of a lay monastery which Augustine and his friends had lost their heads over, and he had promised to subscribe a large sum. Augustine's retreat was a first step towards realizing this plan in a new shape. Romanianus, no doubt, approved of it. In any case, he asked Augustine to keep on giving lessons to his son Licentius. Another young man, Trygetius, begged for the same favour. Augustine therefore did not intend to give up his employment altogether. He had changed, for the present at least, from a Government professor into a private one.

This meant that he had a certain living. All he wanted now was a shelter. A friend, a colleague, the grammarian Verecundus, graciously offered him this. Verecundus thus repaid a favour which Augustine had quite recently done him. It was at Augustine's request that Nebridius, who was a friend of both, agreed to take over the classes of the grammarian, who was obliged to go away. Although rich, full of talent, and very eager for peace and solitude, Nebridius, simply out of good-nature, was willing to take the place of Verecundus in his very modest employment. One cannot too much admire the generosity and kindliness of these ancient and Christian manners. In those days, friendship knew nothing of our narrow and shabby egoisms.

Now Verecundus owned a country house just outside Milan, at Cassicium. He suggested to Augustine to spend the vacation there, and even to live there permanently with all his people, on condition of looking after the property and keeping it up.

Attempts have been made to find traces of this hospitable dwelling where the future monk of Thagaste and Hippo bade farewell to the world. Cassicium has disappeared. The imagination is free to rebuild it fancifully in any part of the rich country which lies about Milan. Still, if the youthful Licentius has not yielded too much to metaphor in the verses wherein he recalls to Augustine "Departed suns among Italian mountain-heights," it is likely that the estate of Verecundus lay upon those first mountain-slopes which roll into the Brianza range. Even today, the rich Milanese have their country houses among those hills.

To Augustine and his companions this flourishing Lombardy must have seemed another promised land. The country, wonderfully fertile and cultivated, is one orchard, where fruit trees cluster, and, in all ways, deep streams wind, slow-flowing and stocked with fish. Everywhere is the tremor of running water—inconceivably fresh music for African ears. A scent of mint and aniseed; fields with grass growing high and straight in which you plunge up to the knees. Here and there, deeply engulfed little valleys with their bunches of green covert, slashed with the rose plumes of the lime trees and the burnished leaves of the hazels, and where already the northern firs lift their black needles. Far off, blended in one violet mass, the Alps, peak upon peak, covered with snow; and nearer in view, sheer cliffs, jutting fastnesses, ploughed through with black gorges which make flare out plainer the bronze-gold of their slopes. Not far off, the enchanted lakes slumber. It seems that an emblazonment fluctuates from their waters, and writhing above the crags which imprison them drifts athwart a sky sometimes a little chill—Leonardo's pensive sky of shadowed amethyst—again of a flushed blue, whereupon float great clouds, silken and ruddy, as in the backgrounds of Veronese's pictures. The beauty of the light lightens and beautifies the over-heavy opulence of the land.

And wherever the country house of Verecundus may be placed, some bit of this triumphal landscape will be found. As for the house itself, Augustine has said enough about it for us to see it fairly well. It was no doubt one of those old rustic buildings, inhabited only some few months of the year, in the warmest season, and for the rest of the time given over to the frolics of mice and rats. Without any pretence to architectural form, it had been enlarged and renovated simply for the greater convenience of those who lived there. There was no attempt at symmetry; the main door was not in the middle of the building, and there was another door on one of the sides. The sole luxury of this country house was perhaps the bath-houses. These baths, however simple they might be, nevertheless reminded Augustine of the decoration of gymnasiums. Does this mean that he found there rich pavements, mosaics, and statues? These were quite usual things in Roman villas. The Italians have always had, at all periods, a great fondness for statues and mosaics. Not very particular about the quality, they made up for it by the quantity. And when they could not treat themselves to the real thing, it was good enough to give themselves the make-believe in painting. I can imagine easily enough Verecundus' house, painted in fresco from top to bottom, inside and out, like those houses at Pompeii, or the modern Milanese villas.

There was no attempt at ornamental gardens at Cassicium. The surroundings must have been kitchen-garden, grazing-land, or ploughed fields, as in a farm. A meadow—not in the least the lawns found in front of a large country house—lay before the dwelling, which was protected from sun and wind by clumps of chestnut trees. There, stretched on the grass under the shade of one of these spreading trees, they chatted gaily while listening to the broken song of the brook, as it flowed under the windows of the baths. They lived very close to nature, almost the life of field-tillers. The whole charm of Cassicium consisted in its silence, its peace, and, above all, its fresh air. Augustine's tired lungs breathed there a purer air than in Milan, where the humid summer heat is crushing. His soul, yearning for retirement, discovered a retreat here in harmony with his new desires, a country solitude of which the Virgilian grace still appealed to his literary imagination. The days he passed there were days of blessedness for him. Long afterwards he was deeply moved when he recalled them, and in an outburst of gratitude towards his host, he prayed God to pay him his debt. "Thou wilt recompense him, O Lord, on the day of the resurrection of the just... For that country house at Cassicium where we found shelter in Thee from the burning summer of our time, Thou wilt repay to Verecundus the coolness and evergreen shade of Thy paradise..."

That was an unequalled moment in Augustine's life. Following immediately upon the mental crisis which had even worn out his body, he seems to be experiencing the pleasure of convalescence. He slackens, and, as he says himself, he rests. His excitement is quenched, but his faith remains as firm as ever. With a cairn and supremely lucid mind he judges his condition; he sees clearly all that he has still to do ere he becomes a thorough Christian. First, he must grow familiar with the Scripture, solve certain urgent questions—that of the soul, for example, its nature and origin—which possessed him just then. Then he must change his conduct, alter his ways of thought, and, if one may so speak, disinfect his mind still all saturated with pagan influences: a delicate work—yes, and an uneasy, at times even painful, which would take more than one day.

After twenty centuries of Christianity, and in spite of our claim to understand all things, we do not yet realize very well what an abyss lies between us and paganism. When by chance we come upon pagan traces in certain primitive regions of the South of Europe, we get muddled, and attribute to Catholicism what is but a survival of old abolished customs, so far from us that we cannot recognize them any more. Augustine, on the contrary, was right next to them. When he strolled over the fields and through the woods around Cassicium, the Fauns and woodland Nymphs of the old mythology haunted his memory, and all but stood before his eyes. He could not take a walk without coming upon one of their chapels, or striking against a boundary-mark still all greasy from the oil with which the superstitious peasants had drenched it. Like himself, the old pagan land had not yet quite put on the Christ of the new era. He was like that Hermes Criophorus, who awkwardly symbolized the Saviour on the walls of the Catacombs. Even as the Bearer of Rams changed little by little into the Good Shepherd, the Bishop of Hippo emerged slowly from the rhetorician Augustine.

He became aware of it during that languid autumn at Cassicium—that autumn heavy with all the rotting of summer, but which already promised the great winter peace. The yellow leaves of the chestnuts were heaped by the roadside. They fell in the brook which flowed near the baths, and the slowed water ceased to sing. Augustine strained his ears for it. His soul also was blocked, choked up by all the deposit of his passions. But he knew that soon the chant of his new life would begin in triumphal fashion, and he said over to himself the words of the psalm: *Cantate mihi canticum novum*—"Sing unto me a new song."

Unfortunately for Augustine, his soul and its salvation was not his only care at Cassicium: he had a thousand others. So it shall be with him throughout his life. Till the very end he will long for solitude, for the life in God, and till the end God will charge him with the care of his brethren. This great spirit shall live above all by charity.

At the house of Verecundus he was not only the head, but he had a complete country estate to direct and supervise. Probably all the guests in the house helped him. They divided the duties. The good Alypius, who was used to business and versed in the twisted ways of the law, took over the foreign affairs—the buying and selling, probably the accounts also. He was continually on the road to Milan. Augustine attended to the correspondence, and every morning appointed their work to the farm-labourers. Monnica looked after the household, no easy work in a house where nine sat down to table every day. But the Saint fulfilled her humble duties with touching kindness and forgetfulness of self: "She took care of us," says Augustine, "as if we had all been her children, and she served us as if each of us had been her father."

Let us look a little at these "children" of Monnica. Besides Alypius, whom we know already, there was the young Adeodatus, the child of sin—"my son Adeodatus, whose gifts gave promise of great things, unless my love for him betrays me." Thus speaks his father. This little boy was, it seems, a prodigy, as shall be the little Blaise Pascal later: "His intelligence filled me with awe"—*horrori mihi erat illud ingenium*—says the father again. What is certain is that he had a soul like an angel. Some sayings of his have been preserved by Augustine. They are fragrant as a bunch of lilies.

The other members of the family are nearer the earth. Navigius, Augustine's brother, an excellent man of whom we know nothing save that he had a bad liver—the icterus of the African colonist—and that on this account he abstained from sweetmeats. Rusticus and Lastidianus, the two cousins, persons as shadowy as the "supers" in a tragedy. Finally, Augustine's pupils, Trygetius and Licentius. The first, who had lately served some time in the army, was passionately fond of history, "like a veteran." Although his master in some of his Dialogues has made him his interlocutor, his character remains for us undeveloped. With Licentius it is different. This son of Romanianus, the Mæcenas of Thagaste, was Augustine's beloved pupil. It is easy to make that out. All the phrases he devotes to Licentius have a warmth of tone, a colour and relief which thrill.

This Licentius comes before us as the type of the spoiled child, the son of a wealthy family, capricious, vain, presuming, unabashed, never hesitating if he sees a chance to have a joke with his master. Forgetful, besides, prone to sudden fancies, superficial, and rather blundering. With all that, the best boy in the world—a bad head, but a good heart. He was a frank pagan, and I believe remained a pagan all his life, in spite of the remonstrances of Augustine and those of the gentle Paulinus of Nola, who lectured him in prose and verse. A great eater and a fine drinker, he found himself obliged to do penance at St. Monnica's rather frugal table. But when the fever of inspiration took hold of him, he forgot eating and drinking, and in his poetical thirst he would would have drained—so his master says—all the fountains of Helicon. Licentius had a passion for versifying: "He is an almost perfect poet," wrote Augustine to Romanianus. The former rhetorician knew the world, and the way to talk to the father of a wealthy pupil, especially if he is your benefactor. At Cassicium, under Augustine's indulgent eyes, the pupil turned into verse the romantic adventure of Pyramus and Thisbe. He declaimed bits of it to the guests in the house, for he had a fine loud voice. Then he flung aside the unfinished poem and suddenly fell in love with Greek tragedies of which, as it happened, he understood nothing at all, though this did not prevent him from boring everybody he met with them. Another day it was the Church music, then quite new, which flung him into enthusiasm. That day they heard Licentius singing canticles from morning till night.

In connection with this, Augustine relates with candid freedom an anecdote which to-day needs the indulgence of the reader to make it acceptable. As it gives light upon that half-pagan, half-Christian way of life which was still Augustine's, I will repeat it in all its plainness.

It happened, then, one evening after dinner, that Licentius went out and took his way to a certain mysterious retreat, and there he suddenly began singing this verse of the Psalm: "Turn us again, O Lord God of hosts, cause Thy face to shine; and we shall be saved." As a matter of fact, he had hardly sung anything else for a long time. He kept on repeating this verse over and over again, as people do with a tune they have just picked up. But the pious Monnica, who heard him, could not tolerate the singing of such holy words in such a place. She spoke sharply to the offender. Upon this the young scatter-brains answered rather flippantly:

"Supposing, good mother, that an enemy had shut me up in that place—do you mean to say that God wouldn't have heard me just the same?"

The next day he thought no more about it, and when Augustine reminded him, he declared that he felt no remorse.

"As far as I am concerned," replied the excellent master, "I am not in the least shocked by it... The truth is, that neither that place, which has so much scandalized my mother, nor the darkness of night, is altogether inappropriate to this canticle. For whence, think you, do we implore

God to drag us, so that we may be converted and gaze upon His face? Is it not from that jakes of the senses wherein our souls are plunged, and from that darkness of which the error is around us?..."

And as they were discussing that day the order established by Providence, Augustine made it a pretext to give a little edifying lecture to his pupil. Having heard the sermon to the end, the sharp Licentius put in with sly maliciousness:

"I say, what a splendid arrangement of events to shew me that nothing happens except in the best way, and for our great good!"

This reply gives us the tone of the conversation between Augustine and his pupils. Nevertheless, however free and merry the talks might be, the purpose was always instructive, and it was always substantial. Let us not forget that the Milanese rhetorician is still a professor. The best part of his days was devoted to these two youths who had been put under his charge. As soon as he had settled the business of the farm, talked to the peasants, and given his orders to the workmen, he fell back upon his business of rhetorician. In the morning they went over Virgil's *Eclogues* together. At night they discussed philosophy. When the weather was fine they walked in the fields, and the discussion continued under the shade of the chestnut trees. If it rained, they took refuge in the withdrawing-room adjoining the baths. Beds were there, cushions, soft chairs convenient for talking, and the equal temperature from the vapour-baths close at hand was good for Augustine's bronchial tubes.

There is no stiffness in these dialogues, nothing which smacks of the school. The discussion starts from things which they had under the eyes, often from some slight accidental happening. One night when Augustine could not sleep—he often suffered from insomnia—the dispute began in bed, for the master and his pupils slept in the same room. Lying there in the dark, he listened to the broken murmur of the stream. He was trying to think out an explanation of the pauses in the sound, when Licentius shifted under the bedclothes, and reaching out for a piece of stick lying on the floor, he rapped with it on the foot of the bed to frighten the mice. So he was not asleep either, nor Trygetius, who was stirring about in his bed. Augustine was delighted: he had two listeners. Immediately he put this question: "Why do those pauses come in the flow of the stream? Do they not follow some secret law?..." They had hit upon a subject for debate. During many days they discussed the order of the world.

Another time, as they were going into the baths, they stopped to look at two cocks fighting. Augustine called the attention of the youths "to a certain order full of propriety in all the movements of these fowls deprived of reason."

"Look at the conqueror," said he. "He crows triumphantly. He struts and plumes himself as a proud sign of victory. And now look at the beaten one, without voice, his neck unfeathered, a look of shame. All that has I know not what beauty, in harmony with the laws of nature..."

New argument in favour of order: the debate of the night before is started rolling again.

For us, too, it is well worth while to pause on this little homely scene. It reveals to us an Augustine not only very sensitive to beauty, but very attentive to the sights of the world surrounding him. Cockfights were still very popular in this Roman society at the ending of the Empire. For a long time sculptors had found many gracious subjects in the sport. Reading this passage of Augustine's, one recalls, among other similar designs, that funeral urn at the Lateran upon which are represented two little boys, one crying over his beaten cock, while the other holds his tenderly in his arms and kisses it—the cock that won, identified by the crown held in its spurs.

Augustine is always very close to these humble realities. Every moment outside things start up in the dialogues between the master and his pupils... They are in bed on a rainy night in November. Gradually, a vague gleam rests on the windows. They ask each other if that can be the moon, or the break of day... Another time, the sun rises in all its splendour, and they decide to go into the meadow and sit on the grass. Or else, the sky darkens and lights are brought in. Or again, it is the appearance of diligent Alyphis, just come back from Milan...

In the same way as he notes these light details in passing, Augustine welcomes all his guests into his dialogues and admits them to the debate: his mother, his brother, the cousins, Alypius between his business journeys, down to the child Adeodatus. He knew the value of ordinary good sense, the second-sight of a pure heart, or of a pious soul strengthened by prayer. Monnica used often to come into the room when they were arguing, to let them know that dinner was ready, or for something of the kind. Her son asked her to remain. Modestly she shewed her astonishment at such an honour.

"Mother," said Augustine, "do you not love truth? Then why should

I blush to give you a place among us? Even if your love for truth were only half-hearted, I ought still to receive you and listen to you. How much more then, since you love it more than you love me, *and I know how much you love me...* Nothing can separate you from truth, neither fear, nor pain of whatever kind it be—no, nor death itself. Do not all agree that this is the highest stage of philosophy? How can I hesitate after that to call myself your disciple?"

And Monnica, utterly confused by such praise, answered with affectionate gruffness:

"Stop talking! You have never told bigger lies."

Most of the time these conversations were simply dialectic games in the taste of the period, games a little pedantic, and fatiguing from subtilty. The boisterous Licentius did not always enjoy himself. He was often inattentive; and his master scolded him. But all the same, the master understood how to amuse his two foster-children while he exercised their intelligence. At the end of one discussion he said to them laughing:

"Just at this hour, the sun warns me to put the playthings I had brought for the children back in the basket..."

Let us remark in passing that this is the last time, before those centuries which are coming of universal intellectual silence or arid scholasticism—the last time that high questions will be discussed in this graceful light way, and with the same freedom of mind. The tradition begun by Socrates under the plane-trees on the banks of the Ilissus, is ending with Augustine under the chestnuts of Cassicium.

And yet, however gay and capricious the form, the substance of these dialogues, "On the Academics," "On Order," and "On the Happy Life," is serious, and even very serious. The best proof of their importance in Augustine's eyes is, that after taking care to have them reported in shorthand, he eventually published them. The *notarii* attended these discussions and let nothing be lost. The rise of the scrivener, of the notary, dates from this period. The administration of the Lower-Empire was frightfully given to scribbling. By contact with it, the Church became so too. Let us not press our complaints about it, since this craze for writing has procured for us, with a good deal of shot-rubbish, some precious historical documents. In Augustine's case, these reports of his lectures at Cassicium have at least the value of shewing us the state of soul of the future Bishop of Hippo at a decisive moment of his life.

For these *Dialogues*, although they look like school exercises, reveal the intimate thoughts of Augustine on the morrow of his conversion. While he seems to be refuting the Academics, he is fighting the errors from which he, personally, had suffered so long. He clarified his new ideal. No; the search for truth, without hope of ever reaching it, cannot give happiness. And genuine happiness is only in God. And if a rhythm is to be found in things, then it is necessary to make the soul rhythmic also and so enable it to contemplate God. It is necessary to still within it the noise of the passions. Hence, the need of inward reformation, and, at a final analysis, of asceticism.

But Augustine knew full well that these truths must be adapted to the weakness of the two lads he was teaching, and also to the common run of mankind. He has not yet in these years the uncompromising attitude which ere long will give him a sterner virtue—an attitude, however, unceasingly tempered by his charity and by the persistent recollections of his reading. It was now that he shaped the rule of conduct in worldly morals and education which the Christian experience of the future will adopt: "If you have always order in your hearts," he said to his pupils, "you must return to your verses. *For a knowledge of liberal sciences, but a controlled and exact knowledge*, forms men who will love the truth... But there are other men, or, to put it better, other souls, who, although held in the body, are sought for the eternal marriage by the best and fairest of spouses. For these souls it is not enough to live; they wish to live happy... But as for you, go, *meanwhile*, and find your Muses!"

"Go and find your Muses!" What a fine saying! How human and how wise! Here is clearly indicated the double ideal of those who continue to live in the world according to the Christian law of restraint and moderation, and of those who yearn to live in God. With Augustine the choice is made. He will never more look back. These Dialogues at Cassicium are his supreme farewell to the pagan Muse.

Chapter 2
THE ECSTASY OF SAINT MONNICA

They stayed through the winter at Cassicium. However taken up he might be by the work of the estate and the care of his pupils, Augustine devoted himself chiefly to the great business of his salvation.

The *Soliloquies*, which he wrote then, render even the passionate tone of the meditations which he perpetually gave way to during his watches and nights of insomnia. He searched for God, moaning: *Fac me, Pater, quærere te*—"Cause me to seek Thee, O my Father." But still, he sought Him more as a philosopher than as a Christian. The old man in him was not dead. He had not quite stripped off the rhetorician or the intellectual. The over-tender heart remained, which had so much sacrificed to human love. In those ardent dialogues between himself and his reason, it is plain to see that reason is not quite the mistress. "I love only God and the soul," Augustine states with a touch of presumption. And his reason, which knows him well, answers: "Do you not then love your friends?"—"I love the soul; how therefore should I not love them?" What does this phrase, of such exquisite sensibility, and even already so aloof from worldly thoughts—what does it lack to give forth a sound entirely Christian? Just a slight change of accent.

He himself began to see that he would do better not to philosophize so much and to draw nearer the Scripture, in listening to the wisdom of that with a contrite and humble heart. Upon the directions of Ambrose, whose advice he had asked by letter, he tried to read the prophet Isaiah, because Isaiah is the clearest foreteller of the Redemption. He found the book so difficult that he lost heart, and he put it aside till later. Meanwhile, he had forwarded his resignation as professor of Rhetoric to the Milan municipality. Then, when the time was come, he sent to Bishop Ambrose a written confession of his errors and faults, and represented to him his very firm intention to be baptized. He was quietly baptized on the twenty-fifth of April, during the Easter season of the year 387, together with his son Adeodatus, and his friend Alypius. Alypius had prepared most piously, disciplining himself with the harshest austerities, to the point of walking barefoot on the frozen soil.

So now the solitaries of Cassicium are back in Milan. Augustine's two pupils were gone. Trygetius doubtless had rejoined the army. Licentius had gone to live in Rome. But another fellow-countryman, an African from Thagaste, Evodius, formerly a clerk in the Ministry of the Interior, came to join the small group of new converts. Evodius, the future Bishop of Uzalis, in Africa, and baptized before Augustine, was a man of scrupulous piety and unquestioning faith. He talked of devout subjects with his friend, who, just fresh from baptism, experienced all the quietude of grace. They spoke of the community which St. Ambrose had either founded or organized at the gates of Milan, and in comparison with a life so austere, Augustine perceived that the life he had led at Cassicium was still stained with paganism. He must carry out his conversion to the end and live as a hermit after the manner of Antony and the solitaries of the Thebaid. Then it occurred to him that he still owned a little property at Thagaste—a house and fields. There they would settle and live in self-denial like the monks. The purity of the young Adeodatus predestined him to this ascetic existence. As for Monnica, who long since had taken the widow's veil, she had to make no change in her ways to lead a saintly life in the company of her son and grandson. It was agreed among them all to go back to Africa, and to start as soon as possible.

Thus, just after his baptism, Augustine shews but one desire: to bury himself in a retreat, to lead a humble and hidden life, divided between the study of the Scripture and the contemplation of God. Later on, his enemies were to accuse him of having become a convert from ambition, in view of the honours and riches of the episcopate. This is sheer calumny. His conversion could not have been more sincere, more disinterested—nor more heroic either: he was thirty-three years old. When we think of all he had loved and all he gave up, we can only bow the head and bend the knee before the lofty virtue of such an example.

In the course of the summer the caravan started and crossed the Apennines to set sail at Ostia. The date of this exodus has never been made quite clear. Perhaps Augustine and his companions fled before the hordes of the usurper Maximus, who, towards the end of August, crossed the Alps and marched on Milan, while the young Valentinian with all his Court took refuge at Aquileia. In any case, it was a trying journey, especially in the hot weather. When Monnica arrived she was very enfeebled. At Ostia they had to wait till a ship was sailing for Africa. Propitious conditions did not offer every day. At this period, travellers were at the mercy of the sea, of the wind, and of a thousand other circumstances. Time did not count; it was wasted freely. The ship sailed short distances at a time, skirting the coasts, where the length of the stay at every point touched depended on the master. On board these ships—feluccas hardly decked over—if the crossing was endless and unsafe, it was, above all, most uncomfortable. People were in no hurry to undergo the tortures of it, and spaced them out as much as possible by frequent stoppages. On account of all these reasons, our Africans made a rather long stay at Ostia. They lodged, no doubt, with Christian brethren, hosts of Augustine or Monnica, in a tranquil house far out of earshot of the cosmopolitan crowd which overflowed in the hotels on the quay.

Ostia, situated at the mouth of the Tiber, was both the port and bond-warehouse of Rome. The Government stores-ships landed the African oil and corn there. It was a junction for commerce, the point where immigrants from all parts of the Mediterranean disbarked. To-day there is only left a wretched little village. But at some distance from this hamlet, the excavations of archæologists have lately brought to light the remains of a large town. They have discovered at the entrance a place of burial with arcosol-tombs; and here perhaps the body of St. Monnica was laid. In this place of graves they came upon also a beautiful statue injured—a funeral Genius, or a Victory, with large folded wings like those of the Christian angels. Further on, the forum with its shops, the guard-house of the night-cohort, baths, a theatre, many large temples, arcaded streets paved with large flags, warehouses for merchandise.

There may still be seen, lining the walls, the holes in which the ends of the amphoræ used to be dropped to keep them upright. All this wreckage gives an idea of a populous centre where the stir of traffic and shipping was intense.

And yet in this noisy town, Augustine and his mother found means to withdraw themselves and join together in meditation and prayer. Amid this rather vulgar activity, in a noise of trade and seafaring, a mystic scene develops where the purified love of mother and son gleams upon us as in a light of apotheosis. They had at Ostia a foretaste, so to speak, of the eternal union in God. This was in the house where they had come on arrival. They talked softly, resting against a window which looked upon the garden... But the scene has been made popular by Ary Scheffer's too well-known painting. You remember it: two faces, pale, bloodless, stripped of flesh, in which live only the burning eyes cast upward to the sky—a dense sky, baffling, heavy with all the secrets of eternity. No visible object, nothing, absolutely nothing, distracts them from their contemplation. The sea itself, although indicated by the painter, almost blends into the blue line of the horizon. Two souls and the sky—there you have the whole subject.

It is living poetry congealed in abstract thought. The attitude of the characters, majestically seated, instead of leaning on the window-ledge, has, in Scheffer's picture, I know not what touch of stiffness, of slightly theatrical. And the general impression is a cold dryness which contrasts with the lyric warmth of the story in the *Confessions*.

For my part, I always thought, perhaps on the testimony of the picture, that the window of the house at Ostia opened above the garden in view of the sea. The sea, symbol of the infinite, ought to be present—so it seemed to me—at the final conversation between Monnica and Augustine. At Ostia itself I was obliged to give up this too literary notion; the sea is not visible there. No doubt at that time the channel was not so silted up as it is to-day. But the coast lies so low, that just hard by the actual mouth of the Tiber, the nearness of the sea can only be guessed by the reflection of the waves in the atmosphere, a sort of pearly halo, trembling on the edge of the sky. At present I am inclined to think that the window of the house at Ostia was very likely turned towards the vast melancholy horizon of the *Agro Romano*. "We passed through, one after another," says Augustine, "all the things of a material order, unto heaven itself." Is it not natural to suppose that these things of a material order—these shapes of the earth with its plantations, its rivers, towns, and mountains—were under their eyes? The bleak spectacle which unrolled before their gaze agreed, at all events, with the disposition of their souls.

This great desolate plain has nothing oppressive, nothing which retains the eyes upon details too material. The colours about it are pale and slight, as if on the point of swooning away. Immense sterile stretches, fawn-coloured throughout, with here and there shining a little pink, a little green; gorse, furze-bushes by the deep banks of the river, or a few *boschetti* with dusty leaves, which feebly stand out upon the blondness of the soil. To the right, a pine forest. To the left, the undulations of the Roman hills expire into an emptiness infinitely sad. Afar, the violet scheme of the Alban mountains, with veiled and dream-like distances, shape indefinitely against the pearl light, limpid and serene, of the sky.

Augustine and Monnica, resting on the window-ledge, looked forth. Doubtless it was towards evening, at the hour when southern windows are thrown open to the cool after a burning day. They looked forth. "We marvelled," says Augustine, "at the beauty of Thy works, O my God!..." Rome was back there beyond the hills, with its palaces, its temples, the gleam of its gilding and its marbles. But the far-off image of the imperial city could not conquer the eternal sadness which rises from the *Agro*. An air of funeral loneliness lay above this plain, ready to be engulfed by the creeping shadows. How easy it was to break free of these vain corporeal appearances which decomposed of themselves! "Then," Augustine resumes, "we soared with glowing hearts still higher." (He speaks as if he and his mother were risen with equal flight to the vision. It is more probable that he was drawn up by Monnica, long since familiar with the ways of the spirit, used to visions, and to mystic talks with God...) Where was this God? All the creatures, questioned by their anguished entreaty, answered: *Quære super nos*—"Seek above us!" They sought; they mounted higher and higher: "And so we came to our own minds, and passed beyond them into the region of unfailing plenty, where Thou feedest Israel for ever with the food of truth... And as we talked, and we strove eagerly towards this divine region, *by a leap with the whole force of our hearts, we touched it for an instant*... Then we sighed, we fell back, and left there fastened the first fruits of the Spirit, and heard again the babble of our own tongues, this mortal speech wherein each word has a beginning and an ending."

"We fell back!" The marvellous vision had vanished. But a great silence was about them, silence of things, silence of the soul. And they said to each other:

"If the tumult of the flesh were hushed; hushed these shadows of earth, sea, sky; suppose this vision endured, and all other far inferior modes of vision were taken away, and this alone were to ravish the beholder, and absorb him, and plunge him in mystic joy, so that eternal life might be like this moment of comprehension which has made us sigh with Love—might not that be the fulfilment of 'Enter thou into the joy of thy Lord'? Ah, when shall this be? Shall it not be, O my God, when we rise again among the dead...?"

Little by little they came down to earth. The dying colours of the sunset-tide smouldered into the white mists of the *Agro*. The world entered into night. Then Monnica, impelled by a certain presentiment, said to Augustine:

"My son, as for me, I find no further pleasure in life. What I am still to do, or why I still linger here, I know not... There was only one thing made me want to tarry a little longer in this life, that I might see you a Christian and a Catholic before I died. My God has granted me this boon far beyond what I hoped for. So what am I doing here?"

She felt it; her work was done. She had exhausted, as Augustine says, all the hope of the century—*consumpta spe sæculi*. For her the parting was near. This ecstasy was that of one dying, who has raised a corner of the veil, and who no longer belongs to this world.

And, in fact, five or six days later she fell ill. She had fever. The climate of Ostia bred fevers, as it does to-day, and it was always unsanitary on account of all the foreigners who brought in every infection of the Orient. Furthermore, the weariness of a long journey in summer had worn out this woman, old before her time. She had to go to bed. Soon she got worse, and then lost consciousness. They believed she was in the agony. They all came round her bed—Augustine, his brother Navigius, Evodius, the two cousins from Thagaste, Rusticus, and Lastidianus. But suddenly she shuddered, raised herself, and asked in a bewildered way:

"Where was I?"

Then, seeing the grief on their faces, she knew that she was lost, and she said in a steady voice:

"You will bury your mother here."

Navigius, frightened by this sight of death, protested with all his affection for her:

"No. You will get well, mother. You will come home again. You won't die in a foreign land."

She looked at him with sorrowful eyes, as if hurt that he spoke so little like a Christian, and turning to Augustine:

"See how he talks," she said.

And after a silence, she went on in a firmer voice, as if to impress on her sons her final wishes:

"Lay this body where you will, and be not anxious about it. Only I beseech you, remember me at the altar of God, wherever you are."

That was the supreme renunciation. How could an African woman, so much attached to her country, agree to be buried in a stranger soil? Pagan notions were still very strong in this community, and the place of burial was an important consideration. Monnica, like all other widows, had settled upon hers. At Thagaste she had had her place prepared beside her husband Patricius. And here now she appeared to give that up. Augustine's companions were astonished at such abnegation. As for himself, he marvelled at the completeness of the change worked in his mother's soul by Grace. And as he thought over all the virtues of her life, the strength of her faith—from that moment, he had no doubt that she was a saint.

She still lingered for some time. Finally, on the ninth day of her illness, she died at the age of fifty-six.

Augustine closed her eyes. A great sorrow surged into his heart. And yet he who was so quick to tears had the courage not to cry... Suddenly a noise of weeping rose in the room of death: it was the young Adeodatus, who lamented at the sight of the corpse. He sobbed in such a heartbroken way that those who were there, demoralized by the distress of it, were obliged to rebuke him. This struck Augustine so deeply, that many years afterwards the broken sound of this sobbing still haunted his ears. "Methought," he says, "that it was my own childish soul which thus broke out in the weeping of my son." As for him, with the whole effort of his reason struggling against his heart, he only wanted to think of the glory which the saint had just entered into. His companions felt likewise. Evodius caught up a psalter, and before Monnica's body, not yet cold, he began to chant the Psalm, "My song shall be of mercy and judgment; unto Thee, O Lord, will I sing." All who were in the house took up the responses.

In the meantime, while the layers-out were preparing the corpse for burial, the brethren drew Augustine into another room. His friends and relations stood round him. He consoled the others and himself. He spoke, as the custom was, upon the deliverance of the faithful soul and the happiness which is promised. They might have imagined that he had no sense of grief, "But in Thy hearing, O my God, where none of them could hear, I was chiding the softness of my heart, and holding back the tide of sorrow... Alas! well did I know what I was choking down in my heart."

Not even at the church, where the sacrifice was offered for Monnica's soul, nor at the cemetery before the coffin, did he weep. From a sense of Christian seemliness, he feared to scandalize his brethren by imitating the desolation of the pagans and of those who die without hope. But this very effort that he made to keep back his tears became another cause of suffering. The day ended in a black sadness, a sadness he could not shake off. It stifled him. Then he remembered the Greek proverb—"The bath drives away sorrow;" and he determined to go and bathe. He went into the *tepidarium* and stretched himself out on the hot slab. Useless remedy! "The bitterness of my trouble was not carried from my heart with the sweat that flowed from my limbs." The attendants rolled him in warm towels and led him to the resting-couch. Worn out by tiredness and so many emotions, he fell into a heavy sleep. The next day, upon awaking, a fresh briskness was in all his being. Some verses came singing into his memory; they were the first words of the confident and joyous hymn of St. Ambrose:

"Creator of the earth and sky,
Ruling the firmament on high,
Clothing the day with robes of light,
Blessing with gracious sleep the night,—

That rest may comfort weary men
To face their usual toil again,

And soothe awhile the harassed mind,
And sorrow's heavy load unbind."

Suddenly, at the word *sorrow*, the thought of his dead mother came back to him, with the regret for that kind heart he had lost. A wave of despair overwhelmed him. He flung himself sobbing on the bed, and at last wept all the tears he had pent up so long.

Chapter 3
THE MONK OF THAGASTE

Almost a year went by before Augustine continued his journey. It is hard to account for this delay. Why should he thus put off his return to Africa, he who was so anxious to fly the world?

It is likely that Monnica's illness, the arrangements about her funeral, and other matters to settle, kept him at Ostia till the beginning of winter. The weather became stormy, the sea dangerous. Navigation was regularly interrupted from November—sometimes even earlier, from the first days of October, if the tempests and the equinox were exceptionally violent. It would then be necessary to wait till spring. Besides, word came that the fleet of the usurper Maximus, then at war with Theodosius, blockaded the African coast. Travellers ran the risk of being captured by the enemy. From all these reasons, Augustine would be prevented from sailing before the end of the following summer. In the meantime, he went to live in Rome. He employed his leisure to work up a case against the Manichees, his brethren of the day before. Once he had adopted Catholicism, he must have expected passionate attacks from his former brothers in religion. To close their mouths, he gathered against them an elaborate mass of documents, bristling with the latest scandals. He busied himself also with a thorough study of their doctrines, the better to refute them: in him the dialectician never slept. Then, when he had an opportunity, he visited the Roman monasteries, studying their rule and organization, so as to decide on a model for the convent which he always intended to establish in his own country. At last, he went back to Ostia some time in August or September, 388, where he found a ship bound for Carthage.

Four years earlier, about the same time of year, he had made the same voyage, coming the opposite way. He had a calm crossing; hardly could one notice the movement of the ship. It is the season of smooth seas in the Mediterranean. Never is it more etherial than in these summer months. The vague blue sky is confused with the bleached sea, spread out in a large sheet without creases—liquid and flexible silk, swept by quivering amber glow and orange saffron when the sun falls. No distinct shape, only strange suffusions of soft light, a pearl-like haze, the wistful blue reaching away indefinably.

At Carthage, Augustine had grown used to the magnificence of this pageantry of the sea. Now, the sea had the same appeased and gleaming face he had seen four years sooner. But how much his soul had since been changed! Instead of the tumult and falsehood which rent his heart and filled it with darkness, the serene light of Truth, and deeper than the sea's peace, the great appeasement of Grace. Augustine dreamed. Far off the Æolian isles were gloomed in the impending shadows, the smoky crater of Stromboli was no more than a black point circled by the double blue of waves and sky. So the remembrance of his passions, of all that earlier life, sank under the triumphant uprising of heavenly peace. He believed that this blissful state was going to continue and fill all the hours of his new life, and he knew of nothing so sweet...

This time, again, he was mistaken about himself. Upon the thin plank of the boat which carried him, he did not feel the force of the immense element, asleep now under his feet, but quick to be unchained at the first gust of wind; and he did not feel either the overflowing energy swelling his heart renewed by Grace—an energy which was going to set in motion one of the most complete and strenuous existences, one of the richest in thought, charity, and works which have enlightened history. Thinking only of the cloister, amidst the friends who surrounded him, no doubt he repeated the words of the Psalm: "Behold, how good and how pleasant it is for brethren to dwell together in unity." He pressed the hands of Alypius and Evodius, and tears came to his eyes.

The sun was gone. All the cold waste of waters, forsaken by the gleam, blurred gradually in vague anguish beneath the fall of night.

After skirting the Sicilian coasts, they arrived at last at Carthage. Augustine did not linger there; he was eager to see Thagaste once more, and to retire finally from the world. Favourable omens drew him to the place, and seemed to hearten him in his resolution. A dream had foretold his return to his former pupil, Elogius, the rhetorician. He was present, too, at the miraculous cure of a Carthage lawyer, Innocentius, in whose house he dwelt with his friends.

Accordingly, he left for Thagaste as soon as he could. There he made himself popular at once by giving to the poor, as the Gospel prescribed, what little remained of his father's heritage. But he does not make clear enough what this voluntary privation exactly meant. He speaks of a house and some little meadows—*paucis agellulis*—that he sequestrated. Still, he did not cease to live in the house all the time he was at Thagaste. The probability is that he did sell the few acres of land he still owned and bestowed the product of the sale on the poor. As to the house, he must have made it over with the outbuildings to the Catholic body of his native town, on condition of keeping the usufruct and of receiving for himself and his brethren the necessities of life. At this period many pious persons acted in this way when they gave their property to the Church. Church goods being unseizable, and exempt from taxation, this was a roundabout way of getting the better of fiscal extortion, whether in the shape of arbitrary confiscations, or eviction by force of arms. In any case, such souls as were tired of the world and longing for repose, found in these bequests an heroic method of saving themselves the trouble of looking after a fortune or a landed estate. When these fortunes and lands were extensive, the generous donors felt, we are told, an actual relief in getting rid of them.

This financial question settled, Augustine took up the task of turning the house into a monastery, like those he had seen at Rome and Milan. His son Adeodatus, his friends Alypius and Evodius, Severus, who became Bishop of Milevia, shared his solitude. But it is certain that he had other solitaries with him whom he alludes to in his letters. Their rule was as yet a little easy, no doubt. The brothers of Thagaste were not confined in a cloister. They were simply obliged to fasts, to a special diet, to prayers and meditations in common.

In this half-rustic retreat (the monastery was situated at the gates of the town) Augustine was happy: he had at last realized the project he had had so long at heart. To enter into himself, pray, above all, to study the Scripture, to fathom even its most obscure places, to comment it with the fervour and piety which the African of all times has brought to *what is written down*—it seemed to him that he had enough there to fill all the minutes of his life. But no man can teach, lecture, discuss, write, during twenty years, in vain. However much Augustine might be converted, he remembered the school at Thagaste, just as he did at Cassicium. Still, it was necessary to finish with this sort of thing once for all. The new monk made what may be called his will as a professor.

He finished, at this time, or revised his school treatises, which he had begun at Milan, comprising all the liberal arts—grammar, dialectic, rhetoric, geometry, arithmetic, philosophy, music. Of all these books he only finished the first, the treatise on grammar. The others were only summaries, and are now lost. On the other hand, we have still the six books on music, likewise begun at Milan, which he finished, almost as an amusement, at Thagaste. They are dialogues between himself and his pupil, the poet Licentius, upon metre and scansion. But we know from himself that he intended to make this book longer, and to write a second part upon melody, that is to say, music, properly so called. He never found the time: "Once," he says, "the burthen of ecclesiastical affairs was placed on my shoulders, *all these pleasant things* slipped from my hands."

Thus, the monk Augustine only rests from prayer and meditation to study music and poetry. He has thought it necessary to excuse himself. "In all that," says he, "I had but one purpose. For, as I did not wish to pluck away too suddenly either young men, or those of another age, on whom God had bestowed good wits, from ideas of the senses and carnal literature, *things it is very hard for them not to be attached to,* I have tried by reasoning lessons to turn them little by little, and by the love of unchanging truth, to attach them to God, sole master of all things... He who reads these books will see that if I have touched upon the poets and grammarians, 'twas more by the exigency of the journey than by any desire to settle among them... Such is the life I have chosen to walk with the feeble, not being very strong myself, rather than to hurl myself out on the void with wings still half-fledged..."

Here again, how human all that is, and wise—yes, and modest too.

Augustine has no whit of the fanatic about him. No straighter conscience than his, or even more persistent in uprooting error. But he knows what man is, that life here below is a voyage among other men weak as himself, and he fits in with the needs of the voyage. Oh, yes, no doubt, for the Christian who has arrived at supreme renunciation—what is poetry, what is knowledge, "what is everything that is not eternal?" But this carnal literature and science are so many steps of a height proportionate to our feebleness, to lead us imperceptibly to the conceptual world. As a prudent guide of souls, Augustine did not wish to make the ascent too rapidly. As for music, he has still more indulgence for that than for any of the other arts, for "it is by sounds that we best perceive the power of numbers in every variety of movement, and their study thus leads us gradually to the closest and highest secrets of truth, and discovers to those who love and seek it the divine Wisdom and Providence in all things..." He is always coming back to it—to this music he loves so much; he comes back to it in spite of himself. Later, in great severity, he will reproach himself for the pleasure he takes in the liturgical chants, but nevertheless the old instinct will remain. He was born a musician. He will remain one to his last gasp.

If he did not break completely with profane art and letters at this present moment of his life, his chief reasons were of a practical order. Still another object may be discerned in these educational treatises—namely, to prove to the pagans that one may be a Christian and yet not be a barbarian and ignorant. Augustine's position in front of his adversaries is very strong indeed. None of them can attempt to cope with him either in breadth of knowledge, or in happy versatility, or in plenitude of intellectual gifts. He had the entire heritage of the ancient world between his hands. Well might he say to the pagans: "What you admire in your orators and philosophers, I have made my own. Behold it! On my lips recognize the accent of your orators... Well, all that, which you deem so high, I despise. The knowledge of this world is nothing without the wisdom of Christ."

Of course, Augustine has paid the price of this all-round knowledge—too far-reaching, perhaps, at certain points. He has often too much paraded his knowledge, his dialectic and oratorical talents. What matters that, if even in this excess he aims solely at the welfare of souls—to edify them and set them aglow with the fire of his charity? At

Thagaste, he disputes with his brethren, with his son Adeodatus. He is always the master—he knows it; but what humility he puts into this dangerous part! The conclusion of his book, *The Master*, which he wrote then, is that all the words of him who teaches are useless, if the hidden Master reveal not the truth to him who listens.

So, under his ungainly monk's habit, he continues his profession of rhetorician. He has come to Thagaste with the intention of retiring from the world and living in God; and here he is disputing, lecturing, writing more than ever. The world pursues him and occupies him even in his retreat. He says to himself that down there at Rome, at Carthage, at Hippo, there are men speaking in the forums or in the basilicas, whispering in secret meetings, seducing poor souls defenceless against error. These impostors must be immediately unmasked, confounded, reduced to silence. With all his heart Augustine throws himself into this work at which he excels. Above all, he attacks his old friends the Manichees... He wrote many tracts against them. From the animosity he put into these, may be judged to what extent Manicheeism filled his thoughts, and also the progress of the sect in Africa.

This campaign was even the cause of a complete change in his way of writing. With the object of reaching the plainest sort of people, he began to employ the popular language, not recoiling before a solecism, when the solecism appeared to him indispensable to explain his thought. This must have been a cruel mortification for him. In his very latest writings he made a point of shewing that no elegance of language was unknown to him. But his real originality is not in that. When he writes the fine style, his period is heavy, entangled, often obscure. On the other hand, nothing is more lively, clear and coloured, and, as we say to-day, more direct, than the familiar language of his sermons and certain of his treatises. This language he has really created. He wanted to clarify, comment, give details, and he felt how awkward classical Latin is to decompose ideas and render shades. And so, in a popular Latin, already very close to the Romance languages, he has thrown out the plan of analytical prose, the instrument of thought of the modern West.

Not only did he battle against the heretics, but his restless friendship continually scaled the walls of his cell to fly to the absent ones dear to his heart. He feels that he must expand to his friends, and make them sharers in his meditations: this nervous man, in poor health, spends a part of his nights meditating. The argument he has hit upon in last night's insomnia—his friends must be told that! He heaps his letters on them. He writes to Nebridius, to Romanianus, to Paulinus of Nola; to people unknown and celebrated, in Africa, Italy, Spain, and Palestine. A time will come when his letters will be real encyclicals, read throughout Christendom. He writes so much that he is often short of paper. He has not tablets enough to put down his notes. He asks Romanianus to give him some. His beautiful tablets, the ivory ones, are used up; he has used the last one for a ceremonial letter, and he asks his friend's pardon for writing to him on a wretched bit of vellum.

Besides all that, he interests himself in the affairs of his fellow-townsmen. Augustine is a personage at Thagaste. The good folk of the free-town are well aware that he is eloquent, that he has a far-reaching acquaintance, and that he has great influence in high quarters. They ask for his protection and his interference. It is even possible that they obliged him to defend them in the courts. They were proud of their Augustine. And as they were afraid that some neighbouring town might steal away their great man, they kept a guard round his house. They prevented him from shewing himself too much in the neighbourhood. Augustine himself agreed with this, and lived retired as far as he could, for he was afraid they would make him a bishop or priest in spite of himself. In those days that was a danger incurred by all Christians who were rich or had talent. The rich gave their goods to the poor when they took orders. The men of talent defended the interests of the community, or attracted opulent benefactors. And because of all these reasons, the needy or badly managed churches stalked as a prey the celebrated Augustine.

In spite of this supervision, this unremitting rush of business, the work of all kinds which he undertook, he experienced at Thagaste a peace which he was never to find again. One might say that he pauses and gathers together all his strength before the great exhausting labour of his apostolate. In this Numidian country, so verdant and cool, where a thousand memories of childhood encompassed him, where he was not able to take a step without encountering the ever-living image of his mother, he soared towards God with more confidence. He who sought in the things of sense ladder-rungs whereby to mount to spiritual realities, still turned kindly eyes on the natural scene. From the windows of his room he saw the forest pines rounding their heads, like little crystal goblets with stems slim and thin. His scarred chest breathed in deliriously the resinous breath of the fine trees. He listened like a musician to the orchestra of birds. The changing scenes of country life always attracted him. It is now that he wrote: "Tell me, does not the nightingale seem to you to modulate her voice delightfully? Is not her song, so harmonious, so suave, so well attuned to the season, the very voice of the spring?..."

Chapter 4
AUGUSTINE A PRIEST

This halt did not last long. Soon was going to begin for Augustine the time of tribulation, that of his struggles and apostolic journeys.

And first, he must mourn his son Adeodatus, that young man who seemed destined to such great things. It is indeed most probable that the young monk died at Thagaste during the three years that his father spent there. Augustine was deeply grieved; but, as in the case of his mother's death, he mastered his sorrow by all the force of his Christian hope. No doubt he loved his son as much as he was proud of him. It will be remembered what words he used to speak of this youthful genius, whose precocity frightened him. Little by little his grief quietened down, and in its place came a mild resignation. Some years later he will write about Adeodatus: "Lord, early didst Thou cut off his life from this earth, but I remember him without a shadow of misgiving. My remembrance is not mixed with any fear for his boyhood, or the youth he was, or the man he would have been." No fear! What a difference between this and the habitual feelings of the Jansenists, who believed themselves his disciples! While Augustine thinks of his son's death with a calm and grave joy which he can scarce hide, those of Port Royal could only think in trembling of the judgment of God. Their faith did not much resemble the luminous and confident faith of Augustine. For him, salvation is the conquest of joy.

At Thagaste he lived in joy. Every morning in awaking before the forest pines, glistening with the dews of the morning, he might well say with a full heart: "My God, give me the grace to live here under the shades of Thy peace, while awaiting that of Thy Paradise." But the Christians continued to watch him. It was to the interest of a number of people that this light should not be hid under a bushel. Perhaps a snare was deliberately laid for him. At any rate, he was imprudent enough to come out of his retreat and travel to Hippo. He thought he might be safe there, because, as the town had a bishop already, they would not have any excuse to get him consecrated in spite of himself.

An inhabitant of Hippo, a clerk of the Imperial Ministry of the Interior, begged his spiritual assistance. Doubts, he maintained, still delayed him on the way to an entire conversion. Augustine alone could help him to get clear of them. So Augustine, counting already on a new recruit for the Thagaste monastery, went over there at the request of this official.

Now, if there was a bishop at Hippo (a certain Valerius), priests were lacking. Furthermore, Valerius was getting on in years. Originally Greek, he knew Latin badly, and not a word of Punic—a great hindrance for him in his duties of judge, administrator, and catechist. The knowledge of the two languages was indispensable to an ecclesiastic in such a country, where the majority of the rural population spoke only the old Carthaginian idiom. All this proves to us that Catholicism was in bad shape in the diocese of Hippo. Not only was there a lack of priests, but the bishop was a foreigner, little familiar with African customs. There was a general demand for a native to take his place—one young, active, and well enough furnished with learning to hold his own against the heretics and the schismatics of the party of Donatus, and also sufficiently able to watch over the interests of the Church at Hippo, and above all, to make it prosperous. Let us not forget that at this time, in the eyes of a crowd of poor wretches, Christianity was first and foremost the religion which gave out bread. Even in those early days, the Church did its best to solve the eternal social question.

While Augustine was at Hippo, Valerius preached a sermon in the basilica in which, precisely, he deplored this lack of priests the community suffered from. Mingled with the congregation, Augustine listened, sure that he would be unrecognized. But the secret of his presence had leaked out. People pointed to him while the bishop was preaching. The next thing was that some furious enthusiasts seized hold of him and dragged him to the foot of the episcopal chair, yelling:

"Augustine a priest! Augustine a priest!"

Such were the democratic ways of the Church in those days. The inconveniences are plain enough. What is certain is, that if Augustine had resisted, he might have lost his life, and that the bishop would have provoked a riot in refusing him the priesthood. In Africa, religious passions are not to be trifled with, especially when they are exasperated by questions of profit or politics. In his heart, the bishop was delighted with this brutal capture which gained him the distinction of such a well-known fellow-worker. There and then he ordained the Thagaste monk. And so, as Augustine's pupil, Possidius, the future Bishop of Guelma, puts it, "This shining lamp, which sought the darkness of solitude, was placed upon the lamp-stand..." Augustine, who saw the finger of God in this adventure, submitted to the popular will. Nevertheless, he was in despair, and he wept at the change they were forcing on him. Then, some of those present, mistaking the significance of his tears, said to console him:

"Yes, you are right. The priesthood is not good enough for your merits. But you may be certain that you will be our bishop."

Augustine well knew all that the crowd meant by that, and what it expected of its bishop. He who only thought of leaving the world, grew frightened at the practical cares he would have to take over. And the spiritual side of his jurisdiction frightened him no less. To speak of God! Proclaim the word of God! He deemed himself unworthy of so high a privilege. He was so ill-prepared! To remedy this fault of preparation, as well as he could, he desired that he might be given a little leisure till the following Easter. In a letter addressed to Valerius, and no doubt intended to be made public, he humbly set forth the reasons why he asked for delay. They were so apposite and so creditable, that very likely the bishop yielded. The new priest received permission to retire to a country house near Hippo. His flock, who did not feel at all sure of their shepherd, would not have let him go too far off.

He took up his duties as soon as possible. Little by little he became, to all intents, the coadjutor of the bishop, who charged him with the preaching and the baptism of catechumens. These were the two most important among the episcopal prerogatives. The bishops made a point of doing these things themselves. Certain colleagues of Valerius even grew scandalized that he should allow a simple priest to preach before him in his own church. But soon other bishops, struck by the advantages of this innovation, followed the example of Valerius, and allowed their clerks to preach even in their presence. The priest of Hippo did not lose his head among so many honours. He felt chiefly the perils of them, and he regarded them as a trial sent by God. "I have been forced into this," he said, "doubtless in punishment of my sins; for from what other motive can I think that the second place at the helm should be given to me—to me who do not even know how to hold an oar..."

Meanwhile, he had not relinquished his purpose of monastic life. Though a priest, he meant to remain a monk. It was heart-breaking for him to be obliged to leave his monastery at Thagaste. He spoke of his regret to Valerius, who, perceiving the usefulness of a convent as a seminary for future priests, gave him an orchard belonging to the church of Hippo, that he might found a new community there. So was established the monastery which was going to supply a great number of clerks and bishops to all the African provinces.

Among the ruins of Hippo, that old Roman and Phoenician city, they search for the place where Augustine's monastery stood, without much hope of ever finding it. Some have thought to locate it upon that hill where the water brought from the near mountains by an aqueduct used to pour into immense reservoirs, and where to-day rises a new basilica which attracts all eyes out at sea. Behind the basilica is a convent where the Little Sisters of the Poor lodge about a hundred old people. So is maintained among the African Mussulmans the remembrance of the grand Christian *marabout*. One might possibly wish to see there a building more in the pure and quiet taste of antiquity. But after all, the piety of the intention is enough. This hospital serves admirably to call up the memory of the illustrious bishop who was charity itself. As for the basilica, Africa has done all she can to make it worthy of him. She has given her most precious marbles, and one of her fairest landscapes as a frame.

It is chiefly in the evening, in the closing dusk, that this landscape reveals all its special charm and its finer values. The roseate glow of the setting sun throws into sharp relief the black profile of the mountains, which command the Seybouse valley. Under the mustering shadows, the pallid river winds slowly to the sea. The gulf, stretching limitless, shines like a slab of salt strangely bespangled. In this atmosphere without mists, the sharp outlines of the coast, the dense movelessness of the aspect, has an indescribable effect. It is like a hitherto unknown and virginal revelation of the earth. Then the stars bloom out, with a flame, an hallucinating palpability. Charles's Wain, burning low on the gorges of the Edough, seems like a golden waggon rolling through the fields of Heaven. A deep peace settles upon farmland and meadow country, only broken by a watch-dog's bark now and then...

But it matters not which spot is chosen in the surroundings of Hippo to place Augustine's monastery, the view will be equally beautiful. From all parts of the plain, mounded by heaps of ruins, the sea can be seen—a wide bay circled in soft bland curves, like at Naples. All around, an arena of mountains—the green ravines of the Edough and its wooded slopes. Along the surbased roads rise the great sonorous pines, and through them wanders the æolian complaint of the sea-winds. Blue of the sea, blue of the sky, noble foliage of Italy's ancient groves—it is one of Lamartine's landscapes under a more burning sun. The gaiety of the mornings there is a physical luxury for heart and eyes, when the new-born light laughs upon the painted cupolas of the houses, and dark blue veils float between the walls, glaring white, of the steep streets.

Among the olives and orange-trees of Hippo, Augustine must have seen happy days pass by, as at Thagaste. The rule he had given the convent, which he himself obeyed like any one else, was neither too slack nor too strict—in a word, such as it should be for men who have lived in the culture of letters and works of the mind. There was no affectation of excessive austerity. Augustine and his monks wore very simple clothes and shoes, but suitable for a bishop and his clerks. Like laymen, they wore the byrrhus, a garment with a hood, which seems very like the ancestor of the Arab burnous. To keep an even line between daintiness and negligence in costume, to have no exaggeration in anything, is what Augustine aimed at. The poet Rutilius Numatianus, who about that time was attacking the sordid and culture-hating monks with sombre irony, would have had a chance to admire a restraint and decorum in the Hippo monastery which recalled what was best in the manners of the ancient world. At table, a like moderation. Vegetables were generally provided, and sometimes meat when any one was sick, or guests arrived. They drank a little wine, contrary to the regulations of St. Jerome, who condemned wine as a drink for devils. When a monk infringed the rule, his share of the wine was stopped.

Through some remains of fastidious habits in Augustine, or perhaps because he had nothing else, the table service he used himself was silver. On the other hand, the pots and dishes were of earthenware, or wood, or common alabaster. Augustine, who was very temperate in eating and drinking, seemed at table to pay attention only to what was being read or talked about. He cared very little what he ate, provided the food was not a stimulant to lubricity. He used to say to those Christians who paraded a Pharisaic severity: "It is the pure heart which makes pure food." Then, with his constant desire for charity, he prohibited all spiteful gossip in the conversation in the refectory. In those times of religious struggle, the clerics ferociously blackened each other's characters. Augustine caused to have written on the walls a distich, which ran thus:

"He who takes pleasure in slandering the life of the absent,
Should know he is unworthy to sit at this table."

"One day," says Possidius, "some of his intimate friends, even other bishops, having forgotten this sentence, he reproached them warmly, and very much perturbed, he cried out that he was going to remove those verses from the refectory, or rise from table and withdraw to his cell. I was present with many others when this happened."

It was not only slanderous talk or interior dissensions which troubled Augustine's peace of mind. He combined the duties of priest, of a head of a convent, and of an apostle. He had to preach, instruct the catechumens, battle against the disaffected. The town of Hippo was very unruly, full of heretics, schismatics, pagans. Those of the party of Donatus were triumphant, driving the Catholics from their churches and lands. When Augustine came into the country, Catholicism was very low. And then the ineradicable Manichees continued to recruit proselytes. He never stopped writing tracts, disputing against them, overwhelming them under the close logic of his arguments. At the request of the Donatists themselves, he had an argument with one of their priests, a certain Fortunatus, in the baths of Sossius at Hippo. He reduced this man to silence and to flight. Not in the least discouraged were the Manichees: they sent another priest.

If the enemies of the Church shewed themselves stubborn, Augustine's own congregation were singularly turbulent, hard to manage. The weakness of old Valerius must have allowed a good many abuses to creep into the community. Ere long the priest of Hippo had a foretaste of the difficulties which awaited him as bishop.

Following the example of Ambrose, he undertook to abolish the custom of feasts in the basilicas and on the tombs of the martyrs. This was a survival of paganism, of which the festivals included gluttonous eating and orgies. At every solemnity, and they were frequent, the pagans ate in the courts and under the porticoes around the temples. In Africa, above all, these public repasts gave an opportunity for repugnant scenes of stuffing and drunkenness. As a rule, the African is very sober; but when he does let himself go he is terrible. This is quite easily seen today, in the great Muslem feasts, when the rich distribute broken bits of meat to the poor of their district. As soon as these people, used to drink water and to eat a little boiled rice, have tasted meat, or drunk only one cup of wine, there is no holding them: there are fights, stabbing matches, a general brawl in the hovels. Just picture this popular debauch in full blast in the cemeteries and the courts of the basilicas, and it will be understood why Augustine did his best to put an end to such scandals.

For this purpose, he joined hands first of all with his bishop, Valerius, and then with the Primate of Carthage, Aurelius, who shall be henceforth his firmest support in his struggle against the schismatics.

During Lent, the subject fitting in naturally with the season, he spoke against these pagan orgies; and this gave rise to a good deal of discontent, outside. Easter went by without trouble. But the day after the Ascension, the people of Hippo were used to celebrate what they called "the Joy-day," by a traditional good feed and drink. The day before, which was the religious festival, Augustine intrepidly spoke against "the Joy-day." They interrupted the preacher. Some of them shouted that as much was done at Rome in St. Peter's basilica. At Carthage, they danced round the tomb of St. Cyprian. To the shrilling of flutes, amid the dull blows of the gongs, mimes gave themselves up to obscene contortions, while the spectators sang to the clapping of their hands... Augustine knew all about that. He declared that these abominations might have been tolerated in former times so as not to discourage the pagans from becoming converts; but that henceforth the people, altogether Christian, should give them up. In the end, he spoke with such touching eloquence that the audience burst into tears. He believed he had won.

The next day it was all to do over again. Agitators had worked among the crowd to such an extent that a riot was feared. Nevertheless, Augustine, preceded by his bishop, entered the basilica at the hour of service. At the same moment the Donatists were banqueting in their church, which was quite near. Through the walls of their own church the Catholics heard the noise of this carouse. It required the coadjutor's most urgent remonstrances to keep them from imitating their neighbours. The last murmurs died down, and the ceremony ended with the singing of the sacred hymns.

Augustine had carried the position. But the conflict had got to the point that he had to threaten the people with his resignation, and, as he wrote to Alypius, "to shake out on them the dust from his clothes." All this promised very ill for the future. He who already considered the priesthood as a trial, saw with terror the bishopric drawing near.

THE APOSTLE OF PEACE AND OF CATHOLIC UNITY

Die eis ista ut plorent... et sic eos rape tecum ad Deum, quia de spiritu ejus hæc dicis eis, si dicis ardens igné caritatis.

Tell them this, O my soul, that they may weep ... and thus carry them up with thyself to God; because by His Spirit thou sayest these things, if Thou speakest burning with the flame of charity.

— *Confessions*, IV, 12.

Chapter 1
THE BISHOP OF HIPPO

In his monastery, Augustine was still spied upon by the neighbouring Churches, who wanted him for their bishop. They would capture him on the first opportunity. The old Valerius, fearing his priest would be taken unawares, urged him to hide himself. But he knew by the very case of Augustine, forced into the priesthood in spite of himself, that the greatest precautions are useless against those determined to gain their ends by any means. It would be safest to anticipate the danger.

He determined therefore to share the bishopric with Augustine, to have him consecrated during his own lifetime, and to indicate him as his successor. This was against the African usage, and what was more, against the Canons of the Council of Nice—though it is true that Valerius, like Augustine himself, was unaware of this latter point. But surely the rule could be waived in view of the exceptional merits of the priest of Hippo. The old bishop began by sounding Aurelius, the Primate of Carthage, and when he was satisfied as to the agreement and support of this high personage, he took the opportunity of a religious solemnity to make known his intentions to the people.

Some of the neighbouring bishops—Megalius, Bishop of Guelma and Primate of Numidia, among them—being gathered at Hippo to consecrate a new bishop, Valerius announced publicly in the basilica that he wished Augustine to be consecrated at the same ceremony. This had been the wish of his people for a long time. Really, in demanding this honour for his priest, the old bishop did no more than follow the wish of the public. Immediately, his words were received with cheers. The faithful with loud shouts demanded Augustine's consecration.

Megalius alone objected. He even made himself the voice of certain calumnies, so as to have the candidate put aside as unworthy. There is nothing astonishing in such an attitude. This Megalius was old (he died a short time after), and, like all old men, he took the gloomiest view of innovations. Already, in the face of settled custom, had Valerius granted Augustine the right to preach in his presence. And see now, by a new sinking, he was attempting to place two bishops at once in the see of Hippo! Whatever this young priest's talents might be, enough, had been done for him—a recent convert into the bargain, and, what was still more serious, a refugee from the Manicheans. What was not related about the abominations committed in the mysteries of those people? Just how far had Augustine dipped into them? They snarled against him everywhere at Hippo, and at Carthage too, where he had compromised himself by his excessive zeal; Catholics and Donatists alike gossiped. Megalius, a punctilious defender of discipline and the hierarchy, no doubt gathered up these malevolent rumours with pleasure. He used them as an excuse for making Augustine mark time, so to speak. Commonplace people always feel a secret delight in humiliating to the common rule those whom they can feel are beings of a different quality from themselves.

One of the slanders set abroad about Valerius' priest, Megalius seems to have believed. He allowed himself to be persuaded that Augustine had given a philtre to a woman, one of his penitents, whom he wished to possess. It was then the fashion among the pious to exchange *eulogies*, or bits of holy bread, to signify a spiritual communion. Augustine was said to have mixed certain magic potions with some of these breads and offered them hypocritically to the woman he was in love with. This accusation started a big scandal, and the remembrance of it persisted long, because five or six years later the Donatist Petilian was still repeating it.

Augustine cleared himself victoriously. Megalius avowed his mistake. He did better: not only did he apologize to him he had slandered, but he solemnly asked forgiveness from his fellow-bishops for having misled them upon false rumours. It is probable that some time during the inquiry he had got to know Valerius' coadjutor better. Augustine's charm, taken with the austerity of his life, acted upon the vexed old man and altered his views. Be that so or not, it was at any rate by Megalius, Bishop of Guelma and Primate of Numidia, that Augustine was consecrated Bishop of Hippo.

He was in consternation over his rise. He has said it again and again. We may take his word for it. Yet the honours and advantages of the episcopate were then so considerable that his enemies were able to describe him as an ambitious man. Nothing could agree less with his character. In his heart, Augustine only wished to live in quiet. Since his retreat at Cassicium, fortune he had given up, as well as literary glory. His sole wish was to live in pondering the divine truths, and to draw nearer to God. *Videte et gustate quam mitis sit Dominus*—"O taste and see that the Lord is good." This perhaps, of the whole Bible, is the verse he liked best, which answered best to the close desire of his soul; and he quotes it oftenest in his sermons. Then, to study the Holy Writings, scan the least syllables of them, since all truth lies there—well, a whole life is not too much for such labour as that! And to do it, one should sever all ties with the world, take refuge forbiddingly in the cloister.

But this sincere Christian analysed himself too skilfully not to perceive that he had a dangerous tendency to isolation. He took too much pleasure in cutting himself off from the society of mankind to enshroud himself in study and meditation. He who acknowledged a secret tendency to the Epicurean indolence—was he going to live a life of the dilettante and the self-indulgent under cover of holiness? Alone could action save him from selfishness. Others doubtless fulfilled the laws of charity in praying, in mortifying themselves for their brethren. But when, like him, a man has exceptional faculties of persuasion and eloquence, such vigour in dialectics, such widespread culture, such power to bring to naught the wrong—would it not be insulting to God to let such gifts lie idle, and a serious failure in charity to deprive his brethren of the support of such an engine?

Besides that, he well knew that no man draws near to truth without a purified heart. Might not his passions, which were so violent, begin to torment him again after this respite with greater frenzy than before his conversion? Against that, too, action was the main antidote. In the duties of the bishopric he saw a means of asceticism—a kind of courageous purification. He would load himself of his own will with so many anxieties and so much work that he would have no time left to listen to the insidious voice of his "old friends." Could he manage to silence them at once? This unheard-of grace—would it be granted to him? Or would not rather the struggle continue in the depths of his conscience? What comes out as certain is that those terrible passions which turned his youth upside down, nevermore play any part in his life. From the moment he fell on his knees under the fig-tree at Milan, his sinful heart is a dead heart. He has been freed from almost all the weaknesses of the old nature, not only from its vices and carnal affections, but from its most pardonable lapses—save, perhaps, some old sediment of intellectual and literary vanity.

His books, at the first glance, shew us him no more save as the doctor, and already the saint. What is seen at once is an entirely bare intelligence, an entirely pure heart, fired only by the divine love. And yet the affectionate and tender heart which his had been, always warms his discussions and his most abstract exegesis. It does not take long to feel the heat of them, the power of pouring forth emotion. Augustine takes no heed of that. Of himself he no longer thinks; he no longer belongs to himself. If he has accepted the episcopate, it is so as to give himself altogether to the Church, to be all things to all men. He is the man-word, the man-pen, the sounding-board of the truth. He becomes the man of the miserable crowds which the Saviour covered with His pity. He is theirs, to convince them and cure them of their errors. He is a machine which works without ever stopping for the greater glory of Christ. Bishop, pastor, leader of souls—he has no desire for anything else.

But it was a heavy labour for this intellectual, who till then had lived only among books and ideas. The day after his consecration, he must have regarded it with more terror than ever. During his nights of insomnia, or at the recreation hour in the monastery garden, he thought over it with great distress. His eyes wide open in the darkness of his cell, he sought to define a theory upon the nature and origin of the soul; or else, at the fall of day, he saw between the olive branches "the sea put on fluctuating shades like veils of a thousand colours, sometimes green, a green of infinite tints; sometimes purple; blue sometimes…" And his soul, easily stirred to poetry, at once arose from these material splendours to the invisible region of ideas. Then, immediately, he caught himself up: it was not a question of all that! He said to himself that he was henceforth the bishop Augustine, that he had charge of souls, that he must work for the needs of his flock. He would have to struggle in a combat without a moment's respite. Thereupon he arranged his plans of attack and defence. With a single glance he gauged the huge work before him.

A crushing work, truly! He was Bishop of Hippo, but a bishop almost without a flock, in comparison with the rival community of Donatists. The bishop of the dissentients, Proculeianus, boasted that he was the true representative of orthodoxy, and as he had on his side the advantage of numbers, he certainly cut a much greater figure in the town than the successor of Valerius, with all his knowledge and all his eloquence. The schismatics' church, as we have seen, was quite near the Catholic church. Their noise interfered with Augustine's sermons. Possibly the situation had become slightly better in Hippo since the edict of Theodosius. But it was not so long ago that those of the Donatist party had the upper hand. A little before the arrival of the new bishop, the Donatist clergy forbade their faithful to bake bread for Catholics. A fanatical baker had even refused a Catholic deacon who was his landlord. These schismatics believed themselves strong enough to put those who did not belong to them under interdict.

The rout of Catholicism appeared to be an accomplished fact from one end to the other of Africa. Quite recently a mere fraction of the Donatist party had been able to send three hundred and ten bishops to the Council of Bagai, who were to judge the recalcitrants of their own sect. Among these bishops, the terrible Optatus of Thimgad became marked on account of his bloody zeal, rambling round Numidia and even the Proconsulate at the head of armed bands, burning farms and villas, rebaptizing the Catholics by main force, spreading terror on all sides.

Augustine knew all this, and when he sought help from the local authorities he was obliged to acknowledge sadly that there was no support to be expected from Count Gildo, who had tyrannized over Carthage and Africa for nearly ten years. This Gildo was a native, a Moor, to whom the ministers of the young Valentinian II had thought it a good stroke of policy to confide the government of the province. Knowing the weakness of the Empire, the Moor only thought of cutting out for himself an independent principality in Africa. He openly favoured Donatism, which was the most numerous and influential party. The Bishop of Thimgad, Optatus, swore only by him, regarding him as his master and his "god." In consequence, he was called "the Gildonian."

Against such enemies, the Imperial authority could only act irregularly. Augustine was well aware of it. He knew that the Western Empire was in a critical position. Theodosius had just died, in the midst of war with the usurper Eugenius. The Barbarians, who made up the greater part of the Roman armies, shewed themselves more and more threatening. Alaric, entrenched in the Peloponnesus, was getting ready to invade Italy. However, the all-powerful minister of the young Honorius, the half-Barbarian Stilicho, did his best to conciliate the Catholics, and assured them that he would continue the protection they had had from Theodosius, Augustine therefore turned to the central power. It alone could bring about a little order in the provinces—and then, besides, the new emperors were firmly attached to the defence of Catholicism. The Catholic Bishop of Hippo did his best, accordingly, to keep on good terms with the representatives of the Metropolitan Government—the proconsuls; the propraetors; the counts; and the tribunes, or the secretaries, sent by the Emperor as Government commissioners.

There was no suspicion of flattery in his attitude, no idolatry of power. At Milan, Augustine had been near enough to the Court to know what the Imperial functionaries were worth. Now, he simply adapted himself as well as he could to the needs of the moment. And with all that, he could have wished in the depths of his heart that this power were stronger, so as to give the Church more effective support. This cultured man, brought up in the respect of the Roman majesty, was by instinct a faithful servant of the Caesars. A man who held to authority and tradition, he maintained that obedience is due to princes: "There is a general agreement," he said, "of human society to obey its Kings." In one of his sermons he compares thought, which commands the body, to the Emperor seated upon his throne, and from the depths of his palace dictating orders which set the whole Empire moving—a purely ideal image of the sovereign of that time, but one which pleased his Latin imagination. Alas! Augustine had no illusions about the effect of Imperial edicts; he knew too well how little they were regarded, especially in Africa.

So he could hardly count upon Government support for the defence of Catholic unity and peace. He found he must trust to himself; and all his strength was in his intelligence, in his charity, in his deeply compassionate soul. Most earnestly did he wish that Catholicism might be a religion of love, open to all the nations of the earth, even as its Divine Founder Himself had wished. A glowing and dominating intelligence, charity which never tired—those were Augustine's arms. And they were enough. These qualities gave him an overwhelming superiority over all the men of his time. Among them, pagans or Christians, he looks like a colossus. From what a height he crushes, not only the professors who had been his colleagues, such as Nectarius of Guelma or Maximus of Madaura, but the most celebrated writers of his time—Symmachus, for instance, and Ammianus Marcellinus. After reading a treatise of Augustine's, one is astounded by the intellectual meagreness of these last pagans. The narrowness of their mind and platitude of thought is a thing that leaves one aghast. Even the illustrious Apuleius, who belonged to the golden age of African literature, the author of *The Doctrine of Plato*, praises philosophy and the Supreme Being in terms which recall the professions of faith of the chemist and druggist, Homais, in *Madame Bovary*.

Nor among those who surrounded Augustine, his fellow-bishops, was there one fit to be compared with him, even at a distance. Except perhaps Nebridius, his dearest friends, Alypius, Severus, or Evodius, are merely disciples, not to say servants of his thought. Aurelius, Primate of Carthage, an energetic administrator, a firm and upright character, if he is not on Augustine's level, is at any rate capable of understanding and supporting him. The others are decent men, like that Samsucius, Bishop of Tours, very nearly illiterate, but full of good sense and experience, and on this ground consulted respectfully by his colleague of Hippo. Or else they are plotters, given to debauch, engaged in business, like Paulus, Bishop of Cataqua, who became involved in risky speculations, swindled the revenue, and by his expensive way of life ruined his diocese. Others, on the Donatist side, are mere swashbucklers, half-brigands, half-fanatics, like the Gildonian Optatus, Bishop of Thimgad, a manifestation in advance of the Mussulman *marabout* who preached the holy war against the Catholics, raiding, killing, burning, converting by sabre blows and bludgeoning.

Amid these insignificant or violent men, Augustine will endeavour to realize to the full the admirable type of bishop, at once spiritual father, protector, and support of his people. He had promised himself to sacrifice no whit of his ideal of Christian perfection. As bishop, he will remain a monk, as he did during his priesthood. Beside the monastery established in Valerius' garden, where it is impossible to receive properly his guests and visitors, he will start another in the episcopal residence.

He will conform to the monastic rule as far as his duties allow. He will pray, study the Scriptures, define dogmas, refute heresies. At the same time, he means to neglect nothing of his material work. He has mouths to feed, property to look after, law-cases to examine. He will labour at all that. For this mystic and theorist it means a never-ceasing immolation.

First, to give the poor their daily bread. Like all the communities of that time, Hippo maintained a population of beggars. Often enough, the diocesan cash-box was empty. Augustine was obliged to hold out the hand, to deliver from the height of his pulpit pathetic appeals for charity. Then, there are hospitals to be built for the sick, a lodging-house for poor wanderers. The bishop started these institutions in houses bequeathed to the church of Hippo. For reasons of economy, he thought better not to build. That would overload his budget. Next came the greatest of all his cares—the administration of Church property. To increase this property, he stipulated that his clergy should give up all they possessed in favour of the community, thus giving the faithful an example of voluntary poverty. He also accepted gifts from private persons. But he also often refused these—for example, the bequest of a father or mother, who, in a moment of anger, disinherited their children. He did not wish to profit by the bad feelings of parents to plunder orphans. On another side, he objected to engage the Church in suits at law with the exchequer upon receiving certain heritages. When a business man at Hippo left to the diocese his share of profits in the service of boats for carrying Government stores, Augustine came to the conclusion that it would be better to refuse. In case of shipwreck, they would be obliged to make good the lost corn to the Treasury, or else to put the captain and surviving sailors to the torture to prove that the crew was not responsible for the loss of the ship. Augustine would not hear tell of it.

"Is it fit," he said, "that a bishop should be a shipowner?... A bishop a torturer? Oh, no; that does not agree at all with a servant of Jesus Christ."

The people of Hippo did not share his views. They blamed Augustine's scruples. They accused him of compromising the interests of the Church. One day he had to explain himself from the pulpit:

"Well I know, my brothers, that you often say between yourselves: 'Why do not people give anything to the Church of Hippo? Why do not the dying make it their heir? The reason is that Bishop Augustine is too easy; he gives all back to the children; he keeps nothing!' I acknowledge it, I only accept gifts which are good and pious. Whoever disinherits his son to make the Church his heir, let him find somebody willing to accept his gifts. It is not I who will do it, and by God's grace, I hope it will not be anybody... Yes, I have refused many legacies, but I have also accepted many. Need I name them to you? I will give only one instance. I accepted the heritage of Julian. Why? Because he died without children..."

The listeners thought that their bishop really put too fine a point on things.

They further reproached him with not knowing how to attract and flatter the rich benefactors. Augustine would not allow, either, that they had any right to force a passing stranger to receive the priesthood and consequently to give up his goods to the poor. All this really was very wise, not only according to the spirit of the Gospel, but according to human prudence. If Augustine, for the sake of the good fame of his Church, did not wish to incur the accusation of grasping and avarice, he dreaded nothing so much as a law-case. To accept lightly the gifts and legacies offered was to lay himself open to expensive pettifogging. Far better to refuse than to lose both his money and reputation. So were reconciled, in this man of prayer and meditation, practical good sense with the high disinterestedness of the Christian teaching.

The bishop was disinterested; his people were covetous. The people of those times wished the Church to grow rich, because they were the first to profit by its riches. Now these riches were principally in houses and land. The diocese of Hippo had to deal with many houses and immense *fundi*, upon which lived an entire population of artisans and freed-men, agricultural labourers, and even art-workers—smelters, embroiderers, chisellers on metals. Upon the Church lands, these small people were protected from taxes and the extortions of the revenue officers, and no doubt they found the episcopal government more fatherly and mild than the civil.

Augustine, who had made a vow of poverty and given his heritage to the poor, became by a cruel irony a great landowner as soon as he was elected Bishop of Hippo. Doubtless he had stewards under him to look after the property of the diocese. This did not save him from going into details of management and supervising his agents. He heard the complaints, not only of his own tenants, but also of those who belonged to other estates and were victimized by dishonest bailiffs. Anyhow, we have a thousand signs to shew that no detail of country life was unfamiliar to him.

On horseback or muleback, he rode for miles through the country about Hippo to visit his vineyards and olivets. He examined, found out things, questioned the workmen, went into the presses and the mills. He knew the grape good to eat, and the grape to make wine with. He pointed out where the ensilage pits had been dug in too marshy land, which endangered the young corn. As a capable landowner he was abreast of the law, careful about the terms of contracts. He knew the formulas employed for sales or benefactions. He saw to it that charcoal was buried around the landmarks in the fields, so that if the post disappeared, its place could be found. And as he was a poet, he gathered on his course a whole booty of rural images which later on went to brighten his sermons. He made ingenious comparisons with the citron-tree, "which is seen to give flowers and fruits all the year if it be watered constantly," or else with the goat "who gets upon her two hind legs to crop the bitter leaves of the wild olive."

These journeys in the open air, however tiring they might be, were after all a rest for his overworked brain. But there was one among his episcopal duties which wearied him to disgust. Every day he had to listen to parties in dispute and give judgment. Following recent Imperial legislation, the bishop became judge in civil cases—a tiresome and endless work in a country where tricky quibbling raged with obstinate fury. The litigants pursued Augustine, overran his house, like those fellahs in dirty burnous who block our law-courts with their rags. In the *secretarium* of the basilica, or under the portico of the court leading to the church, Augustine sat like a Mussulman cadi in the court of the mosque.

The emperors had only regulated an old custom of apostolic times in placing the Christians under the jurisdiction of their bishop. In accordance with St. Paul's advice, the priests did their utmost to settle differences among the faithful. Later, when their number had considerably increased, the Government adopted a system not unlike the "Capitulations" in countries under the Ottoman suzerainty. Lawsuits between clerics and laymen could not be equitably judged by civil servants, who were often pagans. Moreover, the parties based their claims on theological principles or religious laws that the arbitrator generally knew nothing about. In these conditions, it was natural enough that the Imperial authority should say to the disputants, "Fight it out among yourselves".

And it happened, just at the moment when Augustine began to fill the see of Hippo, that Theodosius broadened still more the judicial prerogatives of the bishops. The unhappy judge was overwhelmed with law-cases. Every day he sat till the hour of his meal, and sometimes the whole day when he fasted. To those who accused him of laziness, he answered:

"I can declare on my soul that if it were question of my own convenience, I should like much better to work at some manual labour at certain hours of the day, as the rule is in well-governed monasteries, and have the rest of the time free to read or pray or meditate upon the Holy Scripture, instead of being troubled with all the complications and dull talk of lawsuits."

The rascality of the litigants made him indignant. From the pulpit he gave them advice full of Christian wisdom, but which could not have been much relished. A suit at law, according to him, was a loss of time and a cause of sorrow. It would be better to let the opponent have the money, than to lose time and be filled with uneasiness. Nor was this, added the preacher in all good faith, to encourage injustice; for the robber would be robbed in his turn by a greater robber than himself.

These reasons seemed only moderately convincing. The pettifoggers did not get discouraged. On the contrary, they infested the bishop with their pleas. As soon as he appeared, they rushed up to him in a mob, surrounded him, kissed his hand and his shoulder, protesting their respect and obedience, urging him, constraining him to busy himself about their affairs. Augustine yielded. But the next day in a vehement sermon he cried out to them:

Discedite a me, maligni!—"Go far from me, ye wicked ones, and let me study in peace the commandments of my God!"

Chapter 2
WHAT WAS HEARD IN THE BASILICA OF PEACE

Let us try to see Augustine in his pulpit and in his episcopal city. We cannot do much more than reconstruct them by analogy. Royal Hippo is utterly gone. Bona, which has taken its place, is about a mile and a half away, and the fragments which have been dug out of the soil of the dead city are very inadequate. But Africa is full of Christian ruins, and chiefly of basilicas. Rome has nothing equal to offer. And that is easily understood. The Roman basilicas, always living, have been changed in the course of centuries, and have put on, time after time, the garb forced upon them by the fashion. Those of Africa have remained just as they were—at least in their principal lines—on the morrow of the Arab invasion, as Augustine's eyes had seen them. They are ruins, no doubt, and some very mutilated, but ruins of which no restoration has altered the plan or changed the features.

As the traces of Hippo and its church are swept away or deeply buried, we are obliged, in order to get some approximate idea, to turn towards another African town which has suffered less from time and devastation. Theveste with its basilica, the best preserved, the finest and largest in all Africa, can restore to us a little of the look and colour and atmosphere of Hippo in those final years of the fourth century.

Ancient Theveste was much larger than the present town, the French Tebessa. This, even reduced to the perimeter of the Byzantine fortress built under Justinian, still surprises the traveller by its singularly original aspect. Amid the wide plains of alfa-grass which surround it, with its quadrangular enclosure, its roads on the projection of the walls behind the battlements, its squat turrets, it has a look as archaic, as strange, as our own Aigues-Mortes amid its marshy fen. Nothing can be more rich and joyous to the eye than the rust which covers its ruins—a complete gilding that one would say had been laid on by the hand of man.

It has a little temple which is a wonder and has been compared to the ancient Roman temple—the *Maison Carrée*—at Nîmes. But how much warmer, more living are the stones! The shafts of the columns, and the pilasters of the peristyle, barked by time, seem as scaly and full of sap as the trunks of palm-trees. The carved acanthus-leaves in the capitals of the pillars droop like bunches of palms reddened by the summer.

Quite near, at the end of a narrow street, lined with modern and squalid hovels, the triumphal arch of Septimus Severus and of Caracalla extends its luminous bow; and high above the heavy mass of architecture, resting upon slim aerial little columns, a buoyant *ædiculus* shines like a coral tabernacle or a coffer of yellow ivory.

All about, forms in long draperies are huddled. The Numidian burnous has the whiteness of the toga. It has also the same graceful folds. At the sight of them you suddenly feel yourself to be in a strange land—carried back very far across the centuries. No sooner is the vision of antiquity outlined than it grows firm. Down below there, a horseman, clad in white, is framed with his white horse in the moulded cincture of a door. He passes, and upon the white wall of the near tower his shadow rests a moment, like a bas-relief upon the marble of a frieze.

Beyond the Byzantine enclosure, the basilica, with its minor buildings, forms another town almost as large as the present Theveste, and also closed in by a belt of towers and ramparts. One is immediately struck by the opulent colour of the stones—rose, grown pale and thinner in the sun; and next, by the solid workmanship and the structural finish. The stones, as in the Greek temples, are placed on top of one another in regular layers: the whole holds together by the weight of the blocks and the polish of the surfaces.

The proportions are on a large scale. There was no grudging for the buildings, or the materials, or the land. In front of the basilica is a wide rectangular court bordered with terraces; a portico at the far end; and in the middle four large fountains to water the walk. A flagged avenue, closed by two gateways, divides this court from the basilica, properly so called, which is reached by a staircase between two columns. The staircase leads to the *atrium* decorated by a Corinthian portico. In the centre is the font for purifications, a huge monolithic bason in the shape of a four-leaved clover. Three doors give entrance from the *atrium* to the basilica, which is divided by rows of green marble columns into three aisles. The galleries spread out along the side aisles. The floor was in mosaic. In the apse, behind the altar, stood the bishop's throne.

Around the main building clustered a great number of others: a baptistry; many chapels (one vaulted in the shape of a three-leaved clover) dedicated, probably, to local martyrs; a graveyard; a convent with its cells, and its windows narrow as loop-holes; stables, sheds, and barns. Sheltered within its walls and towers, amid its gardens and outbuildings, the basilica of Theveste thus early resembled one of our great monasteries of the Middle Age, and also in certain ways the great mosques of Islam—the one at Cordova, or that at Damascus, with their vestibules surrounded by arcades, their basons for purification, and their walks bordered with orange-trees. The faithful and the pilgrims were at home there. They might spend the day stretched upon the flags of the porticoes, in loafing or sleeping in the blue shade of the columns and the cool of the fountains. In the full sense of the word, the church was the House of God, open to all.

Very likely the basilicas at Hippo had neither the size nor the splendour of this one. Nor were there very many. At the time Augustine was ordained priest, that is to say, when the Donatists had still a majority in the town, it seems clear that the orthodox community owned but one single church, the *Basilica major*, or Basilica of Peace. Its very name proves this. With the schismatics, "Peace" was the official name for Catholicism. "Basilica of Peace" meant simply "Catholic Basilica." Was not this as much as to say that the others belonged to the dissenters? Doubtless they restored later on, after the promulgations of Honorius, the Leontian Basilica, founded by Leontius, Bishop of Hippo, and a martyr. A third was built by Augustine during his episcopate—the Basilica of the Eight Martyrs of the White Mace.

It was in the Major, or Cathedral, that Augustine generally preached. To preach was not only a duty, but one of the privileges of a bishop. As has been said, the bishop alone had the right to preach in his church. This arose from the fact that the African dioceses, although comparatively widespread, had scarcely more people than one of our large parishes to-day. The position of a bishop was like that of one of our parish priests. There were almost as many as there were villages, and they were counted by hundreds.

However that may be, preaching, the real apostolic ministry, was an exhausting task. Augustine preached almost every day, and often many times a day—rough work for a man with such a fragile chest. Thus it often happened that, to save his voice, he had to ask his audience to keep still. He spoke without study, in a language very near the language of the common people. Stenographers took down his sermons as he improvised them: hence those repetitions and lengthinesses which astonish the reader who does not know the reason for them. There is no plan evident in these addresses. Sometimes the speaker has not enough time to develop his thought. Then he puts off the continuation till the next day. Sometimes he comes with a subject all prepared, and then treats of another, in obedience to a sudden inspiration which has come to him with a verse of Scripture he has just read. Other times, he comments many passages in succession, without the least care for unity or composition.

Let us listen to him in this Basilica of Peace, where during thirty-five years he never failed to announce the Word of God... The chant of the Psalms has just died away. At the far end of the apse, Augustine rises from his throne with its back to the wall, his pale face distinct against the golden hue of the mosaic. From that place, as from the height of a pulpit, he commands the congregation, looking at them above the altar, which is a plain wooden table placed at the end of the great aisle.

The congregation is standing, the men on one side, the women on the other. On the other side of the balustrade which separates them from the crowd, are the widows and consecrated virgins, wrapped in their veils black or purple. Some matrons, rather overdressed, lean forward in the front rank of the galleries. Their cheeks are painted, their eyelashes and eyebrows blackened, their ears and necks overloaded with jewels. Augustine has noticed them; after a while he will read them a lesson. This audience is all alive with sympathy and curiosity before he begins. With all its faith and all its passion it collaborates with the orator. It is turbulent also. It expresses its opinions and emotions with perfect freedom. The democratic customs of those African Churches surprise us to-day. People made a noise as at the theatre or the circus. They applauded; they interrupted the preacher. Certain among them disputed what was said, quoting passages from the Bible.

Augustine is thus in perpetual communication with his audience. Nobody has done less soaring than he. He keeps his eye on the facial expressions and the attitudes of his public. He talks to them familiarly. When his sermon is a little lengthy, he wants to know if his listeners are getting tired—he has kept them standing so long! The time of the morning meal draws near. Bellies are fasting, stomachs wax impatient. Then says he to them with loving good-fellowship:

"Go, my very dear brothers and sisters, go and restore your strength —I do not mean that of your minds, for I see well that they are tireless, but the strength of your bodies which are the servants of your souls. Go then and restore your bodies so that they may do their work well, and when they are restored, come back here and take your spiritual food."

Upon certain days, a blast of the sirocco has passed over the town. The faithful, crowded in the aisles, are stifling, covered with sweat. The preacher himself, who is very much worked up, has his face dripping, and his clothes are all wet. By this he perceives that once more he has been extremely long. He excuses himself modestly. Or again, he jokes like a rough apostle who is not repelled by the odour of a lot of humankind gathered together.

"Oh, what a smell!" says he. "I must have been speaking a long while to-day."

These good-natured ways won the hearts of the simple folk who listened to him. He is aware of the charm he exerts on them, and of the sympathy they give him back in gratitude for his charity.

"You have loved to come and hear me, my brothers," he said to them. "But whom have you loved? If it is me—ah, even that is good, my brothers, for I want to be loved by you, if I do not want to be loved for myself. As for me, I love you in Christ. And you too, do you love me in Him. Let our love for one another moan together up to God—and that is the moaning of the Dove spoken of in the Scripture…"

Although he preaches from the height of his episcopal throne, he is anxious that his hearers should regard him, Christianly, as their equal. So he seems as little of the bishop as possible.

"All Christians are servants of the same master… I have been in the place where you are—you, my brothers, who listen to me. And now, if I give the spiritual bread from the height of this chair to the servants of the Master of us all—well, it is but a few years since I received this spiritual food with them in a lower place. A bishop, I speak to laymen, but I know to how many future bishops I speak..."

So he puts himself on an equal footing with his audience by the brotherly accent in his words. It is not Christendom, the Universal Church, or I know not what abstract listener he addresses, but the Africans, the people of Hippo, the parishioners of the Basilica of Peace. He knows the allusions, the comparisons drawn from local customs, which are likely to impress their minds. The day of the festival of St. Crispina, a martyr of those parts, after he had developed his subject at very great length, he asked pardon in these terms:

"Let us think, brothers, that I have invited you to celebrate the birthday of the blessed Crispina, and that I have kept up the feast a little too long. Well, might not the same thing happen if some soldier were to ask you to dinner and obliged you to drink more than is wise? Let me do as much for the Word of God, with which you should be drunk and surfeited."

Marriages, as well as birthday feasts, supplied the orator with vivid allegories. Thus he says that when a marriage feast is made in a house, organs play upon the threshold, and musicians and dancers begin to sing and to act their songs. And yet how poor are these earthly enjoyments which pass away so soon!... "In the House of God, the feast has no end."

Continually, through the commentaries on the Psalms, like comparisons rise to the surface—parables suited to stir the imagination of Africans. A thousand details borrowed from local habits and daily life enliven the exegesis of the Bishop of Hippo. The mules and horses that buck when one is trying to cure them, are his symbol for the recalcitrant Donatists. The little donkeys, obstinate and cunning, that trot in the narrow lanes of Algerian *casbahs*, appear here and there in his sermons. The gnats bite in them. The unendurable flies plaster themselves in buzzing patches on the tables and walls. Then there are the illnesses and drugs of that country: the ophthalmias and collyrium. What else? The tarentulas that run along the beams on the ceiling; the hares that scurry without warning between the horses' feet on the great Numidian plains. Elsewhere, he reminds his audience of those men who wear an earring as a talisman; of the dealings between traders and sailors—a comparison which would go home to this seafaring people.

The events of the time, the little happenings of the moment, glide into his sermons. At the same time as the service in church to-day, there is going to be horse-racing at the circus, and fights of wild beasts or gladiators at the arena. In consequence, there will not be many people in the Basilica. "So much the better," says Augustine. "My lungs will get some rest." Another time, it is advertised through the town that most sensational attractions will be offered at the theatre—there will be a scene representing the open sea. The preacher laughs at those who have deserted the church to go and see this illusion: "They will have," says he, "the sea on the stage; but we, brothers—ah, we shall have our port in Jesus Christ." This Saturday, while he is preaching, some Jewish women set themselves to dance and sing on the terraces of the near houses, by way of celebrating the Sabbath. In the basilica, the bashing of the crotolos can be heard, and the thuds of the tambourines. "They would do better," says Augustine, "to work and spin their wool."

He dwells upon the catastrophes which were then convulsing the Roman world. The news of them spread with wonderful rapidity. Alaric's Barbarians have taken Rome and put it to fire and sword. At Jerusalem has been an earthquake, and the bishop John organizes a subscription for the sufferers throughout Christendom. At Constantinople, globes of fire have been seen in the sky. The *Serapeum* of Alexandria has just been destroyed in a riot...

All these things follow each other in lively pictures, without any apparent order, throughout Augustine's sermons. It is not he who divides his discourse into three parts, and refrains from passing to the second till he has learnedly expounded the first. Whether he comments upon the Psalms or the Gospels, his sermons are no more than explanations of the Scriptures which he interprets, sometimes in a literal sense, and sometimes in an allegoric. Let us acknowledge it—his allegoric discourses repel us by their extreme subtilty, sometimes by their bad taste; and when he confines himself to the letter of the text, he stumbles among small points of grammar which weary the attention. We follow him no longer. We think his audience was very obliging to listen so long —and on their feet—to these endless dissertations... And then, suddenly, a great lyrical and oratorical outburst which carries us away—a wind which blows from the high mountains, and in the wink of an eye sweeps away like dust all those fine-spun reasonings.

He is fond of certain commonplaces, and also of certain books of the

Bible—for instance, *The Song of Songs* and the Gospel of St. John, the one satisfying in him the intellectual, and the other the mystic of love. He confronts the verse of the Psalm: "Before the morning star have I begotten thee," with the sublime opening of the Fourth Gospel: "In the beginning was the Word." He lingers upon the beauty of Christ: *Speciosus forma præ filiis hominum*, "Thou art fairer than the children of men." This is why he is always repeating with the Psalmist: "Thy face, Lord, have I sought"—*Quæsivi vultum tuum, Domine*. And the orator, carried away by enthusiasm, adds: "Magnificent saying! Nothing more divine could be said. Those feel it who truly love." Another of his favourite subjects is the kindness of God: *Videte et gustate quam mitis sit Dominus*—"O taste and see that the Lord is good." Naught can equal the pleasure of this contemplation, of this life in God. Augustine conceives it as a musician who has fathomed the secret of numbers. "Let your life," he said, "be one prolonged song... We do not sing only with the voice and lips when we intone a canticle, but in us is an inward singing, because there is also in us Some One who listens..."

To live this rhythmic and divine life we must get free of ourselves, give ourselves up utterly in a great outburst of charity.

"Why," he cries—"Oh, why do you hesitate to give yourselves lest you should lose yourselves? It is rather by not giving yourselves that you lose yourselves. Charity herself speaks to you by the mouth of Wisdom and upholds you against the terror which fills you at the sound of those words: 'Give yourself.' If some one wanted to sell you a piece of land, he would say to you: 'Give me your gold.' And for something else, he would say: 'Give me your silver, give me your money.' Listen to what Charity says to you by the mouth of Wisdom: 'My son, give me thy heart.' 'Give me,' quoth she. Give what? 'My son, give me thy heart.'... Thy heart was not happy when it was governed by thee, and was thine, for it turned this way and that way after gawds, after impure and dangerous loves. 'Tis from there thy heart must be drawn. Whither lift it up? Where to place it? 'Give me thy heart,' says Wisdom, 'let it be mine, and it will belong to thee for always.'"

After the chant of love, the chant of the Resurrection. *Cantate mihi canticum novum*—"Sing to me a new song!" Augustine repeats these words over and over again. "We wish to rise from the dead," cry souls craving for eternity. And the Church answers: "Verily, I say unto you, that you shall rise from the dead. Resurrection of bodies, resurrection of souls, ye shall be altogether reborn." Augustine has explained no dogma more passionately. None was more pleasing to the faithful of those times. Ceaselessly they begged to be strengthened in the conviction of immortality and of meeting again brotherlike in God.

With what intrepid delight it rose—this song of the Resurrection in those clear African basilicas swimming in light, with all their brilliant ornamentation of mosaics and marbles of a thousand colours! And what artless and confident language those symbolic figures spoke which peopled their walls—the lambs browsing among clusters of asphodels, the doves, the green trees of Paradise. As in the Gospel parables, the birds of the field and farmyard, the fruits of the earth, figured the Christian truths and virtues. Their purified forms accompanied man in his ascension towards God. Around the mystic chrisms, circled garlands of oranges and pears and pomegranates. Cocks, ducks, partridges, flamingoes, sought their pasture in the Paradisal fields painted upon the walls of churches and cemeteries.

Those young basilicas were truly the temples of the Resurrection, where all the creatures of the Ark saved from the waters had found their refuge. Never more in the centuries to follow shall humanity know this frank joy at having triumphed over death—this youth of hope.

Chapter 3
THE BISHOP'S BURTHEN

Augustine is not only the most human of all the saints, he is also one of the most amiable in all the senses of that hackneyed word—amiable according to the world, amiable according to Christ.

To be convinced of this, he should be observed in his dealings with his hearers, with his correspondents, even with those he attacks—with the bitterest enemies of the faith. Preaching, the administration of property, and sitting in judgment were but a part of that episcopal burthen, *Sarcina episcopatus*, under which he so often groaned. He had furthermore to catechize, baptize, direct consciences, guard the faithful against error, and dispute with all those who threatened Catholicism. Augustine was a light of the Church. He knew it.

Doing his best, with admirable conscientiousness and charity he undertook these tasks. God knows what it must have cost this Intellectual to fulfil precisely all the duties of his ministry, down to the humblest. What he would have liked, above all, was to pass his life in studying the Scriptures and meditating on the dogmas—not from a love of trifling with theories, but because he believed such knowledge necessary to whoever gave forth the Word of God. Most of the priests of that age arrived at the priesthood without any previous study. They had to improvise, as quick as they could, a complete education in religious subjects. We are left astounded before the huge labour which Augustine must have given to acquire his. Before long he even dominated the whole exegetical and theological knowledge of his time. In his zeal for divine letters, he knew sleep no more.

And yet he did not neglect any of his tasks. Like the least of our parish priests, he prepared the neophytes for the Sacraments. He was an incomparable catechist, so clear-sighted and scrupulous that his instructions may still be taken as models by the catechists of to-day. Neither did he, as an aristocrat of the intelligence, only trouble himself with persons of culture, and leave to his deacons the care of God's common people. All had a right to his lessons, the simple peasants as well as the rich and scholarly. One day, a farmer he was teaching walked off and left him there in the middle of his discourse. The poor man, who had fasted, and now listened to his bishop standing, was faint from hunger and felt his legs tremble under him. He thought it better to run away than to fall down exhausted at the feet of the learned preacher.

With his knowledge of men, Augustine carefully studied the kind of people his catechumens were, and adapted his instructions to the character of each. If they were city folk, Carthaginians, used to spending their time in theatres and taverns, drunken and lazy, he took a different tone with them from what he used with rustics who had never left their native *gourbi*. If he were dealing with fashionable people who had a taste for literature, he did not fail to exalt the beauties of the Scripture, although, he would say, they had there a very trifling attraction compared to the truths contained in it. Of all the catechumens, the hardest to deal with, the most fearsome in his eyes, were the professors—the rhetoricians and the grammarians. These men are bloated with vanity, puffed up with intellectual pride. Augustine knew something about that. It will be necessary to rouse them violently, and before anything else, to exhort them to humility of mind.

The good saint goes further. Not only is he anxious about the souls, but also about the bodies of his listeners. Are they comfortable for listening? As soon as they feel tired they must not hesitate to sit down, as is the usage in the basilicas beyond seas.

"Would not our arrogance be unbearable," he asked, "if we forbade men who are our brothers to sit down in our presence, and, much more, men whom we ought to try with all possible care to make our brothers?..."

If they are seen to yawn, "then things ought to be said to them to awaken their attention, or to scatter the sad thoughts which may have come into their minds." The catechist should shew, now a serene joy—the joy of certainty; now a gaiety which charms people into belief; "and always that light-heartedness we should have in teaching." Even if we ourselves are sad from this reason or that, let us remember that Jesus Christ died for those who are listening to us. Is not the thought of bringing Him disciples enough to make us joyful?

Bishop Augustine set the example for his priests. It is not enough to have prepared the conversion of his catechumens with the subtlety of the psychologist, and such perfect Christian charity; but he accompanies them to the very end, and charges them once more before the baptismal piscina.

How he is changed! One thinks of the boon-fellow of Romanianus and of Manlius Theodorus, of the young man who followed the hunts at Thagaste, and who held forth on literature and philosophy in a select company before the beautiful horizons of the lake of Como. Here he is now with peasants, slaves, sailors, and traders. And he takes pleasure in their society. It is his flock. He ought to love it with all his soul in Jesus Christ. What an effort and what a victory upon himself an attitude so strange reveals to us! For really this liking for mean people was not natural to him. He must have put an heroic will-power into it, helped by Grace.

A like sinking of his preferences is evident in the director of consciences he became. Here he was obliged to give himself more thoroughly. He was at the mercy of the souls who questioned him, who consulted him as their physician. He spends his time in advising them, and exercises a never-failing supervision of their morals. It is an almost discouraging enterprise to bend these hardened pagans—above all, these Africans—to Christian discipline. Augustine is continually reproaching their drunkenness, gluttony, and lust. The populace were not the only ones to get drunk and over-eat themselves. The rich at their feasts literally stuffed till they choked. The Bishop of Hippo never lets a chance go by to recall them to sobriety.

Oftener still, he recalls them to chastity. He writes long letters on this subject which are actual treatises. The morals of the age and country are fully disclosed in them. Husbands are found loudly claiming a right to free love for themselves, while they force their wives to conjugal fidelity. The adultery they allow themselves, they punish with death in their wives. They make an abusive practice of divorce. Upon the most futile reasons, they send the wife the *libellus repudii*—the bill repudiating the marriage—as the various peoples of Islam do still. This society in a state of transition was always creating cases of conscience for strict Christians. For example: If a man cast off his wife under pretext of adultery, might he marry again? Augustine held that no marriage can be dissolved as long as both parties are living. But may not this prohibition provoke husbands to kill their adulterous wives, so as to be free to take a new wife? Another problem: A catechumen divorced under the pagan law and since remarried, presents himself for baptism. Is he not an adulterer in the eyes of the Church? A man who lives with a woman and does not hide it, who even declares his firm intention of continuing to live with his concubine—can he be admitted to baptism? Augustine has to answer all these questions, and go into the very smallest details of casuistry.

Is it forbidden to eat the meats consecrated to idols, even when a man or woman is dying of hunger? May one enter into agreements with native camel-drivers and carriers who swear by their gods to keep the bargain? May a lie be told in certain conditions?—say, so as to get among heretics in pretending to be one of themselves, and thus be able to spy on them and denounce them? May adultery be practised with a woman who promises in exchange to point out heretics?... The Bishop of Hippo severely condemns all these devious or shameful ways, all these compromises which are contrary to the pure moral teaching of the Gospel. But he does this without affecting intolerance and rigidity, and with a reminder that the evil of sin lies altogether in the intention, and in the consent of the will. In a word, one must tolerate and put up with what one is powerless to hinder.

Other questions, which it is quite impossible to repeat here, give us a strange idea of the corruption of pagan morals. Augustine had all he could do to maintain the Christian rule in such surroundings, where the Christians themselves were more or less tainted with paganism. But if this troop of sinners and backsliders was hard to drive, the devout were perhaps harder. There were the *continents*—the widowers and widows who had made a vow of chastity and found this vow heavy; the consecrated virgins who lived in too worldly a fashion; the nuns who rebelled against their spiritual director or their superior; the monks, either former slaves who did not want to do another stroke of work, or charlatans who played upon public credulity in selling talismans and miraculous ointments. Then, the married women who refused themselves to their husbands; and those who gave away their goods to the poor without their husbands' consent; and also the proud virgins and widows who despised and condemned marriage.

Then came the crowd of pious souls who questioned Augustine on points of dogma, who wanted to know all, to clear up everything; those who thought they should be able here below to see God face to face, to know how we shall arise, and who asked if the angels had bodies... Augustine complains that they are annoying, when he has so many other things to trouble him, and that they take him from his studies. But he tries charitably to satisfy them all.

Besides all this, he was obliged to keep up a correspondence with a great number of people. In addition to his friends and fellow-bishops, he wrote to unknown people and foreigners; to men in high place and to lowly people; to the proconsuls, the counts and the vicars of Africa; to the very mighty Olympius, Master of the Household to the Emperor Honorius; or again, "to the Right Honourable Lady Maxima," "to the Illustrious Ladies Proba and Juliana," "to the Very Holy Lady Albina"—women who belonged either to the provincial nobility, or to the highest aristocracy of Rome. To whom did he not write?...

And what is admirable in these letters is that he does not answer negligently to get rid of a tiresome duty. Almost all of them are full of substantial teaching, long thought over. Many were intended to be published—they are practically charges. And yet, however grave the tone of them may be, the cultivated man of the world he had been may be traced. His correspondents, after the fashion of the time, overwhelm the bishop with the most fulsome praises. These he accepts, with much ceremony indeed, but he does accept them as evidence of the charity of his brethren. Ingenuously, he does his best to return them. Let us not grow over-scandalized because our men of letters of to-day have debased the value of complimentary language by squandering and exaggerating it. The most austere cotemporaries of Augustine, and Augustine himself, outdid them by a long way in the art and in the abuse of compliments.

Paulinus of Nola, always beflowered and elegant, wrote to Augustine: "Your letters are a luminous collyrium spread over the eyes of my mind." Augustine, who remonstrated with him upon the scarcity of his own letters, replies in language which our own *Précieuses* would not have disowned: "What! You allow me to pass two summers—and two

African summers!—in such thirst?... Would to God that you would allow enter to the opulent banquet of your book, the long fast from your writings which you have put me upon during all a year! If this banquet be not ready, I shall not give over my complaints, unless, indeed, that in the time between, you send me something to keep up my strength." A certain Audax, who begged the honour of a special letter from the great man, calls him "the oracle of the Law"; protests that the whole world celebrates and admires him; and finally, at the end of his arguments, conjures him in verse to "Let fall upon me the dew of thy divine word." Augustine, with modesty and benignity, returns his compliments, but not without slipping into his reply a touch of banter: "Allow me to point out to you that your fifth line has seven feet. Has your ear betrayed you, or did you want to find out if I was still capable of judging these things?"... Truly, he is always capable of judging these things, nor is he sorry to have it known. A young Greek named Dioscorus, who is passing through Carthage, questions him upon the philosophy of Cicero. Augustine exclaims at any one daring to interrupt a bishop about such trifles. Then, little by little, he grows milder, and carried away by his old passion, he ends by sending the young man quite a dissertation on this good subject.

Those are among his innocent whimsicalities. Then, alongside of letters either too literary, or erudite, or profound, there are others which are simply exquisite, such as the one he wrote to a young Carthage girl called Sapida. She had embroidered a tunic for her brother. He was dead, and she asked Augustine kindly to wear this tunic, telling him that if he would do this, it would be a great comfort for her in her grief. The bishop consented very willingly. "I accept this garment," he said to her, "and I have begun to wear it before writing to you..." Then gently he pities her sorrow, and persuades her to resignation and hope.

"We should not rebuke people for weeping over the dead who are dear to them... When we think of them, and through habit we look for them still around us, then the heart breaks, and the tears fall like the blood of our broken heart..."

At the end, in magnificent words, he chants the hymn of the Resurrection:

"My daughter, your brother lives in his soul, if in his body he sleeps. Does not the sleeper wake? God, who has received his soul, will put it again in the body He has taken from him, not to destroy it—oh, no, but some day to give it to him back."

∼

This correspondence, voluminous as it is, is nothing beside his numberless treatises in dogma and polemic. These were the work of his life, and it is by these posterity has known him. The theologian and the disputer ended by hiding the man in Augustine. To-day, the man perhaps interests us more. And this is a mistake. He himself would not have allowed for a moment that his *Confessions* should be preferred to his treatises on Grace. To study, to comment the Scriptures, to draw more exact definitions from the dogmas—he saw no higher employment for his mind, or obligation more important for a bishop. To believe so as to understand, to understand the better to believe—it is a ceaseless movement of the intelligence which goes from faith to God and from God to faith. He throws himself into this great labour without a shade of any attempt to make literature, with a complete sinking of his tastes and his personal opinions, and in it he entirely forgets himself.

One single time he has thought of himself, and it is precisely in the *Confessions*, the spirit of which modern people understand so ill, and where they try to find something quite different from what the author intended. He composed them just after he was raised to the bishopric, to defend himself against the calumnies spread about his conduct. It seems as if he wanted to say to his detractors: "You believe me guilty. Well, I am so, and more perhaps than you think, but not in the way you think." A great religious idea alters this personal defence. It is less a confession, or an excuse for his faults, in the present sense of the word, than a continual glorification of the divine mercy. It is less the shame of his sins he confesses, than the glory of God.

After that, he never thought again of anything but Truth and the Church, and the enemies of Truth and the Church: the Manichees, the Arians, the Pelagians—the Donatists, above all. He lets no error go by without refuting it, no libel without an answer. He is always on the breach. He might well be compared, in much of his writings, to one of our fighting journalists. He put into this generally thankless business a wonderful vigour and dialectical subtlety. Always and everywhere he had to have the last word. He brought eloquence to it, yet more charity—

sometimes even wit. And lastly, he had a patience which nothing could dishearten. He repeats the same things a hundred times over. These tiresome repetitions, into which he was driven by the obstinacy of his opponents, caused him real pain. Every time it became necessary, he took up again the endless demonstration without letting himself grow tired. The moment it became a question of the Truth, Augustine could not see that he had any right to keep quiet.

In Africa and elsewhere they made fun of what they called his craze for scribbling. He himself, in his *Retractations*, is startled by the number of his works. He turns over the Scripture saying which the Donatists amusingly opposed to him: *Væ mullum loquentibus*—"Woe unto them of many words." But calling God to witness, he says to Him: *Væ tacentibus de te*—"Woe unto those who keep silent upon Thee." In the eyes of Augustine, the conditions were such that silence would have been cowardly. And elsewhere he adds: "They may believe me or not as they will, but I like much better to read than to write books..."

In any case, his modesty was evident. "I am myself," he acknowledges, "almost always dissatisfied with what I say." To the heretics he declares, with a glance back at his own errors, "I know by experience how easy it is to be wrong." When there is some doubt in questions of dogma, he does not force his explanations, but suggests them to his readers. How much intellectual humility is in that prayer which ends his great work on the Trinity: "Lord my God, one Trinity, if in these books I have said anything which comes from Thee, may Thou and Thy chosen receive it. But if it is from me it comes, may Thou and Thine forgive me."

And again, how much tolerance and charity in those counsels to the faithful of his diocese who, having been formerly persecuted by the Donatists, now burned to get their revenge:

"It is the voice of your bishop, my brothers, sounding in your ears. He implores you, all of you who are in this church, to keep yourselves from insulting those who are outside, but rather to pray that they may enter with you into communion."

Elsewhere, he reminds his priests that they must preach at the Jews in a spirit of friendliness and loving-kindness, without troubling to know if they listen with gratitude or indignation. "We ought not," said he, "to bear ourselves proudly against these broken branches of Christ's tree."...

This charity and moderation took nothing from the firmness of his character. This he proved in a startling way in the discussion he had with St. Jerome over a passage In the Epistle to the Galatians, and upon the new translation, of the Bible which Jerome had undertaken. The solitary of Bethlehem saw a "feint" on the part of St. Paul in the disputed passage: Augustine said, a "lie." What, then, would become of evangelic truth if in such a place the Apostle had lied? And would not this be a means of authorizing all the exegetical fantasies of heresiarchs, who already rejected as altered or forged all verses of the holy books which conflicted with their own doctrines?...

As to the new translation of the Bible, it would bring about trouble in the African churches, where they were accustomed to the ancient version of the Septuagint. The mistranslations, pointed out by Jerome in the old version, would upset the faithful and lead them to suspect that the entire Scripture was false. In this double matter, Augustine defended at once orthodoxy and tradition from very praiseworthy reasons of prudence.

Jerome retorted in a most aggressive and offensive tone. He flatly accused the Bishop of Hippo of being jealous of him and of wishing to cut out a reputation for learning at his expense. In front of his younger and more supple adversary, he took on the air of an old wrestler who was still capable of knocking out any one who had the audacity to attack him. He hurled at Augustine this phrase heavy with menaces: "The tired ox stands firmer than ever on his four legs."

For all that, Augustine stuck to his opinion, and he confined himself to replying gently: "In anything I say, I am not only always ready to receive your observations upon what you find wounding and contrary to your feelings, but I even ask your advice as earnestly as I can."...

Chapter 4
AGAINST "THE ROARING LIONS"

One day (this was soon after he became bishop) Augustine went to visit a Catholic farmer in the suburbs of Hippo, whose daughter had been lessoned by the Donatists, and had just enrolled herself among their consecrated virgins. The father at first had shouted at the deserter, and flogged her unmercifully by way of improving her state of mind. Augustine, when he heard of the affair, condemned the farmer's brutality and declared that he would never receive the girl back into the community unless she came of her own free will. He then went out to the place to try and settle the matter. On the way, as he was crossing an estate which belonged to a Catholic matron, he fell in with a priest of the Donatist Church at Hippo. The priest at once began to insult him and his companions, and yelled:

"Down with the traitors! Down with the persecutors!"

And he vomited out abominations against the matron herself who owned the land. As much from prudence as from Christian charity, Augustine did not answer. He even prevented those with him from falling upon the insulter.

Incidents of this kind happened almost every day. About the same time, the Donatists of Hippo made a great noise over the rebaptizing of another apostate from the Catholic community. This was a good-for-nothing loafer who beat his old mother, and the bishop severely rebuked his monstrous conduct.

"Well, as you talk in that tone of voice," said the loafer, "I'm going to be a Donatist."

Through bravado, he continued to ill-treat the poor old woman, and to make the worst kind of threats. He roared in savage fury:

"Yes, I'll become a Donatist, and I'll have your blood."

And the young ruffian did really go over to the Donatist party. In accordance with the custom among the heretics, he was solemnly rebaptized in their basilica, and he exhibited himself on the platform clad in the white robe of the purified. People in Hippo were much shocked. Augustine, full of indignation, addressed his protests to Proculeianus, the Donatist bishop. "What! is this man, all bloody with a murder in his conscience, to walk about for eight days in white robes as a model of innocence and purity?" But Proculeianus did not condescend to reply.

These cynical proceedings were trifling compared to the vexations which the Donatists daily inflicted on their opponents. Not only did they tamper with Augustine's people, but the country dwellers of the Catholic Church were continually interfered with on their lands, pillaged, ravaged, and burned out by mobs of fanatical brigands who organized a rule of terror from one end of Numidia to the other. Supported in secret by the Donatists, they called themselves "the Athletes of Christ." The Catholics had given them the contemptuous name of "Circoncelliones," or prowlers around cellars, because they generally plundered cellars and grain-houses. Troops of fanaticized and hysterical women rambled round with them, scouring the country like your true bacchantes, clawing the unfortunate wretches who fell into their hands, burning farms and harvests, broaching barrels of wine and oil, and crowning these exploits by orgies with "the Athletes of Christ." When they saw a haystack blazing in the fields, the country-folk were panic-stricken—the "Circoncelliones" were not far off. Soon they appeared, brandishing their clubs and bellowing their war cry: *Deo laudes!*—"Praise be to God." "Your shout," said Augustine to them, "is more dreaded by our people than the roaring of lions."

Something had to be done to quell these furious monsters, and to resist the encroachments and forcible acts of the heretics. These, by way of frightening the Catholic bishops, told them roundly:

"We don't want any of your disputes, and we are going to rebaptize just as it suits us. We are going to lay snares for your sheep and to rend them like wolves. As for you, if you are good shepherds, keep quiet!"

Augustine was not a man to keep quiet, nor yet to spend his strength in small local quarrels. He saw big; he did not imprison himself within the limits of his diocese. He knew that Numidia and a good part of Africa were in the hands of the Donatists; that they had a rival primate to the Catholic primate at Carthage; that they had even sent a Pope of their community to Rome. In a word, they were in the majority. Everywhere a dissenting Church rose above the orthodox Church, when it did not succeed in stifling it altogether. At all costs the progress of this sect must be stopped. In Augustine's eyes there was no more urgent work. For him and his flock it was a question of insuring their lives, since they were attacked even in their fields and houses. From the moment he first came to Hippo, as a simple priest, he had thrown himself intrepidly into this struggle. He never ceased till Donatism was conquered and trampled underfoot. To establish peace and Catholic unity everywhere was the great labour of his episcopate.

Who, then, were these terrible Donatists whom we have been continually striking against since the beginning of this history?

It would soon be a century since they had been disturbing and desolating Africa. Just after the great persecution of Diocletian, the sect was born, and it increased with amazing rapidity. During this persecution, evidence had not been wanting of the moral slackness in the African Church. A large number of lay people apostatized, and a good number of bishops and priests handed over to the pagan authorities, besides the devotional objects, the Scriptures and the muniments of their communities. In Numidia, and especially at Constantine, scandalous scenes took place. The cowardice of the clergy was lamentable. Public opinion branded with the names of *traditors*, or traitors, those who had weakened and given over the sacred books to the pagans.

The danger once over, the Numidians, whose behaviour had been so little brilliant, determined to redeem themselves by audacity, and to prove with superb impudence that they had been braver than the others. So they set themselves to shout *traditor* against whoever displeased them, and particularly against those of Carthage and the Proconsulate. At bottom it was the old rivalry between the two Africas, East and West.

Under the reign of Constantine a peace had been patched up, when it fell out that a new Bishop of Carthage had to be elected, and the Archdeacon Cæcilianus, whose name was put forward, was accused of preventing the faithful from visiting the martyrs in their prisons. The zealots contended that in collusion with his bishop, Mensurius, he had given up the Holy Scriptures to the Roman authorities to be burned. The election promised to be stormy. The supporters of the Archdeacon, who feared the hostility of the Numidian bishops, did not wait for their arrival. They hurried things over. Cæcilianus was elected and consecrated by three bishops of the district, of whom one was a certain Felix of Abthugni.

At once the opposite clan, backed up by the Numidians, objected. At their head was a wealthy Spanish woman named Lucilla, an unbalanced devotee, who, it seemed, always carried about her person a bone of a martyr, and a doubtful one at that. She would ostentatiously kiss her relic before receiving the Eucharist. The Archdeacon Cæcilianus forbade this devotion as superstitious, and thus made a relentless enemy of the fanatical Spaniard. All the former accusations were renewed against him, and it was added that Felix of Abthugni, who had consecrated him, was a *traditor*. Hence the election was void, by the single fact of the unworthiness of the consecrating bishops. Lucilla, having bribed a section of the bishops assembled in council, Cæcilianus was deposed, and the deacon Majorinus elected in his room. He himself was soon after succeeded by Donatus, an active, clever, and energetic man, who organized resistance so ably, and who represented so well the spirit of the sect, that he left it his name. Henceforth, Donatism enters into history.

But Cæcilianus had on his side the bishops overseas and the Imperial Government. The Pope of Rome and the Emperor recognized him as legitimately elected. Besides that, he cleared himself of all the grievances urged against him. Finally, an inquiry, conducted by laymen, proved that Felix of Abthugni was not a *traditor*. The Donatists appealed to Constantine, then to two Councils convoked successively at Rome and Arles. Everywhere they were condemned. Moreover, the Council of Arles declared that the character of him who confers the Sacraments has no influence whatever on their validity. Thus, baptism and ordination, even conferred by a *traditor*, were canonically sound.

This decision was regarded as an abominable heresy by the Donatists. As a matter of fact, there was an old African tradition, accepted by St. Cyprian himself, that an unworthy priest could not administer the Sacraments. The local prejudice would not yield: all were rebaptized who had been baptized by the Catholics—that is to say, by the supporters of the *traditors*.

The theological question was complicated with a question of property which was all but insoluble. Since the Donatist bishops were resolved to separate from the Catholic communion, did they mean to give up, with their title, their basilicas and the property belonging to their churches? Supposing that they themselves were disinterested, they had behind them the crowd of clients and land-tillers who got their living out of the Church, and dwelt on Church property. Never would these people allow a rival party to alter the direction of the charities, to plant themselves in their fields and their *gourbis*, to expel them from their cemeteries and basilicas. Other reasons, still deeper perhaps, induced the Donatists to persevere in the schism. These religious dissensions were agreeable to that old spirit of division which at all times has been the evil genius of Africa. The Africans have always felt the need of segregating themselves from one another in hostile *cofs*. They hate each other from one village to another—for nothing, just, for the pleasure of hating and felling each other to the ground.

At bottom, here is what Donatism really was: It was an extra sharp attack of African individualism. These rebels brought in nothing new in dogma. They would not even have been heretics without their claim to rebaptize. They limited themselves to retain a position gained long ago; to keep their churches and properties, or to seize those of the Catholics upon the pretence that they were themselves the legitimate owners. With that, they affected a respect for tradition, an austerity in morals and discipline, which made them perfect puritans. Yes, they were the pure, the irreconcilables, who alone had not bent before the Roman officials. All this was very pleasing to the discontented and quarrelsome, and caressed the popular instinct in its tendency to particularism.

That is why the sect became, little by little, mistress of almost the whole country. Then it subdivided, crumbled up into little churches which excommunicated each other. In Southern Numidia, the citadels of orthodox Donatism, so to speak, were Thimgad and Bagai. Carthage, with its primate, was the official centre. But in the Byzacena and Tripolitana Regio, there were the Maximianists, and the Rogatists in Mauretania, who had cut themselves off from the Great Church. These divisions of the schism corresponded closely enough to the natural compartments of North Africa. There must be some incompatibility of temper between these various regions. To this day, Algiers prides itself on not thinking like Constantine, which does not think like Bona or like Tunis.

Are we to see in Donatism a nationalist or separatist movement directed against the Roman occupation? That would be to transport quite modern ideas into antiquity. No more in Augustine's time than in our own was there such a thing as African nationality. But if the sectaries had no least thought of separating from Rome, it is none the less true that they were in rebellion against her representatives, temporal as well as spiritual. Supposing that Rome had yielded to them—an impossible event, of course—that would have meant a surrender to the claims of Africans who wished to be masters of their property as well as of their religious beliefs in their own country. What more could they have wanted? It little mattered to them who was the nominal master, provided that they had the realities of government in their hands. Altogether, Donatism is a regionalist revindication, very strongly characterized. It is a remarkable fact that it was among the indigenous population, ignorant of Latin, that the most of its adherents were recruited.

Such was the position of the Church in Africa when Augustine was named Bishop of Hippo. He judged it at once, with his clear-sightedness, his strong good sense, his broad outlook of a Roman citizen freed from the smallnesses of a local spirit, his Christian idealism which took no heed of the accidents or considerations of worldly prosperity. What! was Catholicism to become an African religion, a restricted sect, wretchedly tied to the letter of tradition, to the exterior practices of worship? To reign in a little corner of the world—did Christ die for that? Never! Christ died for the wide world. The only limits of His Church are the limits of the universe. And besides, in this resolution to exclude, what becomes of the great principle of Charity? It is by charity, above all, that we are Christians. Faith without love is a faith stagnant and dead...

Augustine also foresaw the consequences of spiritual separation; he had them already under his eyes. The Church is the great spring, not only of love, but of intelligence. Once cut away from this reviving spring, Donatism would become dry and stunted like a branch stripped from a tree. The deep sense of its dogmas would become impoverished as its works emptied themselves of the spirit of charity. Obstinacy, narrowness, lack of understanding, fanaticism, and cruelty—there you had the inevitable fruits of schism. Augustine knew the rudeness and ignorance of his opponents, even of the most cultivated among them: he might well ask himself in anguish what would become of the African Church deprived of the benefit of Roman culture, isolated from the great intellectual current which united all the churches beyond seas. Finally, he knew his fellow-countrymen; he knew that the Donatists, even victorious, even sole masters of the land, would turn against themselves the fury they now satisfied against the Catholics, and never stop tearing each other in pieces. Here was now nearly a hundred years that they had kept Africa in fire and blood. This meant before very long a return to barbarism. Separated from Catholicism, they would really separate from the Empire and even from civilization. And so it was that in fighting for Catholic unity, Augustine fought for the Empire and for civilization.

Confronted with these barbarians and sectaries, his attitude could not be doubtful for a single moment. He must do his best to bring them back to the Church. It was only a matter of hitting upon the most effectual means.

Preaching, for an orator such as he was, should be an excellent weapon. His eloquence, his dialectic, his profane and sacred learning, gave him an immense superiority over the defenders of the opposite side. He certainly kept in the Church many Catholics who were ready to apostatize. But before the crowd of schismatics, all these high gifts were as good as lost. The people were in no wise anxious to know upon which side truth was to be found. They were Donatists, as they were Numidians or Carthaginians, without knowing why—because everybody about them was. Many might have answered like that grammarian of Constantine, who told the Inquisitors with astute simplicity:

"I am a professor of Roman literature, a teacher of Latin grammar. My father was a decurion at Constantine; my grandfather was a soldier and had served in the guard. Our family is of Moorish blood... As for me, I am quite ignorant about the origin of the schism: I am just one of the ordinary faithful of the people called Christians. When I was at Carthage, Bishop Secundus came there one day. I heard tell that they found out that Bishop Cæcilianus had been ordained irregularly by I don't know who, and they elected another bishop against him. That's how the schism began at Carthage. I have no means of knowing much about the origin of the schism, because there has never been more than one church in our city. If there has been a schism here, we know nothing about it."

When a grammarian talked thus, what could have been the thoughts of agricultural labourers, city workmen, and slaves? They belonged to an estate, or a quarter of a town, where no other faith than theirs had ever been professed. They were Donatists like their employers, like their neighbours, like the other people of the *cof* to which they had belonged from father to son. The theological side of the question left them absolutely indifferent. If Augustine tried to debate with them, they refused to listen and referred him to their bishops. That was the word of command.

The bishops, on their side, avoided all discussion. Augustine tried in vain to arrange an argument with Proculeianus, his Donatist colleague at Hippo. And if some of them shewed themselves more obliging, the evasions and reticences of the antagonist, and sometimes outside circumstances, made the debate utterly futile. At Thubursicum the audience raised such a noise in the place where Augustine was debating with the bishop Fortunius, that they were no longer able to hear each other. At other times, the meeting sank to an oratorical joust, wherein they tired themselves out passading against words, instead of attacking the matters at issue. Augustine felt that he was losing his time. Besides, the Donatist bishops presented an obstinate front against which everything smashed.

"Leave us in our errors," they said ironically. "If we are lost in your eyes, why follow us about? We don't want to be saved."

And they prohibited their flocks from saluting Catholics, from speaking to them, from going into their churches or into their houses, from sitting down in the midst of them. They laid an interdict on their adversaries. Primanius, the Donatist Primate of Carthage, upon being invited to a conference, answered proudly:

"The sons of the martyrs can have nothing to do with the race of traitors."

This being the state of the case, no method of pacification was left but written controversy. Augustine shewed himself tireless at it. It was chiefly in these letters and treatises against the Donatists that he was not afraid to repeat himself. He knew that he was dealing with the deaf, and with the deaf who did not want to hear: he was obliged to raise his voice. With admirable self-denial he reiterated the same arguments a hundred times over, a hundred times took up the history of the quarrel from the beginning, spreading such a light over the quibbles and refinings of his contradictors, that it should have brought conviction to the bluntest minds. "No," he repeated, "Cæcilianus was not a *traditor*, nor Felix of Abthugni either who consecrated him bishop. The documents are there to prove this. And even supposing they were, can the fault of a single man be charged to the whole Church?... Then why do you baptize the Catholics under the pretence that their priests are *traditors* and as such unworthy to administer the Sacraments? It is the sacrifice of Jesus Christ and not the virtue of the priest which renders baptism efficacious. If it were otherwise, what was the good of the Redemption? It is the fact that by the voluntary death of Christ, all men have been called to salvation. Salvation is not the privilege of Africans only. Being Catholic, the Church should take in the whole world..."

In the long run, these continual repetitions end by seeming wearisome to modern readers: for us there arises out of all these discussions a dense and intolerable boredom. But let us remember that all this was singularly living for Augustine's cotemporaries, that these thankless developments were read with passion. And then, too, it was a question of the unity of the Church which involved, as we cannot too often repeat, the interest of the Empire and civilization.

Against so persuasive a power the Donatists opposed a conspiracy of silence. Their bishops forbade the people to read what Augustine wrote. They did more—they concealed their own libels so that it was impossible to reply to them. But Augustine used all his skill to unearth them. He refuted them, and had his refutations recopied and posted on the walls of the basilicas. The copies circulated through the province and the whole Roman world.

This would have had an excellent result if the quarrel had been entirely over questions of theory. But immense property interests came into it, and rancours and terrible hates. Augustine was forced to pass from verbal polemics to direct action—defensive action, at first, and then attack.

While he and his fellow-bishops did their utmost to preach peace, the Donatist bishops urged their followers to the holy war. Augustine even received threats on his life. During one of his visitations, he was nearly assassinated. Men in ambush lay in wait for him. By a providential chance, he took the wrong road, and owed his life to this mistake. His pupil Possidius, who was then Bishop of Guelma, was not so lucky.

Brought to bay in a house by the Donatist bishop Crispinus, he defended himself desperately. They set fire to the house to turn him out. When there was nothing else left but to be burned alive, he did come out. The band of Donatists seized him, and would have beaten his brains out, if Crispinus himself, fearing a prosecution for murder, had not interfered. But the assailants sacked the property and slaughtered all the horses and mules in the stables. At Bagai, Bishop Maximianus was stabbed in his basilica. A furious mob smashed the altar and began to strike the victim with the fragments, and left him for dead on the flags. The Catholics lifted up his body, but the Donatists plucked him out of their hands and flung him from the top of a tower, and he fell on a dunghill which broke the fall. The unhappy man still breathed, and by a miracle he recovered.

Meanwhile, the Circoncelliones, armed with their bludgeons, continued to pillage and burn the farms. They tortured the owners to extract their money from them. They made them toil round the mill-path like beasts of burthen, while they lashed at them with whips. At their back, the Donatist priests invaded the Catholic churches and lands. There and then they rebaptized the labourers. These doings were, indeed, very like the practices of the African Mussulmans to-day, who, in like circumstances, always begin by converting the Christian farm-hands by main force. Then they purified the basilicas by scraping down the walls and washing the floors with big douches of water; and after demolishing the altar, they scattered salt where it had stood. It was a perfect disinfection. The Donatists treated the Catholics like the plague-stricken.

Such acts cried out for vengeance. Augustine, who up till this time had recoiled from asking the public authorities to prosecute, who, as an observer of the apostolic tradition, did not recognize the interference of the civil power in Church matters—well, Augustine had to give way to circumstances, and also to the pressure brought to bear on him by his colleagues. Councils assembled at Carthage petitioned the Emperor to take exceptional measures against the Donatists, who laughed at all the laws directed against heretics. When they were summoned before the courts they demonstrated to the judges, who were often pagans incompetent to decide in these questions, that it was they who really belonged to the only orthodox Church. Something must be done to end this equivocal position, and to bring about once for all a categorical condemnation of the schism. Augustine, acting in concert with the primate Aurelius, was the ruling spirit of these meetings.

Let us not judge his conduct by modern ideas, or be in a hurry to exclaim against his intolerance. He and the Catholic bishops, in acting thus, were complying with the old tradition which had influenced all the pagan governments. Rome, particularly, though it recognized all the local sects, all the foreign religions, never allowed any of its subjects to refuse to fall in with the official religion. The persecutions of the Christians and the Jews had no other motive. Now that it was become the State religion, Christianity, willingly or unwillingly, had to summon people to the same obedience. The Emperors made a special point of this from political reasons easy to understand—to prevent riots and maintain public order. Even if the bishops had refrained from all complaint, the Imperial Government would have acted without them and suppressed the disturbances caused by the heretics.

Just look at the situation and the men as they were at that moment in Africa. It was the Catholics who were persecuted, and that with revolting fury and cruelty. They were obliged to defend themselves. In the next place, the distribution of property in those countries made conversions in batches singularly easy. Multitudes of farm tenants, workmen, and agricultural slaves, lived upon the immense estates of one owner. Without any interest in dogmatic questions, they were Donatists simply because their master was. To change these devouring wolves into tranquil sheep, it was often quite enough if the master got converted. The great blessing of peace depended upon pressure being brought to bear on certain persons. When all day and every day there was a risk of being murdered or burned out by irresponsible ruffians, the temptation was very strong to fall back on such a prompt and simple remedy. Augustine and his colleagues ended by making up their minds to do so. For that matter, they had no choice. They were bound to strike, or be themselves suppressed by their enemies.

However, before resorting to rigorous measures, they resolved to send forth a supreme appeal for reconciliation. The Catholics proposed a meeting to the Donatists in which they would loyally examine one another's grievances. As personal or material questions made the great bar to an understanding, they promised that every Donatist bishop who turned convert should keep his see. In places where a schismatic and an orthodox bishop were found together, they would come to a friendly agreement to govern the diocese by turns. Where it was impossible for this to be done, it was proposed that the Catholic should resign in favour of the other. Augustine lent all his eloquence to carry this motion, which was sufficiently heroic for a good number of bishops who were not so detached as he from the goods of this world. And one must allow that it was difficult to go much further in the way of self-denial.

After a good deal of skirmishing and hesitation on the side of the schismatics, the Conference met at Carthage in June of the year 411, under the presidency of an Imperial commissioner, the tribune Marcellinus. Once again, the Donatists saw themselves condemned. Upon the report of the commissioner, a decree of Honorius classed them definitely among heretics. They were forbidden to rebaptize or to assemble together, under penalties of fine and confiscation. Refractory countrymen and slaves would be liable to corporal punishment, and as for the clerics, they would be banished.

The effect of these new laws was not long in appearing, and it fully answered the wishes of the orthodox bishops. Many populations returned, or pretended to return, to the Catholic communion. This result was largely the work of Augustine, who for twenty years had worked to bring it about by preaching and controversy. But, as might be expected, he did not overdo his triumph. Without delay, he set himself to preach moderation to the conquerors. Nor had he waited till the enemy was defeated to do that. Ten years before, while the Donatists were besetting the Catholics everywhere, he said to the priests of his communion:

"Remember this, my brothers, so as to practise and preach it with never-varying gentleness. Love the men; kill the lie! Lean on truth without pride; fight for it without cruelty. Pray for those whom you chide, and for those to whom you shew their error."

However, the victory of the party of peace was not so thorough as it had seemed at first. A good many fanatics here and there grew obstinate in their resistance. The Circoncelliones, maddened, distinguished themselves by a new outbreak of ravages and cruelties. They tortured and mutilated all the Catholics who fell into their hands. They had invented an unheard-of refinement of torture, which was to cover with lime diluted with vinegar the eyes of their victims. The priest Restitutus was assassinated in the suburbs of Hippo. A bishop had his tongue and his hand cut off. If the towns were pretty quiet, terror began to reign once more in the country places.

The Roman authorities exerted themselves to put an end to these bloody scenes. They heavily chastised the offenders whenever they could catch them. In his charity, Augustine interceded for them with the judges. He wrote to the tribune Marcellinus:

"We would not that the servants of God should be revenged by hurts like to those they suffered. Surely, we are not against depriving the guilty of the means to do harm, but we consider it will be enough, without taking their lives or wrenching any limb from them, to turn them from their senseless tumult by the restraining power of the laws, in bringing them back to calm and reason; or, in a last resort, to take away the opportunity for criminal actions by employing them in some useful work... Christian judge, in this matter fulfil the duty of a father, and while repressing injustice, do not forget humanity."

This compassion of Augustine was shewn particularly in his meeting with Emeritus, the Donatist Bishop of Cherchell (or as it was then called, Mauretanian Cæsarea), one of the most stubborn among the irreconcilables. His attitude in dealing with this uncompromising enemy was not only humane, but courteous, full of graciousness, and of the most sensitive charity.

This fell out in the autumn of the year 418, seven years after the great Conference at Carthage. Augustine was sixty-four years old. How was it that he who had always had such feeble health undertook at this age the long journey from Hippo to Cæsarea? We know that the Pope, Zozimus, had entrusted him with a mission to the Church of that town. With his tireless zeal, always ready to march for the glory of Christ, the old bishop doubtless saw in this journey a fresh opportunity for an apostle. So he started off, in spite of the roads, which were very unsafe in those troublous times, in spite of the crushing heat of the season—the end of September. He travelled six hundred miles across the endless Numidian plain and the mountainous regions of the Atlas, preaching in the churches, halting in the towns and the hamlets to decide questions of private interest, ever pursued by a thousand business worries and by the squabbles of litigants and the discontented. At last, after many weeks of fatigue and tribulation, he reached Cherchell, where he was the guest of Deuterius, the metropolitan Bishop of Mauretania.

Now Emeritus, the deposed bishop, lived mysteriously in the suburbs, in constant fear of some forcible action on the part of the authorities. When he learned the friendly intentions of Augustine, he came out of his hiding-place and shewed himself in the town. In one of the squares of Cæsarea the two prelates met. Augustine, who had formerly seen Emeritus at Carthage, recognized him, hurried over to him, saluted him, and at once suggested a friendly talk.

"Let us go into the church," he said. "This square is hardly suitable for a talk between two bishops."

Emeritus, flattered, agreed. The conversation continued in such a cordial tone that Augustine was already rejoicing upon having won back the schismatic. Deuterius, following the line of conduct which the Catholic bishops had adopted, spoke of resigning and handing over the see to the other. It was agreed that within two days Emeritus should come to the cathedral for a public discussion with his colleague of Hippo. At the appointed hour he appeared. A great crowd of people gathered to hear the two orators. The basilica was full. Then Augustine, turning to the impenitent Donatist, said to him mildly:

"Emeritus, my brother, you are here. You were also at our Conference at Carthage. If you were beaten there, why do you come here now? If, on the other hand, you think that you were not beaten, tell us what leads you to believe that you had the advantage..."

What change had Emeritus undergone in two days? Whatever it was, he disappointed the hopes of Augustine and the people of Cæsarea. He returned only ambiguous phrases to the most pressing and brotherly urging. Finally, he took refuge in an angry silence from which it was found impossible to draw him.

Augustine went home without having converted the heretic. No doubt he was sorely disappointed. Nevertheless, he shewed no resentment; he even took measures to ensure the safety of the recalcitrant, in a charitable fear less the roused people might do him a bad turn. With all that, when he looked back at the results of nearly thirty years of struggle against schism, he might well say to himself that he had done good work for the Church. Donatism, in fact, was conquered, and conquered by him. Was he at last to have a chance to rest himself, with the only rest suitable to a soul like his, in a steady meditation and study of the Scriptures? Henceforth, would he be allowed to live a little less as a bishop and a little more as a monk? This was always the strong desire of his heart...

But new and worse trials awaited him at Hippo.

FACE TO FACE WITH THE BARBARIANS

Et nunc veniant omnes quicumque amant Paradisum, iocum quietis, locum securitatis, locicm perpetuæ felicitatis, locum in quo non pertimescas Barbarum...
And now let all those come who love Paradise, the place of quiet, the place of safety, the place of eternal happiness, the place where the Barbarian need be feared no more...

— *Sermon sur la Persécution des Barbares,*
VII, 9.

Chapter 1
THE SACK OF ROME

During June of the year 403, an astonishing event convulsed the former capital of the Empire. The youthful Honorius, attended by the regent Stilicho, came there to celebrate his triumph over Alaric and the Gothic army, defeated at Pollentia.

The pageantry of a triumph was indeed a very astonishing sight for the Romans of that period. They had got so unused to them! And no less wonderful was the presence of the Emperor at the Palatine. Since Constantine's reign, the Imperial palaces had been deserted. They had hardly been visited four times in a century by their master.

Rome had never got reconciled to the desertion of her princes. When the Court was moved to Milan, and then to Ravenna, she felt she had been uncrowned. Time after time the Senate appealed to Honorius to shew himself, at least, to his Roman subjects, since political reasons were against his dwelling among them. This journey was always put off. The truth is, the Christian Cæsars did not like Rome, and mistrusted her still half-pagan Senate and people. It needed this unhoped-for victory to bring Honorius and his councillors to make up their minds. The feeling of a common danger had for the moment drawn the two opposing religions together, and here they were apparently making friends in the same patriotic delight. Old hates were forgotten. In fact, the pagan aristocracy had hopes of better treatment from Stilicho. On account of all these reasons, the triumphant Cæsar was received at Rome with delirious joy.

The Court, upon leaving Ravenna, had crossed the Apennines. A halt was called on the banks of the Clitumnus, where in ancient times the great white herds were found which were sacrificed at the Capitol during a triumph. But the gods of the land had fallen; there would be no opiman bull this time on their altars. The pagans felt bitter about it.

Thence, by Narnia and the Tiber valley, they made their way down into the plain. The measured step of the legions rang upon the large flags of the Flaminian way. They crossed the Mulvius bridge—and old Rome rose like a new city. In anticipation of a siege, the regent had repaired the Aurelian wall. The red bricks of the enclosure and the fresh masonwork of the towers gleamed in the sun. Finally, striking into the *Via lata*, the procession marched to the Palatine.

The crowd was packed in this long, narrow street, and overflowed into the nearest alleys. Women, elaborately dressed, thronged the balconies, and even the terraces of the palace. All at once the people remarked that the Senate was not walking before the Imperial chariot. Stilicho, who wished to conciliate their good graces, had, contrary to custom, dispensed them from marching on foot before the conqueror. People talked with approval of this wily measure in which they saw a promise of new liberties. But applause and enthusiastic cheers greeted the young Honorius as he passed by, sharing with Stilicho the honour of the triumphal car.

The unequalled splendour of his *trabea*, of which the embroideries disappeared under the number and flash of colour of the jewels, left the populace gaping. The diadem, a masterpiece of goldsmith's work, pressed heavily on his temples. Emerald pendants twinkled on each side of his neck, which, as it was rather fat, with almost feminine curves, suggested at once to the onlookers a comparison with Bacchus. They found he had an agreeable face, and even a soldierly air with his square shoulders and stocky neck. Matrons gazed with tender eyes on this Cæsar of nineteen, who had, at that time, a certain beauty, and the brilliance, so to speak, of youth. This degenerate Spaniard, who was really a crowned eunuch, and was to spend his life in the society of the palace eunuchs and die of dropsy—this son of Theodosius was just then fond of violent exercise, of hunting and horses. But he was even now becoming ponderous with unhealthy fat. His build and bloated flesh gave those who saw him at a distance a false notion of his strength. The Romans were most favourably impressed by him, especially the young men.

But the army, the safeguard of the country, was perhaps even more admired than the Emperor. The legions, following the ruler, had almost deserted the capital. The flower of the troops were almost unknown there. In consequence, the march past of the cavalry was quite a new sight for the people. A great murmur of admiration sounded as the *cataphracti* appeared, gleaming in the coats of mail which covered them from head to foot. Upon their horses, caparisoned in defensive armour, they looked like equestrian, statues—like silver horsemen on bronze horses. Childish cries greeted each *draconarius* as he marched by carrying his ensign—a dragon embroidered on a long piece of cloth which flapped in the wind. And the crowd pointed at the crests of the helmets plumed with peacock feathers, and the scarfs of scarlet silk flowing over the camber of the gilded cuirasses...

The military show poured into the Forum, swept up the *Via Sacra*, and when it had passed under the triumphal arches of the old emperors, halted at the Palace of Septimus Severus. In the Stadium, the crowd awaited Honorius. When he appeared on the balcony of the Imperial box, wild cheering burst out on all the rows of seats. The Emperor, diadem on head, bowed to the people. Upon that the cheers became a tempest. Rome did not know how to express her happiness at having at last got her master back.

On the eve of the worst catastrophes she had this supreme day of glory, of desperate pride, of unconquerable faith in her destiny. The public frenzy encouraged them in the maddest hopes. The poet Claudian, who had followed the Court, became the mouthpiece of these perilous illusions. "Arise!" he cried to Rome, "I prithee arise, O venerable queen! Trust in the goodwill of the gods. O city, fling away the mean fears of age, *thou who art immortal as the heavens!*..."

For all that, the Barbarian danger continued to threaten. The victory of Pollentia, which, moreover, was not a complete victory, had settled nothing. Alaric was in flight in the Alps, but he kept his eye open for a favourable chance to fall back upon Italy and wrench concessions of money and honours from the Court of Ravenna. Supported by his army of mercenaries and adventurers in the pay of the Empire like himself, his dealings with Honorius were a kind of continual blackmail. If the Imperial Government refused to pay the sums which he protested it owed him for the maintenance of his troops, he would pay himself by force. Rome, where fabulous riches had accumulated for so many centuries, was an obvious prey for him and his men. He had coveted it for a long time; and to get up his courage for this daring exploit, as well as to work upon his soldiers, he pretended that he had a mission from Heaven to chastise and destroy the new Babylon. In his Pannonian forests it would seem he had heard mysterious voices which said to him: "Advance, and thou shalt destroy the city!"

This leader of clans had nothing of the conqueror about him. He understood that he was in no wise cut out to wear the purple; he himself felt the Barbarian's cureless inferiority. But he also felt that neither was he born to obey. If he asked for the title of Prefect of the City, and if he persisted in offering his services to the Empire, it was as a means to get the upper hand of it more surely. Repulsed, disdained by the Court, he tried to raise himself in his own eyes and in the eyes of the common people by giving himself the airs of an instrument of justice, a man designed by fate, who marches blindly to a terrible purpose indicated by the divine wrath. It often happened that he was duped by his own mummery. This turbid Barbarian soul was prone to the most superstitious terrors.

Notwithstanding his rodomontades, it is certain that in his heart he was scared by Rome. He hardly dared to attack it. In the first place, it was not at all a convenient operation for him. His army of mercenaries had no proper implements to undertake the siege of this huge city, of which the defence lines were thrown out in so wide a perimeter. He had to come back to it twice, before he could make up his mind to invest it seriously. The first time, in 408, he was satisfied with starving the Romans by cutting off the food supply. He had pitched his camp on the banks of the Tiber in such a way as to capture the shipping between the capital and the great store-houses built near the mouth of the river. From the ramparts, the Romans could see the Barbarian soldiers moving about, with their sheepskin coats dyed to a crude red. Panic-stricken, the aristocracy fled to its villas in Campania, or Sicily, or Africa. They took with them whatever they were able to carry. They sought refuge in the nearest islands, even in Sardinia and Corsica, despite their reputation for unhealthiness. They even hid among the rocks of the seashore. The terror was so great that the Senate agreed to everything demanded by Alaric. He was paid an enormous indemnity which he claimed as a condition of his withdrawal.

The following year he used the same method of intimidation to force on the people an emperor he had chosen, and to get conferred on him the title of Prefect of the City which he had desired so long. Finally, in the year 410, he struck the supreme blow.

The Barbarian knew what he was about, and that he did not risk much in blockading Rome. Famine would open the gates to him sooner or later. All who were able had left the city, especially the rich. There was no garrison to defend it. Only a lazy populace remained behind the walls, unused to arms, and still more enfeebled by long starvation. And yet this wretched and decimated population, in an outburst of patriotism, resisted with desperate energy. The siege was long. Doubtless it began before the spring; it ended only at the end of the summer. In the night of the twenty-fourth of August, 410, amid the glare of lightning and crashes of thunder, Alaric entered Rome by the Salarian gate. It is certain that he only managed it even then by treachery. The prey was handed to him.

The sack of Rome seems to have lasted for three days and three nights. Part of the town was burned. The conquered people underwent all the horrors which accompany such events—violent and stupid destruction, rapes, murders of individuals, wholesale slaughter, torture, and mutilation. But in reality the Barbarians only wanted the Roman gold. They acted like perfect highway robbers. If they tortured their victims without distinction of age or sex, it was to pluck the secret of their treasure-houses out of them. It is even said that in these conditions the Roman avarice produced some admirable examples of firmness. Some let themselves be tortured to their last gasp rather than reveal where their treasures were hid. At last, when Alaric decided that his army was gorged enough with spoil, he gave the order to evacuate the city, and took to the roads with his baggage-waggons full.

Let us be careful not to judge these doings after our modern notions. The capture of Rome by Alaric was not a national disaster. It was plundering on a huge scale. The Goth had no thought at all of destroying the Empire. He was only a mercenary in rebellion—an ambitious mercenary, no doubt—but, above all, a looter.

As a consequence of this attack on the Eternal City, one after another caught the disease of plunder, which contaminated even the functionaries and the subjects of Rome. Amid the general anarchy, where impunity seemed certain, nobody restrained himself any longer. In Africa especially, where the old instinct of piracy is always half-awake, they applied themselves to ransack the fugitive Romans and Italians. Many rich people were come there, seeking a place of safety in the belief that they would be more secure when they had put the sea between themselves and the Barbarians. The report of their riches had preceded them, exaggerated out of all measure by popular rumour. Among them were mentioned patricians such as the Anicii, whose property was so immense and their palaces so splendid that they could not find purchasers. These multi-millionaires in flight were a miraculous windfall for the country. They were bled without mercy.

Quicker than any one else, the military governor of Africa, Count Heraclianus, was on the spot to pick the pockets of the Italian immigrants. No sooner were they off the boat than he had very distinguished ladies seized, and only released them when he had extorted a large ransom. He sold those unable to pay to the Greek and Syrian slave-merchants who provided human flesh for the Oriental harems. When the example came from such a height, the subordinates doubtless said to themselves that they would be very wrong to have the least shame. From one end of the province to the other, everybody struggled to extract as much as possible from the unfortunate fugitives. Augustine's own parishioners at Hippo undertook to tear a donation from one of those gorgeous Anicii, whose lands stretched further than a kite could fly— from Pinian, the husband of St. Melania the younger. They wanted to force him to be ordained priest in spite of himself, which, as has been explained, involved the handing over of his goods to the Catholic community. Augustine, who opposed this, had to give in to the crowd. There was almost a riot in the basilica.

Such were the far-off reverberations of the capture of Rome by Alaric. Carthaginians and Numidians pillaged the Romans just like the Barbarians.

Now, how did it come about that this monstrous loot took on before the eyes of contemporaries the magnitude of a world-catastrophe? For really nothing was utterly lost. The Empire remained standing. After Alaric's retreat, the Romans had come back to their city and they worked to build up the ruins. Ere long, the populace were crying out loud that if the circus and amphitheatre games were given back to them, they would look upon the descent of the Goths as a bad dream.

It is no less certain that this sensational occurrence had struck the whole Mediterranean world into a perfect stupor. It seized upon the imaginations of all. The idea that Rome could not be taken, that it was integral and almost sacred, had such a hold on people's minds, that they refused to credit the sinister news. Nobody reflected that the sack of Rome by the Barbarians should have been long ago foreseen—that Rome, deprived of a garrison, abandoned by the Imperial army, was bound to attract the covetousness of the Goths, and that the pillage of a place without defence, already enfeebled by famine, was not a very glorious feat, very difficult, or very extraordinary. People only saw the brutal fact: the Eternal City had been captured and burned by the mercenaries. All were under the influence of the shock caused by the narratives of the refugees. In one of his sermons, Augustine has transmitted to us an echo of the general panic:

"Horrible things," said he, "have been told us. There have been ruins, and fires, and rapine, and murder, and torture. That is true; we have heard it many times; we have shuddered at all this disaster; we have often wept, and we have hardly been able to console ourselves."

This capture of Rome was plainly a terrible warning for the future. But party spirit strangely exaggerated the importance and meaning of the calamity. For pagans and Christians alike it became a subject for speeches, a commonplace of religious polemic. Both saw the event as a manifestation of the wrath of Heaven.

"While we sacrificed to our gods," the pagan said, "Rome was standing, Rome was happy. Now that our sacrifices are forbidden, you see what has become of Rome..."

And they went about repeating that Christianism was responsible for the ruin of the Empire. On their side, the Christians answered: In the first place, Rome has not fallen: it is always standing. It has been only chastised, and this happened because it is still half pagan. By this frightful punishment (and they heightened the description of the horrors committed), God has given it a warning. Let it be converted, let it return to the virtues of its ancestors, and it will become again the mistress of nations.

There is what Augustine and the bishops said. Still, the flock of the faithful were only half convinced. It was all well enough to remonstrate to them that the Christians of Rome, and even a good number of pagans, had been spared at the name of Christ, and that the Barbarian leader had bestowed a quite special protection and respect upon the basilicas of the holy apostles; it was impossible to prevent their thinking that many Christians had perished in the sack of the city, that consecrated virgins had experienced the last outrages, and that, as a matter of fact, all the inhabitants had been robbed of their property... Was it thus that God protected His chosen? What advantage was there in being Christian if they had the same treatment as the idolaters?

This state of mind became extremely favourable for paganism to come back again on the offensive. Since the very hard laws of Theodosius, which forbade the worship of the ancient gods, even within the house, the pagans had not overlooked any chance to protest against the Imperial severity. At Carthage there were always fights in the streets between pagans and Christians, not to say riots. In the colony of Suffetula, sixty Christians had been massacred. The year before the capture of Rome, there had been trouble with the pagans at Guelma. Houses belonging to the Church were burned, a monk killed in a brawl. Whenever the Government inspection relaxed, or the political situation appeared favourable, the pagans hurried to proclaim their belief. Only just lately, in Rome beleaguered by Alaric, the new consul, Tertullus, had thought fit to revive the old customs. Before assuming office, he studied gravely the sacred fowls in their cages, traced circles in the sky with the augur's wand, and marked the flight of birds. Besides, a pagan oracle circulated persistently among the people, promising that after a reign of three hundred and sixty-five years Christianity would be conquered. The centuries of the great desolation were fulfilled; the era of revenge was about to begin for the outcast gods.

These warlike symptoms did not escape Augustine's vigilance. His indignation no longer arose only from the fact that paganism was so slow in dying; he was now afraid that the feebleness of the Empire might allow it to take on an appearance of life. It must be ended, as Donatism had been ended. The old apostle was summoned to a new campaign, and in it he would spend the best of his strength to the eve of his death.

Chapter 2
THE CITY OF GOD

For thirteen or fourteen years, through a thousand employments and a thousand cares, amid the panics and continual alarums which kept the Africans on the alert in those times, Augustine worked at his *City of God*, the most formidable machine of war ever directed against paganism, and also the arsenal fullest of proofs and refutations which the disputants and defenders of Catholicism have ever had at their disposal.

It is not for us to examine the details of this immense work, for our sole aim is to study Augustine's soul, and we quote scarcely anything from his books save those parts wherein a little of this ardent soul pulsates—those which are still living for us of the twentieth century, which contain teachings and ways of feeling still likely to move us. Now, Augustine's attitude towards paganism is one of those which throw the greatest light on his nature and character. And it may even yet come to be our own attitude when we find opposed to us a conception of life and the world which may indeed be ruined for a time, but is reborn as soon as the sense of spirituality disappears or grows feeble.

> "Immortal Paganism, art thou dead? So they say.
> But Pan scoffs under his breath, and the Chimæra
>   laughs."
>
> — Sainte-Beuve.

Like ourselves, Augustine, brought up by a Christian mother, knew it only through literature, and, so to speak, æsthetically. Recollections of school, the emotions and admirations of a cultivated man—there is what the old religion meant for him. Nevertheless, he had one great advantage over us for knowing it well: the sight of the pagan customs and superstitions was still under his eyes.

That the lascivious, romantic, and poetic adventures of the ancient gods, their statues, their temples, and all the arts arising from their religion, had beguiled him and filled him with enthusiasm before his conversion, is only too certain. But all this mythology and plastic art were looked upon as secondary things then, even by pagans. The serious, the essential part of the religion was not in that. Paganism, a religion of Beauty, is an invention of our modern æsthetes; it was hardly thought of in that way in Augustine's time.

Long before this, the Roman Varro, the great compiler of the religious antiquities of paganism, made a threefold distinction of the doctrine concerning the gods. The first—that of the theatre, as he calls it, or fabulous mythology, adapted to poets, dramatists, sculptors, and jesters. Invented by these, it is only a fantasy, a play of imagination, an ornament of life. The third is civil theology, serious and solid, which claims the respect and piety of all. "It is that which men in cities, and chiefly the priests, *ought to be* cunning in. It teaches which gods to worship in public, and with what ceremonies and sacrifices each one must be served." Finally, the second, physical or metaphysical theology, is reserved for philosophers and exceptional minds; it is altogether theoretical. The only important and truly religious one, which puts an obligation on the believer, is the third—the civil theology.

Now, we never take account of this. What we persist in regarding as paganism is what Varro himself called "a religion for the theatre"—matter of opera, pretext for ballets, for scenery, and for dance postures. Transposed into another key by our poets, this mythology is inflated now and then by mysticism, or by a vague symbolism. Playthings of our pretty wits! The living paganism, which Augustine struggled against, which crowds defended at the price of their blood, in which the poor believed and the wisest statesmen deemed indispensable as a safeguard of cities—that paganism is quite another matter. Like all religions which are possible, it implied and it *enforced* not only beliefs, but ritual, sacrifices, festivals. And this is what Augustine, with the other

Christians of that time, spurned with disgust and declared to be unbearable.

He saw, or he had seen with his own eyes, the reality of the pagan worship, and the most repellent of all to our modern delicacy—the sacrifices. At the period when he wrote *The City of God*, private sacrifices, as well as public, were forbidden. This did not prevent the devout from breaking the law whenever a chance offered. They hid themselves more or less when they sacrificed before a temple, a chapel, or on some private estate. The rites could not be carried out according to all the minute instructions of the pontifical books. It was no more than a shadow of the ceremonies of former times. But in his childhood, in the reign of Julian, for instance, Augustine could have attended sacrifices which were celebrated with full pomp and according to all the ritual forms. They were veritable scenes of butchery. For Heaven's sake let us forget the frieze of the Parthenon, and its sacrificers with their graceful lines! If we want to have a literal translation of this sculpture, and find the modern representation of a hecatomb, we must go to the slaughter-houses at La Villette.

Among the heaps of broken flesh, the puddles of blood, the mystic Julian was attacked by a kind of drunkenness. There were never enough beasts strangled or slaughtered to suit him. Nothing satisfied his fury for sacred carnage. The pagans themselves made fun of this craze for sacrificing. During the three years his reign lasted the altars streamed with blood. Oxen by hundreds were slain upon the floors of the temples, and the butchers throttled so many sheep and other domestic animals that they gave up keeping count of them. Thousands of white birds, pigeons or sea-gulls, were destroyed day by day by the piety of the prince. He was called the *Victimarius*, and when he started upon his campaign against the Persians, an epigram was circulated once more which had been formerly composed against Marcus Aurelius (the philosophic emperor!) who was equally generous of hecatombs: "To Marcus Cæsar from the white oxen. It will be all over with us if you come back a conqueror." People said that Julian, on his return, would depopulate stables and pasture-lands.

The populace, who gathered their very considerable profit from these butcheries, naturally encouraged such an excess of devotion. At Rome, under Caligula, more than a hundred and sixty thousand victims were immolated in three months—nearly two thousand a day. And these massacres took place upon the approaches of the temples; in the middle of the city; on the forums; in narrow squares crowded with public buildings and statues. Just try to call up the scene in summer, between walls at a white heat, with the smells and the flies. Spectators and victims rubbed against one another, pressed close in the restricted space. One day, Caligula, while he was attending a sacrifice, was splashed all over by the blood of a flamingo as they cut its neck. But the august Cæsar was not so fastidious; he himself operated in these ceremonies armed with a mallet and clad in the short shirt of the killers. The ignominy of all this revolted the Christians, and whoever had nerves at all sensitive. The bloody mud in which passers slipped, the hissing of the fat, the heavy odour of flesh, were sickening. Tertullian held his nose before the "stinking fires" on which the victims were roasting. And St. Ambrose complained that in the Roman Curia the senators who were Christians were obliged to breathe in the smoke and receive full in the face the ashes of the altar raised before the statue of Victory.

The manipulations of the *haruspicina* seemed an even worse abomination in the eyes of the Christians. Dissection of bowels, examination of entrails, were practices very much in fashion in all classes of society. The pagans generally took more or less interest in magic. One was scarcely a philosopher without being a miracle-worker. In this there was a kind of perfidious rivalry to the Christian miracles. The ambitious or the discontented opened the bellies of animals to learn when the Emperor was going to die, and who would succeed him. But although it did not pretend to magic, the *haruspicina* made an essential part of the sacrifices. As soon as the dismemberment was done, the diviners examined the appearance of the entrails. Consulting together, they turned them over frequently with anxious attention. This business might continue for a long time. Plutarch relates that Philip, King of Macedonia, when sacrificing an ox on the Ithomæa, with Aratus of Sicyon and Demetrius of Pharos, wished to inquire out from the entrails of the victim concerning the wisdom of a piece of strategy. The *haruspex* put the smoking mass in his hands. The King shewed it to his companions, who derived contradictory presages from it. He listened to one side and the other, holding meanwhile the ox's entrails in his hands. Eventually, he decided for the opinion of Aratus, and then tranquilly gave the handful back to the sacrificer...

No doubt in Augustine's time these rites were no longer practised openly. For all that, they were of the first importance in the ancient religion, which desired nothing better than to restore them. It is easy to understand the repulsion they caused in the author of *The City of God*. He who would not have a fly killed to make sure of the gold crown in the contest of poets, looked with horror on these sacred butchers, and manglers, and cooks. He flung the garbage of the sacrifices into the sewer, and shewed proudly to the pagans the pure oblation of the eucharistic Bread and Wine.

But what, above all, he attacked, because it was a present and permanent scandal, was the gluttony, the drunkenness, and lust of the pagans. Let us not exaggerate these vices—not the two first, at least. Augustine could not judge them as we can. It is certain that the Africans of his time —and for that matter, those of to-day—would have struck us modern people as very sober. The outbursts of intemperance which he accuses them of only happened at intervals, at times of public festivity or some family celebration. But as soon as they did begin they were terrible. When one thinks of the orgies of our Arabs behind locked doors!

But it is no less true that the pagan vices spread themselves out cynically under the protecting shadow of religion. Popular souses of eating and drinking were the obligatory accompaniments of the festivals and sacrifices. A religious festival meant a carouse, loads of victuals, barrels of wine broached in the street. These were called the Dishes, *Fercula*, or else, the Rejoicing, *Lætitia*. The poor people, who knew meat only by sight, ate it on these days, and they drank wine. The effect of this unaccustomed plenty was felt at once. The whole populace were drunk. The rich in their houses possibly did it with more ceremony, but it was really the same brutishness. The elegant Ovid, who in the *Art of Love* teaches fine manners to the beginners in love, advises them not to vomit at table, and to avoid getting drunk like the husbands of their mistresses.

Plainly, religion was only an excuse for these excesses. Augustine goes too far when he makes the gods responsible for this riot of sensuality. What is true is that they did nothing to hinder it. And it is also true that the lechery, which he flings so acridly in the face of the pagans, the gross stage-plays, the songs, dances, and even prostitution, were all more or less included in the essence of paganism. The theatre, like the games of the arena and circus, was a divine institution. At certain feasts, and in certain temples, fornication became sacred. All the world knew what took place at Carthage in the courts and under the porticoes of the Celestial Virgin, and what the ears of the most chaste matrons were obliged to hear, and also what the use was of the castrated priests of the Great Mother of the gods. Augustine, who declaims against these filthy sports, has not forced the note of his denunciation to make out a good case. If anybody wants to know in more detail the sights enjoyed at the theatre, or what were the habits of certain pious confraternities, he has only to read what is told by Apuleius, the most devout of pagans. He takes evident pleasure in these stories, or, if he sometimes waxes indignant, it is the depravity of men he accuses. The gods soar at a great height above these wretched trifles. To Augustine, on the contrary, the gods are unclean devils who fill their bellies with lust and obscenities, as if they were hankering for the blood and grease of sacrifices.

And so he puts his finger on the open wound of paganism—its basic immorality, or, if you like, its unmorality. Like our scientism of to-day, it was unable to lay down a system of morals. It did not even try to. What Augustine has written on this subject in *The City of God*, is perhaps the strongest argument ever objected to polytheism. Anyhow, pages like this are very timely indeed to consider:

"But such friends and such worshippers of those gods, whom they rejoice to follow and imitate in all villainies and mischiefs—do they trouble themselves about the corruption and great decay of the Republic? Not so. Let it but stand, say they; let it but prosper by the number of its troops and be glorious by its victories; or, *which is best of all, let it but enjoy security and peace*, and what care we? Yes, what we care for above all is that every one may have the means to increase his wealth, to pay the expenses of his usual luxury, and that the powerful may still keep under the weak. Let the poor crouch to the rich to be fed, or to live at ease under their protection; let the rich abuse the poor as things at their service, and to shew how many they have soliciting them. Let the people applaud such as provide them with pleasures, not such as have a care for their interests. *Let naught that is hard be enjoined, nothing impure be prohibited...* Let not subdued provinces obey their governors as supervisors of their morality, but as masters of their fortune and the procurers of their pleasures. What matters it if this submission has no sincerity, but rests upon a bad and servile fear! *Let the law protect estates rather than fair justice.* Let there be a good number of public harlots, either for all that please to enjoy themselves in their company, or for those that cannot keep private ones. Let stately and sumptuous houses be erected, so that night and day each one according to his liking or his means may gamble and drink and revel and vomit. Let the rhythmed tinkling of dances be ordinary, the cries, the uncontrolled delights, the uproar of all pleasures, even the bloodiest and most shameful in the theatres. He who shall assay to dissuade from these pleasures, let him be condemned as a public enemy. And if any one try to alter or suppress them—let the people stifle his voice, let them banish him, let them kill him. On the other hand, those that shall procure the people these pleasures, and authorize their enjoyment, let them be eternized for the true gods."...

However, Augustine acknowledges a number of praiseworthy minds among pagans—those philosophers, with Plato in the first rank, who have done their best to put morality into the religion. The Christian teacher renders a magnificent tribute to Platonism. But these high doctrines have scarcely got beyond the portals of the schools, and this moral teaching which paganism vaunts of, is practically limited to the sanctuaries. "Let them not talk," says he, "of some closely muttered instructions, taught in secret, and whispered in the ear of a few adepts, which hold I know not what lessons of uprightness and virtue. But let them shew the temples ordained for such pious meetings, wherein were no sports with lascivious gestures and loose songs... Let them shew us the places where the gods' doctrine was heard against covetousness, the suppression of ambition, the bridling of luxury, and where wretches might learn what the poet Persius thunders unto them, saying:

'Learn, wretches, and conceive the course of things,
What man is, and why nature forth him brings;...
How to use money; how to help a friend;
What we on earth, and God in us, intend.'

Let them shew where their instructing gods were used to give such lessons; and where their worshippers used to go *often* to hear these matters. As for us, we can point to our churches, built for this sole purpose, wheresoever the religion of Christ is diffused."

Can it surprise, then, if men so ignorant of high morality, and so deeply embedded in matter, were also plunged in the grossest superstitions? Materialism in morals always ends by producing a low credulity. Here Augustine triumphs. He sends marching under our eyes, in a burlesque array, the innumerable army of gods whom the Romans believed in. There are so many that he compares them to swarms of gnats. Although he explains that he is not able to mention them all, he amuses himself by stupefying us with the prodigious number of those he discovers. Dragged into open day by him, a whole divine population is brought out of the darkness and forgetfulness where it had been sleeping perhaps for centuries: the little gods who work in the fields, who make the corn grow and keep off the blight, those who watch over children, who aid women in labour, who protect the hearth, who guard the house. It was impossible to take a step among the pagans, to make a movement, without the help of a god or goddess. Men and things were as if fettered and imprisoned by the gods.

"In a house," says Augustine scoffingly, "there is but one porter. He is but a mere man, yet he is sufficient for that office. But it takes three gods, Forculus for the door, Cardea for the hinge, Limentinus for the threshold. Doubtless, Forculus all alone could not possibly look after threshold, door and hinges." And if it is a case of a man and woman retiring to the bridal chamber after the wedding, a whole squadron of divinities are set in motion for an act so simple and natural. "I beseech you," cries Augustine, "leave something for the husband to do!"

This African, who had such a strong sense of the unity and fathomless infinity of God, waxed indignant at this sacrilegious parcelling of the divine substance. But the pagans, following Varro, would answer that it was necessary to distinguish, among all these gods, those who were just the imagination of poets, and those who were real beings—between the gods of fable and the gods of religion. "Then," as Tertullian had said already, "if the gods be chosen as onions are roped, it is obvious that what is not chosen is condemned." "Tertullian carries his fancy too far," comments Augustine. The gods refused as fabulous are not held reprobate on that account. The truth is, they are a cut of the same piece as the admitted gods. "Have not the pontiffs, like the poets, a bearded Jupiter and a Mercury without beard?... Are the old Saturn and the young Apollo so much the property of the poets that we do not see their statues too in the temples?..."

And the philosophers, in their turn, however much they may protest against the heap of fabulous gods and, like Plato and Porphyry, declare that there exists but one God, soul of the universe, yet they no less accepted the minor gods, and intermediaries or messengers betwixt gods and men, whom they called demons. These hybrid beings, who pertained to humanity by their passions, and to the divinity by the privilege of immortality, had to be appeased by sacrifices, questioned and gratified by magic spells. And there is what the highest pagan wisdom ended in—yes, in calling up spirits, and the shady operations of wizards and wonder-smiths. That is what the pagans defended, and demanded the continuation of with so much obstinacy and fanaticism.

By no means, replied Augustine. It does not deserve to survive. It is not the forsaking of these beliefs and superstitious practices which has brought about the decay of the Empire. If you are asking for the temples of your gods to be opened, it is because they are easy to your passions. At heart, you scoff at them and the Empire; all you want is freedom and impunity for your vices. There we have the real cause of the decadence! Little matter the idle grimaces before altars and statues. Become chaste, sober, brave, and poor, as your ancestors were. Have children, agree to compulsory military service, and you will conquer as they did. Now, all these virtues are enjoined and encouraged by Christianity. Whatever certain heretics may say, the religion of Christ is not contrary to marriage or the soldier's profession. The Patriarchs of the old law were blest in marriage, and there are just and holy wars.

And even supposing, that in spite of all efforts to save it, the Empire is condemned, must we therefore despair? We should be prepared for the end of the Roman city. Like all the things of this world, it is liable to old age and death. It will die then, one day. Far from being cast down, let us strengthen ourselves against this disaster by the realization of the eternal. Let us strengthen our hold upon that which passes not. Above the earthly city, rises the City of God, which is the communion of holy souls, the only one which gives complete and never-failing joy. Let us try to be the citizens of that city, and to live the only life worth calling life. For the life here below is but the shadow of a shadow...

The people of those times were wonderfully prepared to hearken to such exhortations. On the eve of the Barbarian invasions, these Christians, for whom the dogma of the Resurrection was perhaps the chief reason of their faith, these people, sick at heart, who looked on in torture at the ending of a world, must have considered this present life as a bad dream, from which there should be no delay in escaping.

At the very moment even that Augustine began to write *The City of God*, his friend Evodius, Bishop of Uzalis, told him this story.

He had as secretary a very young man, the son of a priest in the neighbourhood. This young man had begun by obtaining a post as stenographer in the office of the Proconsul of Africa. Evodius, who was alarmed at what might happen to his virtue in such surroundings, having first made certain of his absolute chastity, offered to take him into his service. In the bishop's house, where he had scarcely anything to do but read the Holy Scripture, his faith became so enthusiastic that he longed for nothing now but death. To go out of this life, "to be with Christ," was his eager wish. It was heard. After sixteen days of illness he died in the house of his parents.

"Now, two days after his funeral, a virtuous woman of Figes, a servant of God, a widow for twelve years, had a dream, and in her dream she saw a deacon who had been dead some four years, together with men, and women too, virgins and widows—she saw these servants of God getting ready a palace. This dwelling was so rich that it shone with light, and you would have believed it was all made of silver. And when the widow asked whom these preparations were for, the deacon replied that they were for a young man, dead the evening before, the son of a priest. In the same palace, she saw an old man, all robed in white, and he told two other persons, also robed in white, to go to the tomb of this young man, and lift out the body, and carry it to Heaven. When the body had been drawn from the tomb and carried to Heaven, there arose (said she) out of the tomb a bush of virgin-roses, which are thus named because they never open…"

So the son of the priest had chosen the better part. What was the good of remaining in this abominable world, where there was always a risk of being burned or murdered by Goths and Vandals, when, in the other world, angels were preparing for you palaces of light?

Chapter 3
THE BARBARIAN DESOLATION

Augustine was seventy-two years old when he finished the *City of God*. This was in 426. That year, an event of much importance occurred at Hippo, and the report of it was inserted in the public acts of the community.

"The sixth of the calends of October," *The Acts* set forth, "the very glorious Theodosius being consul for the twelfth time, and Valentinian Augustus for the second, Augustine the bishop, accompanied by Religianus and Martinianus, his fellow-bishops, having taken his place in the Basilica of Peace at Hippo, and the priests Saturnius, Leporius, Barnaby, Fortunatianus, Lazarus, and Heraclius, being present, with all the clergy and a vast crowd of people—Augustine the bishop said:

"'Let us without delay look to the business which I declared yesterday to your charity, and for which I desired you to gather here in large numbers, as I see you have done. If I were to talk to you of anything else, you might be less attentive, seeing the expectation you are in.

"'My brothers, we are all mortal in this life, and no man knows his last day. God willed that I should come to dwell in this town in the force of my age. But, as I was a young man then—see, I am old now, and as I know that at the death of bishops, peace is troubled by rivalry or ambition (this have I often seen and bewailed it)—I ought, so far as it rests with me, to turn away so great a mischief from your city... I am going then to tell you that my will, which I believe also to be the will of God, is that I have as successor the priest Heraclius.'

"At these words all the people cried out:

"'Thanks be to God! Praise be to Christ!'

"And this cry they repeated three-and-twenty times.

"'Christ, hear us! Preserve us Augustine!'

"This cry they repeated sixteen times.

"'Be our father! Be our bishop!'

"This cry they repeated eight times.

"When the people became silent, the bishop Augustine spoke again in these words:

"'There is no need for me to praise Heraclius. As much as I do justice to his wisdom, in equal measure should I spare his modesty... As you perceive, the secretaries of the church gather up what we say and what you say. My words and your shouts do not fall to the ground. To put it briefly, these are ecclesiastical decrees that we are now drawing up, and I desire by these means, as far as it is in the power of man, to confirm what I have declared to you.'

"Here the people cried out:

"'Thanks be to God! Praise be to Christ!'

"'Be our father, and let Heraclius be our bishop!'

"When silence was made again, Augustine the bishop thus spoke:

"'I understand what you would say. But I do not wish that it happen to him as it happened to me. Many of you know what was done at that time... I was consecrated bishop during the lifetime of my father and bishop, the aged Valerius, of blessed memory, and with him I shared the see. I was ignorant, as he was, that this was forbidden by the Council of Nice. I would not therefore that men should blame in Heraclius, my son, what they blamed in me.'

"With that the people cried out thirteen times:

"'Thanks be to God! Praise be to Christ!'

"After a little silence, Augustine the bishop said again:

"'So he will remain a priest till it shall please God for him to be a bishop. But with the aid and mercy of Christ, I shall do in future what up to now I have not been able to do... You will remember what I wanted to do some years ago, and you have not allowed me. For a work upon the Holy Scriptures, with which my brothers and my fathers the bishops had deigned to charge me in the two Councils of Numidia and Carthage, *I was not to be disturbed by anybody during five days of the week*. That was a thing agreed upon between you and me. The act was drawn up, and you all approved of it after hearing it read. But your promise did not last long. I was soon encroached upon and overrun by you all. I am no longer free to study as I desire. Morning and afternoon, I am entangled in your worldly affairs. I beg of you and supplicate you in Christ's name to suffer me to shift the burthen of all these cares upon this young man, the priest Heraclius, whom I signal, in His name, as my successor in the bishopric.'

"Upon this the people cried out six-and-twenty times:

"'We thank thee for thy choice!'

"And the people having become silent, Augustine the bishop said:

"'I thank you for your charity and goodwill, or rather, I thank God for them. So, my brothers, you will address yourselves to Heraclius upon all the points you are used to submit to me. Whenever he needs counsel, my care and my help will not be wanting... In this way, without any loss to you, I shall be able to devote the remainder of life which it may please God still to leave me, not to laziness and rest, but to the study of the Holy Scriptures. This work will be useful to Heraclius, and hence to yourselves. Let nobody then envy my leisure, for this leisure will be very busy...

"'It only remains for me to ask you, at least those who can, to sign these acts. Your agreement I cannot do without; so kindly let me learn it by your voices.'

"At these words the people shouted:

"'Let it be so! Let it be so!'

~

"When all there became silent, Augustine the bishop made an end, saying:

"'It is well. Now let us fulfil our duty to God. While we offer Him the Sacrifice, and during this hour of supplication, I would urge of your charity to lay aside all business and personal cares, and to pray the Lord God for this church, for me, and for the priest Heraclius.'"

The dryness and official wording of the document do not succeed in stifling the vividness and colour of this crowded scene. Through the piety of the formal cries, it is easy to see that Augustine's hearers were hard to manage. This flock, which he loved and scolded so much, was no easier to lead now than when he first became bishop. Truly it was no sinecure to rule and administer the diocese of Hippo! The bishop was literally the servant of the faithful. Not only had he to feed and clothe them, to spend his time over their business and quarrels and lawsuits, but he belonged to them body and soul. They kept a jealous eye on the employment of his time; if he went away, they asked for an explanation. Whenever Augustine went to preach at Carthage or Utica, he apologized to his own people. And before he can undertake a commentary on the Scriptures, a commentary, moreover, which he has been asked by two Councils to prepare, he must get their permission, or, at any rate, their agreement.

At last, at seventy-two years old, after he had been a bishop for thirty-one years, he got their leave to take a little rest. But what a rest! He himself said: "This leisure will be very busy"—this leisure which is going to fill the five holidays in the week. He intends to study and fathom the Scripture, and this, besides, to the profit of his people and clergy and the whole Church. It is the fondest dream of his life—the plan he was never able to realize. All that, at first sight, astonishes us. We ask ourselves, "What else had he been doing up to this time in his treatises and letters and sermons, in all that sea of words and writings which his enemies threw up at him, if he was not studying and explaining the Holy Scriptures?" The fact is, that in most of these writings and sermons he elucidates the truth only in part, or else he is confuting heresiarchs. What he wanted to do was to study the truth for its own sake, without having to think of and be hindered by the exposure of errors; and above all, to seize it in all its breadth and all its depths, to have done with this blighting and irritating eristic, and to reflect in a vast *Mirror* the whole and purest light of the sacred dogmas.

He never found the time for it. He had to limit himself to a handbook of practical morals, published under this title before his death, and now lost. Once more the heresiarchs prevented him from leading a life of speculation. During his last years, amid the cruellest anxieties, he had to battle with the enemies of Grace and the enemies of the Trinity, with Arius and Pelagius. Pelagius had found an able disciple in a young

Italian bishop, Julian of Eclanum, who was a formidable opponent to the aged Augustine. As for Arianism, which had seemed extinguished in the West, here it was given a new life by the Barbarian invasion.

It was a grave moment for Catholicism, as it was for the Empire. The Goths, the Alani, and the Vandals, after having laid waste Gaul and Spain, were taking measures to pass over into Africa. Should they renew the attempts of Alaric and Radagaisus against Italy, they would soon be masters of the entire Occident. Now these Barbarians were Arians. Supposing (and it seemed more and more likely) that Africa and Italy were vanquished after Gaul and Spain, then it was all over with Western Catholicism. For the invaders carried their religion in their baggage, and forced it on the conquered. Augustine, who had cherished the hope of equalling the earthly kingdom of Christ to that of the Cæsars, was going to see the ruin of both. His terrified imagination exaggerated still more the only too real and threatening peril. He must have lived hours of agony, expecting a disaster.

If only the truth might be saved, might swim in this sea of errors which spread like a flood in the wake of the Barbarian onflow! It was from this wish, no doubt, that sprang the tireless persistence which the old bishop put into a last battle with heresy. If he selected Pelagius specially to fall upon with fury, if he forced his principles to their last consequences in his theory of Grace, the dread of the Barbarian peril had perhaps something to do with it. This soul, so mild, so moderate, so tenderly human, promulgated a pitiless doctrine which does not agree with his character. But he reasoned, no doubt, that it was impossible to drive home too hard the need of the Redemption and the divinity of the Redeemer in front of these Arians, these Pelagians, these enemies of Christ, who to-morrow perhaps would be masters of the Empire.

Therefore, Augustine continued to write, and discuss, and disprove. There came a time when he had to think of fighting otherwise than with the pen. His life, the lives of his flock, were threatened. He had to see to the bodily defence of his country and city. The fact was, that some time before the great drive of the Vandals, forerunners of them, in the shape of hordes of African Barbarians, had begun to lay waste the provinces. The Circoncelliones were not dead, nor their good friends the Donatists either. These sectaries, encouraged by the widespread anarchy, came out of their hiding-places and shewed themselves more insolent and aggressive than ever. Possibly they hoped for some effective support against the Roman Church from the Arian Vandals who were drawing near, or at least a recognition of what they believed to be their rights. Day after day, bands of Barbarians were landing from Spain. In the rear of these wandering troops of brigands or irregular soldiers, the old enemies of the Roman peace and civilization, the Nomads of the South, the Moors of the Atlas, the Kabylian mountaineers, flung themselves upon country and town, pillaging, killing, and burning everything that got in their way. All was laid desolate. "Countries but lately prosperous and populated have been changed into solitudes," said Augustine.

At last, in the spring of the year 429, the Vandals and the Alani, having joined forces on the Spanish coast under their King, Genseric, crossed the Straits of Gibraltar. It was devastation on a large scale this time. An army of eighty thousand men set themselves methodically to plunder the African provinces. Cherchell, which had already been sorely tried during the revolt of Firmus the Moor, was captured again and burned. All the towns and fortified places on the coast fell, one after another. Constantine alone, from the height of its rock, kept the invaders at bay. To starve out those who fled from towns and farms and took refuge in the fastnesses of the Atlas, the Barbarians destroyed the harvest, burned the grain-houses, and cut down the vines and fruit trees. And they set fire to the forests which covered the slopes of the mountains, to force the refugees out of their hiding-places.

This stupid ravaging was against the interest of the Vandals themselves, because they were injuring the natural riches of Africa, the report of which had brought them there. Africa was for them the land of plenty, where people could drink more wine than they wanted and eat wheaten bread. It was the country where life was comfortable, easy, and happy. It was the granary of the Mediterranean, the great supply-store of Rome. But their senseless craving for gold led them to ruin provinces, in which, nevertheless, they counted upon settling. They behaved in Africa as they had behaved in Rome under Alaric. By way of tearing gold out of the inhabitants, they tortured them as they had tortured the wealthy Romans. They invented worse ones. Children, before their parents' eyes, were sliced in two like animals in a slaughterhouse. Or else their skulls were smashed against the pavements and walls of houses.

The Church was believed to be very rich; and perhaps, as it had managed to comprise in its domains the greatest part of the landed estates, it was upon it chiefly that the Barbarians flung themselves. The priests and bishops were tortured with unheard-of improvements of cruelty. They were dragged in the rear of the army like slaves, so that heavy ransoms might be extracted from the faithful in exchange for their pastors. They were obliged to carry the baggage like the camels and mules, and when they gave out the Barbarians prodded them with lances. Many sank down beside the road and never rose more. But it is certain that fanaticism added to the covetousness and ferocity of the Vandals. These Arians bore a special grudge against Catholicism, which was, besides, in their eyes, the religion of the Roman domination. This is why they made their chief attacks on basilicas, convents, hospitals, and all the property of the Church. And throughout the country public worship was stopped.

In Hippo, these atrocities were known before the Barbarians arrived. The people must have awaited them and prepared to receive them with gloomy resignation. Africa had not been tranquil for a century. After the risings of Firmus and Gildo, came the lootings of the southern Nomads and the Berber mountaineers. And it was not so long since the Circoncelliones were keeping people constantly on the alert. But this time everybody felt that the great ruin was at hand. They were stunned by the news that some town or fortified place had been captured by the Vandals, or that some farm or villa in the neighbourhood was on fire.

Amid the general dismay, Augustine did his best to keep calm. He, indeed, saw beyond the material destruction, and at every new rumour of massacre or burning he would repeat to his clerics and people the words of the Wise Man:

"Doth the firm of heart grieve to see fall the stones and beams, and death seize the children of men?"

They accused him of being callous. They did not understand him. While all about him mourned the present misfortunes, he was already lamenting over the evil to come, and this clear-sightedness pained him more than the shock of the daily horrors committed by the Barbarians. His disciple Possidius, the Bishop of Guelma, who was with him in these sad days, naively applied to him the saying out of *Ecclesiastes*: "In much wisdom is much grief." Augustine did really suffer more than others, because he thought more profoundly on the disaster. He foresaw that Africa was going to be lost to the Empire, and consequently to the Church. They were bound together in his mind. What was there to do against brutal strength? All the eloquence and all the charity in the world would be as nothing against that unchained elemental mass of Vandals. It was as impossible to convert the Barbarians as it had been to convert the Donatists. Force was the only resource against force.

Then in despair the man of God turned once more to Cæsar. The monk appealed to the soldier. He charged Boniface, Count of Africa, to save Rome and the Church.

This Boniface, a rather ambiguous personage, was a fine type of the swashbuckler and official of the Lower-Empire. Thracian by origin, he joined the trickery of the Oriental to all the vices of the Barbarian. He was strong, clever in all bodily exercises like the soldiers of those days, overflowing with vigour and health, and even brave at times. In addition, he was fond of wine and women, and ate and drank like a true pagan. He was married twice, and after his second marriage he kept in the sight and knowledge of everybody a harem of concubines. He was sent, first of all, to Africa as a Tribune—that is to say, as Commissioner of the Imperial Government, probably to carry out the decrees of Honorius against the Donatists; and ere long he was made commander of the military forces of the province, with the title of Count.

In reality, while seeming to protect the country, he set himself to plunder it, as the tradition was among the Roman officials. His *officium*, still more grasping than himself, persuaded him to deeds which the Bishop of Hippo, who was, however, anxious to remain on the right side of him, protested against by hints. Boniface was obliged to overlook much robbery and pillage on the part of his subordinates so as to keep them faithful. Moreover, he himself stole. He was bound to close his eyes to the depredations of others, that his own might be winked at. Once become the accomplice of this band of robbers, he had no longer the authority to control them.

How did Augustine ever believe in the goodwill and good faith of this adventurer full of coarse passions, so far as to put his final hopes in him? Augustine knew men very well; he could detect low and hypocritical natures at a distance. How came it that he was taken in by Boniface?

Well, Augustine wanted his support, first of all, when he came as Imperial Commissioner to Carthage to bring the Donatists into line. Generally, we see only the good points of people who do us good turns. Besides, in order to propitiate the bishop, and the devout Court at Ravenna, the Tribune advertised his great zeal in favour of Catholicism. His first wife, a very pious woman whom he seems to have loved much, encouraged him in this. When she died, he was so overcome by despair that he took refuge in the extremest practices of religion—and in this, perhaps, he was quite sincere. It is also possible that he was becoming discredited at Ravenna, where they must have known about his oppressions and suspected his ambitious intrigues. Anyhow, whether he was really disgusted with the world, or whether he deemed it prudent to throw a little oblivion over himself just then, he spoke on all hands of resigning his post and living in retreat like a monk. It was just at this moment that Augustine and Alypius begged him not to desert the African army.

They met the Commander-in-Chief at Thubunæ, in Southern Numidia, where, no doubt, he was reducing the Nomads. We must remark once more Augustine's energy in travelling, to the very eve of his death. It was a long and dangerous road from Hippo to Thubunæ. Before making up his mind to so much fatigue, the old bishop must have judged the situation to be very serious. At Thubunæ, was Boniface playing a game, or was he, indeed, so crushed by his grief that the world had become unbearable and he pondered genuine thoughts of changing his way of life? What is sure is, that he gave the two prelates the most edifying talk. When they heard the Count of Africa speaking with unction of the cloister and of his desire to retire there, they were a little astonished at so much piety in a soldier. Besides, these excellent resolutions were most inconvenient for their plans. They remonstrated with him that it was quite possible to save one's soul in the army, and quoted the example of David, the warrior king. They ended by telling him all the expectations they founded upon his resource and firmness. They begged him to protect the churches and convents against fresh attacks of the Donatists, and especially against the Barbarians of Africa. These were at this moment breaking down all the old defence lines and laying waste the territories of the Empire.

Boniface allowed himself to be easily convinced—promised whatever he was asked. But he never budged. From now on, his conduct becomes most singular. He is in command of all the military strength of the province, and he takes no steps to suppress the African looters. It would seem as if he only thought of filling the coffers of himself and his friends. The country was so systematically scoured by them that, as Augustine said, there was nothing more left to take.

This inactivity lent colour to the rumours of treason. Nor is it impossible that he had cherished a plan from the beginning of his command to cut out an independent principality for himself in Africa. Was this the reason that he dealt softly with the native tribes, so as to make certain of their help in case of a conflict with the Imperial army? However that may be, his behaviour was not frank. Some years later, he landed on the Spanish coast to war against the Vandals under the command of the Prefect Castinus, and there he married a Barbarian princess who was by religion an Arian. It is true that the new Countess of Africa became a convert to Catholicism. But her first child was baptized by Arian priests, who rebaptized, at the same time, the Catholic slaves of Boniface's household. This marriage with a Vandal, these concessions to Arianism, gave immense scandal to the orthodox. Rumours of treason began to float about again.

No doubt Boniface took great advantage of his fidelity to the Empress Placidia. But he was standing between the all-powerful Barbarians and the undermined Empire. He wanted to remain on good terms with both, and then, when the hour came, to go over to the stronger. This double-faced diplomacy caused his downfall. His rival Aëtius accused him of high treason before Placidia. The Court of Ravenna declared him an enemy of the Empire, and an army was sent against him. Boniface did not hesitate; he went into open rebellion against Rome.

Augustine was thunderstruck by his desertion. But what way was there to make this violent man listen to reason, who had at least the appearances of right on his side, since there was a chance they had slandered him to the Empress, and who thought it quite natural to take vengeance on his enemies? His recent successes had still more intoxicated him. He had just defeated the two generals who had been sent to reduce him, and he was accordingly master of the situation in Africa. What was he going to do? The worst resolutions were to be feared from this conqueror, all smarting, and hungry for revenge... Nevertheless, Augustine resolved to write to him. His letter is a masterpiece of tact, of prudence, and also of Christian and episcopal firmness.

It would have been dangerous to declare to this triumphant rebel: "You are in the wrong. Your duty is to submit to the Emperor, your master." Boniface was quite capable of answering: "What are you interfering for? Politics are no business of yours. Look after your Church!" This is why Augustine very cleverly speaks to him from beginning to end of his letter simply as a bishop, eager for the salvation of a very dear son in Jesus Christ. And so, by keeping strictly to his office of spiritual director, he gained his end more surely and entirely; and, as a doctor of souls, he ventured to remind Boniface of certain truths which he would never have dared to mention as counsellor.

According to Augustine, the disgrace of the Count, and the evils which this event had brought on Africa, came principally from his attachment to worldly benefits. It was the ambition and covetousness of himself and his followers which had done all the harm. Let him free himself from perishable things, let him prevent the thefts and plundering of those under him. Let him, who some time ago wished to live in perfect celibacy, now keep at least to his wife and no other. Finally, let him remember his sworn allegiance. Augustine did not mean to go into the quarrel between Boniface and Placidia, and he gave no opinion as to the grievances of either. He confined himself to saying to the general in rebellion: "If you have received so many benefits from the Roman Empire, do not render evil for good. If, on the other hand, you have received evil, do not render evil for evil."

It is clear that the Bishop of Hippo could scarcely have given any other advice to the Count of Africa. To play the part of political counsellor in the very entangled state of affairs was extremely risky. How was it possible to exhort a victorious general to lay down his arms before the conquered? And yet, in estimating the situation from the Christian standpoint alone, Augustine had found a way to say everything essential, all that could profitably be said at the moment.

How did Boniface take a letter which was, in the circumstances, so courageous? What we know is that he did not alter his plans. It would indeed have been very difficult for him to withdraw and yield; and more than ever since a new army under Sigisvultus had been sent against him in all haste. A real fatality compelled him to remain in revolt against Rome. Did he believe he was ruined, as has been stated, or else, through his family connections—let us remember that his wife was a Barbarian—had he been for a long time plotting with Genseric to divide Africa? He has been accused of that. What comes out is, that as soon as he heard of the arrival of Sigisvultus and the new expeditionary force, he called in the Vandals to his aid. This was the great invasion of 429.

Ere long, the Barbarians entered Numidia. The borderlands about Hippo were threatened. Stricken with terror, the inhabitants in a mass fled before the enemy, leaving the towns empty. Those who were caught in them rushed into the churches, imploring the bishops and priests to help them. Or else, giving up all hope of life, they cried out to be baptized, confessed, did penance in public. The Vandals, as we have seen, aimed specially at the clergy; they believed that the Catholic priests were the soul of the resistance. Should not these priests, then, in the very interest of the Church, save themselves for quieter times, and escape the persecution by flight? Many sheltered themselves behind the words of Christ: "When they persecute you in this city, flee ye into another."

But Augustine strongly condemned the cowardliness of the deserters. In a letter addressed to his fellow-bishop, Honoratus, and intended to be read by all the clergy in Africa, he declares that bishops and priests should not abandon their churches and dioceses, but stay at their post till the end—till death and till martyrdom—to fulfil the duties of their ministry. If the faithful were able to withdraw into a safe place, their pastors might accompany them; if not, they should die in the midst of them. Thus they would have at least the consolation of lending aid to the dying in their last moments, and especially of preventing the apostasies which readily took place under the shock of the terror. For Augustine, who foresaw the future, the essential thing was that later, when the Vandal wave had swept away, Catholicism might flourish again in Africa. To this end, the Catholics must be made to remain in the country, and the greatest possible number be strengthened in their faith. Otherwise, the work of three centuries would have to be done all over again.

We must admire this courage and clear-mindedness in an old man of seventy-five, who was being continually harassed by the complaints and lamentations of a crowd of demoralized fugitives. The position became more and more critical. The siege lines were drawing closer. But in the midst of all this dread, Augustine was given a gleam of hope: Boniface made his peace with the Empire. Henceforward, his army, turning against the Barbarians, might protect Hippo and perhaps save Africa.

Had Augustine a hand in this reconciliation? There is not the least doubt that he desired it most earnestly. In a letter to Count Darius, the special envoy sent from Ravenna to treat with the rebel general, he warmly congratulates the Imperial plenipotentiary on his mission of peace. "You are sent," he said to him, "to stop the shedding of blood.

Therefore rejoice, illustrious and very dear son in Jesus Christ, rejoice in this great and real blessing, and rejoice upon it in the Lord, Who has made you what you are, and entrusted to you a task so beautiful and important. May God seal the good work He has done for us through you!" ... And Darius answered: "May you be spared to pray such prayers for the Empire and the Roman State a long time yet, my Father."

But the Empire was lost in Africa. If the reconciliation of the rebellious Count had given some illusions to Augustine, they did not last long. Boniface, having failed in his endeavours to negotiate the retreat of the Vandals, was defeated by Genseric, and obliged to fall back into Hippo with an army of mercenary Goths. Thus it came about that Barbarians held against other Barbarians one of the last Roman citadels in Africa. From the end of May, 430, Hippo was blockaded on the land side and on the side of the sea.

In great tribulation, Augustine resigned himself to this supreme humiliation, and to all the horrors which would have to be endured if the city were captured. As a Christian, he left all to the will of God, and he would repeat to those about him the words of the Psalm: "Righteous art Thou, O Lord, and upright are Thy judgments." A number of fugitive priests, and among them Possidius, Bishop of Guelma, had taken refuge in the episcopal residence. One day, when he lost heart, Augustine, who was at table with them, said:

"In front of all these disasters, I ask God to deliver this city from the siege, or, if that be not His decree, to give His servants the necessary strength to do His will, or at least to take me from this world and receive me into His bosom."

But it is more than probable that discouragement of that kind was only momentary with him, and that in his sermons, as well as in his conversations with Boniface, he did his utmost to stimulate the courage of the people and the general. His correspondence includes a series of letters written about this time to the Count of Africa, which manifest here and there a very warlike spirit. These letters are most certainly apocryphal. Yet they do reveal something of what must have been the sentiments just then of the people of Hippo and of Augustine himself. One of these letters emphatically congratulates Boniface upon an advantage gained over the Barbarians.

"Your Excellency knows, I believe, that I am stretched upon my bed, and that I long for my last day to come. I am overjoyed at your victory. I urge you to save the Roman city. Rule your soldiers like a good Count. Do not trust too much to your own strength. Put your glory in Him Who gives courage, and you will never fear any enemy. Farewell!"

The words do not matter much. Whatever may have been Augustine's last farewell to the defender of Hippo, it was no doubt couched in language not unlike this. In any case, posterity has wished to believe that the dying bishop maintained to the end his unyielding demeanour face to face with the Barbarians. It would be a misuse of words to represent him as a patriot in the present sense of the term. It is no less true that this African, this Christian, was an admirable servant of Rome. Until his death he kept his respect for it, because in his eyes the Empire meant order, peace, civilization, the unity of faith in the unity of rule.

Chapter 4
SAINT AUGUSTINE

I n the third month of the siege, he fell ill. He had a fever—no doubt an infectious fever. The country people, the wounded soldiers who had taken refuge in Hippo after the rout of Boniface, must have brought in the germs of disease. It was, moreover, the end of August, the season of epidemics, of damp heats and oppressive evenings, the time of the year most dangerous and trying for sick people.

All at once, Augustine took to his bed. But even there, upon the bed in which he was going to die, he was not left in quiet. People came to ask his prayers for some possessed by devils. The old bishop was touched; he wept and asked God to give him this grace, and the devils went out of those poor crazy men. This cure, as may well be thought, made a great noise in the city. A man brought him another one sick to be healed. Augustine, being most weary, said to the man:

"My son, you see the state I am in. If I had any power over illnesses, I should begin by curing myself."

But the man had no idea of being put off: he had had a dream. A mysterious voice had said to him, "Go and see Augustine: he will put his hands on the sick person, who will rise up cured." And, in fact, he did. I think these are the only miracles the saint made in his life. But what matters that, when the continual miracle of his charity and his apostolate is considered?

Soon the bishop's illness grew worse. Eventually, he succeeded in persuading them not to disturb him any more, and that they would let him prepare for death in silence and recollection. During the ten days that he still lingered, nobody entered his cell save the physicians, and the servants who brought him a little food. He availed himself of the quiet to repent of his faults. For he was used to say to his clergy that "even after baptism, Christians—nay, priests, however holy they might be, ought never go out of life without having made a general confession." And the better to rouse his contrition, he had desired them to copy out on leaves the Penitential Psalms, and to put these leaves on the wall of his room. He read them continually from his pillow.

Here, then, he is alone with himself and God. A solemn moment for the great old man!

He called up his past life, and what struck him most, and saddened him, was the foundering of all his human hopes. The enemies of the Church, whom he had battled with almost without ceasing for forty years, and had reason to believe conquered—all these enemies were raising their heads: Donatists, Arians, Barbarians. With the Barbarians' help, the Arians were going to be the masters of Africa. The churches, reformed at the price of such long efforts, would be once more destroyed. And see now! the authority which might have supported them, which he had perhaps too much relied upon—well, the Empire was sinking too. It was the end of order, of substantial peace, of that minimum of safety which is indispensable for all spiritual effort. From one end to the other of the Western world, Barbarism triumphed.

Sometimes, amid these sad thoughts of the dying man, the clangour of clarions blared out—there was a call to arms on the ramparts. And these musics came to him in his half-delirious state very mournfully, like the trumpets proclaiming the Judgment Day. Yes, it might well be feared that the Day of Wrath was here! Was it really the end of the world, or only the end of a world?... Truly, there were then enough horrors and calamities to make people think of the morrow with dismay. Many of the signs predicted by Scripture dazed the imagination: desolations, wars, persecutions of the Church, increased with terrific steadiness and cruelty. Yet all the signs foretold were not there. How many times already had humanity been deceived in its fear and its hope! In reality, though all seemed to shew that the end of time was drawing nigh, no one could tell the day nor the hour of the Judgment. Hence, men should watch always, according to the words of Christ... But if this trial of

Barbarian war was to pass like the others, how woeful it was while it endured! How hard for Augustine, above all, who saw nearly the whole of his work thrown down.

One thought at least consoled him, that since his conversion, for forty years and more, he had done all he was able—he had worked for Christ even beyond his strength. He said to himself that he left behind him the fruit of a huge labour, a whole body of doctrine and apology which would safeguard against error whatever was left of his flock and of the African Church. He himself had founded a Church which might serve as an example, his dear Church of Hippo, that he had done his best to fashion after the divine plan. And he had also founded convents, and a library full of books, which had become still larger recently through the generosity of Count Darius. He had lessoned his clergy who, once the disasters were past, would scatter the good seed of Truth. Books, monasteries, priests, a sure and solid nourishment for the mind, shelters and guides for souls—there is what he bequeathed to the workers of the future. And with a little joy mingling with his sorrow, he read on the corner of the wall where his bed was, this verse of the Psalm: *Exibit homo ad opus suum et operationem suam usque ad vesperum*—"Man goeth forth unto his work and to his labour until the evening." He, too, had worked until evening.

If the earthly reward seemed to slip from him now, if all was sinking around him, if his episcopal city was beleaguered, if he himself, although still a strong man—"he had the use of all his limbs," says Possidius; "a keen ear and perfect sight"—if he himself was dying too soon, it was doubtless in expiation for the sins of his youth. At this remembrance of his disorders, the tears fell over his face... And yet, however wild had been his conduct at that time, he could descry in it the sure marks of his vocation. He recalled the despair and tears of his mother, but also his enthusiasm when he read the *Hortensius*; his disgust for the world and all things when he lost his friend. In the old man he recognized the new. And he said to himself: "Nay! but that was myself. I have not changed. I have only found myself. I have only changed my ways. In my youth, in the strongest time of my mistakes, I had already risen to turn to Thee, my God!"

His worst foolishness had been the desire to understand all things. He had failed in humility of mind. Then God had given him the grace to submit his intelligence to the faith. He had believed, and then he had understood, as well as he could, as much as he could. In the beginning, he acknowledged very plainly that he did not understand. And then faith had thrown open the roads of understanding. He had splendidly employed his reason, within the limits laid down against mortal weakness. Had that not been the proud desire of his youth? To understand! What greater destiny?

To love also. After he had freed himself from carnal passions, he had much employed his heart. He thought of all the charity he had poured out upon his people and the Church, upon all he had loved in God— upon all he had done, upon all the consequence of his labour, inspired and strengthened by the divine love... Yes, to love—all was in that! Let the Barbarians come! Had not Christ said: "Lo, I am with you alway, even unto the end of the world"? So long as there shall be two men gathered together for love of Him, the world will not be entirely lost, the Church and civilization will be saved. The religion of Christ is a leaven of action, understanding, sacrifice, and charity. If the world be not at this hour already condemned, if the Day of Judgment be still far off, it is from this religion that shall arise the new influences of the future...

And so Augustine forgot his sufferings and his human disappointments in the thought that, in spite of all, the Church is eternal. The City of God gathered in the wreckage of the earthly city: "The Goth cannot capture what Christ protects"—*Non tollit Gothus quod custodit Christus*. And as his sufferings increased, he turned all his thoughts on this unending City, "where we rest, where we see, where we love," where we find again all the beloved ones who have gone away. All—he called them all in this supreme moment: Monnica, Adeodatus, and her who had nearly lost herself for him, and all those he had held dear...

On the fifth day of the calends of September, Augustine, the bishop, was very low. They were praying for him in the churches at Hippo, and especially in the Basilica of Peace, where he had preached and worked for others so long. Possidius of Guelma was in the bishop's room, and the priests and monks. They sent up their prayers with those of the dying man. And no doubt they sang for the last time before him one of those liturgical chants which long ago at Milan had touched him even to tears, and now, since the siege, in the panic caused by the Barbarians, they dared not sing any more. Augustine, guarding himself even now against the too poignant sweetness of the melody, attended only to the sense of the words. And he said:

"My soul thirsts after the living God. When shall I appear before His face?"

Or again:

"He Who is Life has come down into this world. He has suffered our death, and He has caused it to die by the fullness of His life... Life has come down to you—and will you not ascend towards Him and live?..."

He was passing into Life and into Glory. He was going very quietly, amid the chanting of hymns and the murmur of prayers... Little by little his eyes were veiled, the lines of his face became rigid. His lips moved no more. Possidius, the faithful disciple, bent over him. Like a patriarch of the Scriptures, Augustine of Thagaste "slept with his fathers."...

And now, whatever may be the worth of this book, which has been planned and carried out in a spirit of veneration and love for the saint, for the great heart and the great intellect that Augustine was, for this unique type of the Christian, the most perfect and the most admirable perhaps that has ever been seen—the author can only repeat in all humility what was said fifteen hundred years ago by the Bishop of Guelma, Augustine's first biographer:

"I do desire of the charity of those into whose hands this work shall fall, to join with me in thanksgiving and blessing to Our Lord, Who has inspired me to make known this life to those present and those absent, and has given me the strength to do it. Pray for me and with me, that I may try here below to follow in the steps of this peerless man, whom, by God's goodness, I have had the happiness of living with for such a long time..."

THE END

Copyright © 2024 by Alicia ÉDITIONS

Credits: www.canva.com ; Alicia Éditions

Public Domain: Saint Augustine of Hippo Receiving the Sacred Heart of Jesus by Philippe de Champaigne, between 1645 and 1650, Los Angeles County Museum of Art.

https://commons.wikimedia.org/wiki/File:Saint_Augustinee_by_Philippe_de_Champaigne.jpg

Painting of Saint Augustine in His Study by Sandro Botticelli (1480), Ognissanti Church (Florence).

https://commons.wikimedia.org/wiki/File:Sandro_Botticelli_050.jpg

ISBN EBOOK: 9782384554430

ISBN PAPERBACK: 9782384554447

ISBN HARDCOVER: 9782384554454

All rights reserved.

www.ingramcontent.com/pod-product-compliance
Lightning Source LLC
LaVergne TN
LVHW092011090526
838202LV00002B/102